EXPANSION MASTERY

EXPANSION
MASTERY

*The Practical Guide
to Living a Fully Engaged Life*

ROBERT D. BESSLER

NEW YORK

EXPANSION MASTERY

The Practical Guide to Living a Fully Engaged Life

ISBN 978-1-61448-342-7 paperback
ISBN 978-1-61448-343-4 eBook
Library of Congress Control Number: 2012945352

Morgan James Publishing
The Entrepreneurial Publisher
5 Penn Plaza, 23rd Floor,
New York City, New York 10001
(212) 655-5470 office • (516) 908-4496 fax
www.MorganJamesPublishing.com

Cover Design by:
Rachel Lopez
www.r2cdesign.com

Interior Design by:
Bonnie Bushman
bonnie@caboodlegraphics.com

In an effort to support local communities, raise awareness and funds, Morgan James Publishing donates a percentage of all book sales for the life of each book to Habitat for Humanity Peninsula and Greater Williamsburg.

Get involved today, visit
www.MorganJamesBuilds.com.

Habitat
for Humanity®
Peninsula and
Greater Williamsburg
Building Partner

To my Grandfather,

Doyle Short

You were, and always will be,
the most special and
influential person in my life.
I am so blessed to have had
so many great years with
you and honored to have
learned so much from you.
You are forever in my heart.
I love you and miss you.

CONTENTS

SPECIAL THANKS

I WOULD LIKE TO OFFER an extra-special thought of appreciation for the immense assistance with this project, without which, it would not have come into reality.

Thank you so much to my proof-reader and initial editor, Amy Ehrman, for all the long hours you spent alongside me on this project and for the massive amounts of red ink you gave me; great corrections that helped this book become something truly special. Thank you so much for believing in me and standing beside me while I brought it into reality. I love you, baby.

Thank you so very much to an amazing editor and author, Solala Towler. You did a wonderful job and you did it very quickly. Your suggestions and guidance are always valued and greatly appreciated. A lot of hard work and dedication went into this book and I am so grateful to have had your knowledge and experience to guide me. Words are not adequate for expressing my appreciation.

APPRECIATION

I WOULD LIKE TO EXPRESS my sincere and heartfelt appreciation for the many amazing Beings in my life, who have made my experience here in this lifetime a truly special adventure. I love you all.

To my fiancé, Amy. You have opened my heart more than I ever thought possible and you allow me to feel the unconditional love and support that you so generously give. You are my Sunshine, my Angel, the light of my life and I love you more than words could ever express. I am so grateful that you can feel my heart, so you can know the depths of my love. Life with you is truly Heaven on Earth! You are my bliss and you have my eternal appreciation. I love you so much.

To my daughters, Lacey and Amanda. You are both so precious to me and you are always in my heart and on my mind. I am so proud of both of my girls and I hope that you have the most amazing lives imaginable. I am so fortunate to be your dad. You have brought more joy into my life than you will ever know and for that I thank you both. I love you girls very much.

To my grandson, Jordan. You are now and always will be Grandpa's "Bestest Buddy." You have been an amazing little man since the day you were born and I am so grateful that I received the second chance of life that I was given in order to assist in your birth, let you sleep on my chest, play cars with you on the kitchen floor and play trains with you. I am always here for you. I love you buddy.

To my new grandson, Dallas. You are new to our lives and I don't get to see you often, but I love you just the same. You have the biggest smile I have ever seen a baby give and you light up the room with your giggles. It makes me smile when you crawl up to see me on the computer screen during the Skype calls. I look forward to being your Grandpa. I love you.

To my grandfather, Doyle Short (1914–2008). My best friend, my mentor, my "father" and my grandpa – you filled all of these roles in my life. I owe so much to you that I could never repay you in a thousand lifetimes. I would not be half the man I am today without your love, support and guidance. Thank you so much for being the most wonderful Grandpa anyone ever had.

To my brother, Michael. A better younger brother could not be asked for. You are very accomplished in life as a retiree of the United States Navy. Although I didn't say it aloud often enough, I have always been so proud of you. You were a great companion in childhood as a little brother and you are more special to me now as not only my brother, but as a friend. I love you.

To my greatest teachers. Bujinkan Soke Masaaki Hatsumi, Enbukan Soke Kenshinsai Machida, Enbukan So-Shihan Takeshi Machida, Wudang Taoist Master Yun Long Zhong, Qigong Master Michael Winn, Grandmaster Mantak Chia, Brendon Burchard, John Beaman, Rick Frishman, Solala Towler. I am so blessed to have the ability to train directly with each one of you. You are truly masters of the highest caliber and I owe you all so much. Thank you for pointing the Way along the path of life; you have made my journey very special. You have my unconditional love, respect and appreciation.

PREFACE

THE HUMAN RACE IS facing a time of intense change, unlike any other in recorded history. We all notice the signs in the world around us; at this point they are undeniable. They are evident in every country and in every corner of the world. There is nowhere and no one left unaffected. We can even feel this within ourselves at a deep soul level if we pay close enough attention. This time is not easy for any of us; there are overwhelming struggles that we all face in one form or another. I know now, more than ever, people are experiencing the feelings of being lost, unfulfilled, empty and are suffering from despair. Every person is doing the best they can in these times and together we can help each other to overcome these struggles, emerging forever changed for the better. Now is when we must consider every other person on the planet to be family. We must be willing to open our hearts and love one another without condition or judgment. The call for change can no longer be ignored or suppressed. It is time to summon a courageous spirit in order to acknowledge the changes, to embrace and fully engage them. You can sense this calling, you can feel it, and you can hear it in your thoughts. You are not alone; we are all experiencing this.

The time of singularity and individuality has faded into the mists of times past. We must now join together as a unified race of beings and unite as one family, one voice and one heart. We can no longer afford to see each other as "different" because of race, creed, culture or belief. The time has arrived when we must rise above the ego-motivated mentality, rising to our higher sense of purpose, a higher sense of being. We are *all* in this together, and together we can not only endure this time of colossal change but thrive in spite of it. Right now is a time of immeasurable human potential for positive personal growth as well as technological growth. Balance is crucial. Human beings are learning faster, developing a deeper understanding and breaking through mental barriers like never before. Just as the lotus blossom perseveres through the murky waters to unfold in the glory of the sunlight, so too must we wade through our limiting beliefs and excuses to give birth to our true potential.

I place a challenge before each of you to rise to meet your Highest Self, living from that place with every new breath. Will you rise to this occasion, freeing yourself from the cage of your comfort zone, from your comfy couch where you have been lounging for so long, hypnotically staring at the screen in front of you? Instead of wasting your life away, can you take action and participate in your life? Will you cease "just getting by" and begin to engage life fully with enthusiasm, passion and presence? It's not a question of *can* you; it's a question of *will* you. Every one of us has the personal power to make this choice. It is time to be reunited with the world around you, to know yourself as a being of Heaven and Earth. It's time to reunite with others, to know your connection to every heart on the planet. It's time to know yourself as a child of the Divine, living a life in harmony with Nature, reclaiming your rightful heritage. We must celebrate our own unique nature, remembering the identity of our innermost self as we courageously face the boundless new landscape of changes before us. We must be willing to abandon the complacency of our comfort zones for the thrilling prospect of a new adventure, in order to experience a life that is nothing less than Heaven on Earth!

Now is the moment for unparalleled human Expansion. It is the moment for all beings to expand upwards toward the Heavens while connecting more deeply than ever to the Earth. This is the Expansion I am referring to in the pages of this book, and this is what we are being called to do. This *is* happening. There is hope for the human species and planet Earth, all is *not* lost. Accept the challenge and participate in your own Expansion, just as I have, and embrace the amazing gift of your own life! And remember to have the time of your life, because that's exactly what you are doing!

Love, bliss & appreciation,

Robert D. Bessler

This auspicious day of March 3rd, 2011

INTRODUCTION

The Tao gives birth to one. One gives birth to two.
Two gives birth to three. Three gives birth to
the ten thousand beings.
All beings carry yin and yang to create harmony.
Here is what people loath: Orphans, desolate and worthless.
Yet great lords use these titles to describe themselves.
Some lose yet also gain. Others gain yet end up losing.
What others teach, I also teach. Those who are
forceful and aggressive will not die a natural death.
This is the essence of my teaching.
— Lao Tzu / Solala Towler —
The 42nd verse of the Tao Te Ching

The book you're holding in your hands is designed to serve and guide you along your life path, facilitating the launch and guidance of your Expansion. While it will not be providing you with the "three easy steps to this or that," it will provide practical and effective practices to assist those who are serious about mastering their personal growth. This book is about mastery; its focus is leaving behind a life of unconscious, powerless, undisciplined and uninspired living. It will help you trade in mediocrity for excellence, where you take charge and consciously create the life you know in your heart you desire. I have put together some of the best, most powerful practices I have learned over 30 plus years to create a very unique system, that when followed correctly can produce amazing results in your life. I am openly sharing the secrets that have made a tremendously positive impact in my life and the lives of my students and friends in the hopes that it will elevate you as well. However, I worked diligently for decades on this material and have achieved results due to consistent, perfect practice. You will have to do the same, but believe me when I say that it is so worth your efforts. If I can do it, so can you, because we are from the same Source and ultimately we are one.

It has become all too common for people to accept living far below their level of capability, mostly due to severely deteriorating mental attention spans and insanely fast paced lives. People are giving up. Don't allow yourself to give up when the greatest opportunity for personal growth is happening all around you, right here and now. We are living in a time where so many things are possible and human beings have the ability to be extraordinary! It's time to leave the excuses behind; no one is buying them anymore, and they are more transparent than you may think. It's time to step up to the amazing potential that you know in your heart you have, reclaiming your rightful place as a powerful human being fully engaged in your life. I know there are hundreds of thousands or even millions of people out there at this moment feeling disconnected, empty, lost, depressed, easily overwhelmed and even suicidal. I suspect there are also an equal number of people out there who feel a strange compulsion deep in their soul to make huge modifications in their lives. You may feel the need to change what you are doing for a living, your relationship or even where you live. You are not alone, as many of us possess these yearnings and are struggling to gather the courage to act on them. These feelings cannot be ignored, as they get more and more intense with each passing day. They are but a few of the symptoms created by the evolutionary shift, which I will explain further in later chapters.

You can transform these sensations through conscious action to feel fully engaged and filled with overflowing love, appreciation and joy. Living with a revived sense of passion and purpose that is clearer than ever before, I want you to feel so enthusiastic about your life that you are excited to awaken every morning to have another glorious day. Are you ready to become a master of your own Expansion? I have faith in you and your ability to succeed, because I know the awesome potential you have within your being, even if you don't realize it yet. You are a truly beautiful person, brimming with the potential for greatness and a power that is extraordinary. It's time for you to know and accept that fact in your own heart.

When you turn and look back upon the path you have chosen, you can begin to see the Divine nature in the unfolding of your life's events. They are like delicate cherry blossoms as they bud, bloom and then fall away, only to be whisked off into the void by the cool spring breeze. Each is perfect and happens at the perfect moment. You can begin to glimpse the totality of the choices you've made and the people and events that were placed there for you by unseen forces. Some of them you seem to have created or attracted for yourself; others clearly showed up out of some Divine cosmic design with the purpose of supporting you on your life's journey.

Upon looking back on my own path, I have been relatively intuitive since I was a teenager but I still possessed the immaturity of youth and did not always listen to the callings of my Higher Self. What I can say with certainty is that after my *first* near-death experience at age 14, I've had a heightened awareness for my sensitivity to the subtle forces of Nature. It began one evening as I was seated on our living room sofa enjoying a fireball jawbreaker with my younger brother. As I laughed at his antics, the candy slid down my throat to become securely lodged in my windpipe. I franticly tried to cough it up and even swallow it down, but neither one offered me the ability to draw a breath. We bolted into the kitchen to alert my mother and grandfather, who were relaxing at the dining room table drinking coffee. As I tried to communicate without being able to speak, my grandfather instantly picked up on the message I was desperately trying to convey. I'm sure the unnatural color of my face was a big indication of the situation. He sprang from the chair, violently knocking me to the floor on my hands and knees where he tried to get the jawbreaker dislodged. I can remember the look of sheer terror on his face and I unquestionably knew the situation was serious. He proceeded to strike me in the back, massage my throat, and even tried digging it out with his fingers. Nothing was working. This was before the Heimlich maneuver became widely known and commonly taught to the public.

As it became increasingly more difficult to breathe, I recall being somewhat surprised at how calm I was over the whole thing. My mother had managed to call for an ambulance through her hysteria and I felt bad for making everyone so frightened. It was the middle of winter in Michigan; the roads had not yet been plowed and the ambulance ended up firmly entrenched in a snow bank at the end of my street. I later learned that the good neighbors living around us rushed outdoors with their snow shovels to lend a hand as the paramedic hurried to the house to work on me. I can remember seeing the burly paramedic enter through the front door, the concerned look on his face when he saw me, and hearing my brother yelling in the background that I was dying. I felt my consciousness starting to slip away before everything faded into darkness.

I recall regaining some degree of consciousness for a very brief moment as I felt my body brutally and repeatedly lifted off the floor with a crushing sensation in my midsection. I could actually feel how concerned and frightened my grandfather was without seeing his face, and he was always one to keep his cool; we always had a deep connection and were very close. Then the blackness enveloped me again. I regained consciousness one more time, long enough to hear the paramedic saying that I hadn't been breathing and they didn't have much time, but they couldn't get it out. Then the blackness reclaimed me once again, its grasp was a little tighter this time. I could no longer feel the terrible punishment my body was taking as the paramedic tried his best to save my life, nor could I hear the voices of those around me or sense their presence. This time, I felt myself slip further away from what I had come to know as my life. I saw no bright lights or angels, religious figures or anything of the sort. What I did experience was the feeling of complete unimaginable comfort and love, a sensation of being where I was supposed to be. It was almost a feeling of being home. Everything was black, yet there was absolutely no fear or concern at all. I had left behind any sense of earthly connection and I knew that I had never felt so free and so peaceful. My consciousness was intact so there was still a sense of "me," yet I was very, very different. There was no image like that of my physical self, just my consciousness and a serene sense of "being."

Suddenly I found myself gasping for breath, in immense pain. The brawny paramedic was kneeling over me and yelling to someone that I was breathing again, as the jawbreaker had dissolved and slid down my throat. They seemed awfully worried about how long it had been. He collapsed back against the wall, exhausted, while I just lay there on the floor in a fetal heap, gulping air like a fish washed ashore. I was trying to connect with my body once again and figure out what the hell had happened. My ribs were cracked and bruised and my throat was severely strained, I had ruptured blood vessels in my face and neck and damaged my vocal cords, but I was alive. It hurt to breath, it hurt to swallow and it felt like my eyes had bugged out of my head. I can very clearly recall the extreme relief to be alive, but at the same time I missed that feeling I had when I was so close to death. It was at that moment that I lost any fear of dying. I had a strong sense of recognition for the feeling a baby has the moment it emerges from its mother. Please understand that I am not calling into question the near death or after death experiences of others, I am merely sharing what I experienced. It's amazing what you learn about yourself when you are standing at death's door.

After that, things began to get a bit more interesting. I can very clearly call to mind when I was 15, stepping out the back door of my childhood home in Michigan one spring morning to let out our Samoyed puppy Snowflake. At that moment I noticed things felt out of the ordinary, and I was compelled to look up at the sky. I couldn't explain it then, but I had a bad feeling that something horrific was coming involving the weather. At that time of the morning it was still sunny and mild with no dark clouds in sight. Later that afternoon, Kalamazoo had a powerful F3 tornado rip through the downtown area, causing massive devastation that took the lives of five people, injured 79 others and caused $50 million of damage. I remember helping one of my childhood friends clean debris from their small local church. I was in awe of the sheer power of nature as I pulled blades of grass out of the pews and walls like tiny daggers. This is what I had felt earlier that morning. I spent a lot of contemplating how I'd known it was coming, but all I knew for certain was I'd felt it in the air.

I tend to perceive these types of things in two ways at the same time. I will feel a positive or negative sensation in my body, as well as have a sense of knowing, almost a kind of thought, that will be encouraging or provide a warning. After years of study and refinement, I have come to understand that the thought-sense of knowing is actually the voice of my *Higher Self* and the feeling that goes with it is the sensory perception of my *Lower Self*. By Higher Self I am referring to the Divine spirit or soul. By Lower Self I am talking about the physical, mental and emotional body. Please note that lower does not mean "lesser," as physical reality is an important part of our experience. It is the unification of the Higher and Lower Selves that brings about the activation of a fully actualized being. Some people are in tune to the Higher Self and Lower Self, while others have simply not awakened to it yet. I believe this is something that can be effectively taught to people who are willing and open to the encounter, without the need for a near-death experience. I don't recommend that route if you can help it!

Here is another example of this type of intuition. In 1982, when I was 18 and practicing Tae Kwon Do, it didn't take long to realize that it was not the right fit for me. I contacted Stephen K. Hayes regarding a Ninjutsu training event and received a response letter from his lovely wife Rumiko, but this training was not easily accessible to me at that time both geographically and financially. The letter shed some serious light on what martial art I needed to study, but I was still too young to grasp the importance of it and take full responsibility for my life. I stuck it out with my Tae Kwon Do training and attained my first-degree black belt, but I immediately left after completing my test. I could not rationally explain it, but I had a sense of knowing that the martial arts contained much more than the sports mentality and competition present in Tae Kwon Do. I began speaking with various masters and trying different arts to see if they resonated with what I knew deep down I needed. I stopped making excuses for myself and did what was necessary to attain the training I was guided towards, eventually becoming a student of Ninjutsu.

What I needed for my own path was an art that provided the means of subduing one's ego. Sport martial arts serve well to build self-esteem, but in the process often bolster the ego. While I did need to improve my self-esteem, the last thing I needed was for my ego to be reinforced. Many of the older, complete fighting arts serve to boost self-esteem while overcoming the ego. While this may seem to be a contradiction on the surface, it's the paradox that shows its depth, value, and authenticity. I was oblivious of it at the time, but I needed this type of training in the worst way. In order to begin my diligent training in Ninjutsu, I drove four hours round trip two to three times a week, additionally attending seminars whenever available that required an eleven hour round trip trek. I adhered to this routine for over seven years. This is the training that soon began to develop my intuition to much higher degrees while helping me in a myriad of additional ways.

The second near-death experience came in 2006 when I was 42 years old; it was at this point in my life that everything decided to hit the proverbial fan. I was working 12-hour shifts at a chemical factory, then going to my martial arts school to teach classes, as I had done for more than 15 years. Eighteen to twenty-hour workdays were the norm for me. I started to slowly spin out of control, thinking I could just keep pushing through, but I was wrong—dead wrong! Near the end of the last class for the evening, I felt a strange sensation in my neck, but it wasn't pain or any other typical heart attack symptom. I knew something was out of the ordinary, but it didn't seem to be getting worse. I managed a few hours of restless sleep and went into work the next day for overtime before heading to the dojo for a two-hour private lesson. My neck still felt uncomfortable and my chest felt a bit odd. Then I noticed I was sweating more than usual and I began to feel short of breath. I finished teaching the private lesson, cleaned up at home and went straight to the hospital.

I lay in a hospital bed in the emergency room for over four hours while they ran various tests. My vital signs were normal and I was devoid of chest pain or numbness in my arm. The doctors were not even certain I was having a cardiac episode. However, the results of the blood work showed my cardiac enzymes were elevated, indicating that I was indeed in the middle of a mild heart attack. They rushed me to the "cath lab" where they assembled a team to prep me. They wanted to put a catheter in to see how bad the blockage was in my heart. This would help them to determine whether either a stent or surgery was necessary. The procedure revealed a collapsed blood vessel, and as the catheter struck the resulting blockage, it pierced through the heart vessel. This allowed it to jump across the heart to puncture another vessel on the other side. It had turned into a very serious situation that required immediate open-heart surgery. Once again I was to come face to face with death. They gave me medication to keep my heart rate as low as possible until they could operate.

I was very clear about what was happening, but I had no fear for whether I lived or died. Maybe it was because this wasn't the first time I had faced death, or maybe it was because at this stage in my life I was pretty unhappy, unclear what to do about it and just didn't care anymore. I remember saying to myself on a few occasions, "If this is going to be my life, I don't care about living." Bam! How's that for attraction!? I didn't fully realize it then, but I had been vibrating at a very low emotional level due to my apathy. I truly didn't understand why I was so unhappy, but I had a feeling I could not go on the way I was living. I could no longer ignore these peculiar feelings that my life needed to change in some very big ways. I felt discontent with my job, with teaching at the martial arts school, and with my home life. Of course, as is the case with many men, I was not good at communicating these things. I made the big mistake of keeping everything bottled up inside, going about my life while ignoring my feelings. Bad move.

Into the operating room I went, smiling as I joked around with the surgeon for a moment. After the anesthesia was given I can recall hearing the surgeon teasing about playing country music that nobody else in the room enjoyed. I very briefly had a sense of awareness of someone pulling my arms in a strange way and then of being ripped in two down the middle. This was not something I was seeing, but something I was feeling and experiencing; yet it was not something that was happening to "me." Then I welcomed that same comforting darkness that enveloped me as it did when I was 14 years old. There was only silence, peace, tranquility and a sense of incredible comfort. There was no dreaming, no mental picture show. I felt no attachments to earthly concerns such as my physical body, my loved ones, my possessions or responsibilities. This time I began to have a sense of spreading out, a feeling of being a part of everything, becoming aware of everywhere, all at once. Not flying around from place to place, but dissolving into the blackness and becoming part of the all. Just as before, I felt as though my consciousness was still mostly intact, like I was still me for the most part. I had the awareness—not really the memories as such – but the feelings of all the experiences in my life. It was like they were part of me and I had taken them with me. I don't recall any thought forms during this time, only feeling-awareness that seemed to be a sort of consciousness of its own.

After I awoke in the ICU, I was trying to reconnect to my body but I wasn't so sure I really wanted to. I felt like I had no choice in the matter so I pushed on. My mouth and throat were painfully dry and my body felt like it had been hit by a very large truck that decided to back up and hit me a few more times for good measure. The angelic nurse showed me mercy and brought me a few ice chips. She told me that I had to stay awake and that she was going to begin pulling out all the tubes, wires and other gadgets that were attached to me. This was not a pleasant experience, especially since there were copper wires inserted into my chest, touching my heart, in case they needed to shock me should my heart decide to stop.

After this type of surgery you have to learn to walk all over again, which is agonizing at first. I refused to use the morphine drip; I wanted to feel my body to know I was alive, to stay present, even though that meant feeling the pain of having my chest split in two and wired back together. Three days later I was walking laps around the unit at a record pace and standing on my own, getting out of bed and assuming the fighting postures of the *Gyokko ryu* martial lineage. One of the postures, *Hicho no Kamae* (the posture of the flying bird) requires standing on one leg. I was able to do this and maintain my balance for five minutes or so. I could hear the nurses speaking at the desk in the hall about how they didn't know what the heck I was doing but they were impressed that I could do it. Six days later I was in my front yard practicing the *Bujinkan Sanshin no Kata* set of exercises and walking to the end of the block and back, although very slowly. It felt so good to move and to be alive. I had a new sense of wanting to enjoy this lifetime, yet there was still a strange voice inside desperately urging me to make modifications if I was going to achieve the spiritual growth I was meant to experience. I knew beyond any possible doubt I had been given a second chance at life and I better not waste it. I would have to shake some bad habits that developed due to my unacknowledged unhappiness and make some major lifestyle changes.

Throughout the next couple years, everything was about to become very apparent as I collided with yet more intense situations. I was incredibly close to my grandparents on my mother's side. They were both very special people who I loved with all of my heart. I lost my grandmother to Alzheimer's and my grandfather followed behind her a year later at 94 years of age. His name was Doyle, one of the finest men I have ever known. He was not just my grandfather, but my best friend, mentor and "father"—not to mention a hero in my eyes for many reasons. The following year I lost my step-father, followed by my mother passing away after a four-month struggle with cancer. Hell, I even had to have the family dog put down due to old age and ill health a few days after getting out of the hospital. Within this same timeframe I went through a divorce, closed my martial arts school of 16 years and left my factory job of 23 years. I had to start over! This was not just my conscious decision, but the universe shoving me from behind with both hands. It was during these highly turbulent years of change and tremendous soul-crushing loss that I also decided to listen to Divine guidance. I began a deep study and practice of the most potent and powerful techniques I had been taught over a period of 30 years. I decided to put it all to the test, to see if I could actually live according to the principles that I had believed in my whole life. In order to begin a new, inspired life led by these principles, I left the States to live and study in China to recharge and refresh my mind, body and spirit.

Part of this sense of being drawn toward something deeper included having a concept placed before me time and time again. The concept was pertaining to Heaven, Earth and Mankind (Being). I've had the 42nd verse of the *Tao Te Ching* show up in my life in one form or another since I was quite young, long before I had ever heard of Lao Tzu or the Tao. This led me to have a fascination with the concept of Heaven, Earth and Being and it is this concept that has significantly influenced the creation of the Expansion Mastery System and the material within these pages. During my month in China, living on Wudang Mountain and studying Tai Chi, Tai Chi Sword and Qigong (Chi Kung) and journeying up the mountain to meditate at some of the breathtaking temples. I chose Wudang as I'd experienced a strange familiarity and comfort when I visited a couple years earlier that convinced me I would have to return. Most of the ideas came at night during some very restful sleep, and I was once again presented with the push to present the concept of the 42nd verse to people in a big way. There was a sense of urgency associated with it, indicating this information needed to be out there now to offer its benefits. I returned to the United States ready to delve into a life of renewed spirituality.

The process I went through was arduous at the time, there is no question about that. It was messy and painful in more ways than I could count. However, upon looking back at it now, it reminds me of the growth process of a lotus flower. The lotus bulb is nothing special to look at, yet it contains the potential to become a beautiful flower. There is no guarantee that it will survive and blossom. The lotus struggles to grow out of the mud and muck, through the water which cleanses it, to finally break the water's surface and expose a flower that opens into an incredibly gorgeous blossom. The remarkable flower then basks in the fresh air and sunlight. This colorful blossom reaches out in all directions as it opens and presents its beauty to the world. So too did I manage to grow out of these difficult times to eventually expand into someone much better than who I had been, opening my heart in the process. It is my understanding that this symbolism of the lotus is one reason it is so revered by spiritual schools and religions throughout the world.

The story of the phoenix seems to apply here as well. The stories of this mythical bird originated in ancient Egypt and spread throughout the world. The phoenix is a bird that tragically dies only to be reborn from its own ashes, transformed into a magnificent, majestic creature. The phoenix is larger, more stunning and dynamic then when it was an average bird. This is why the phoenix is a symbol associated with divinity, royalty and greatness. It also symbolizes the indomitable spirit, the warrior's heart of perseverance and victory. This is not a product of the ego, but instead the result of amazing life-changing transformation— transformation and spiritual awakening that every human being is capable of undergoing. I am not arrogantly comparing myself to the lotus or phoenix directly; I am just acknowledging the similarity of the process of personal transformation and Expansion that I underwent and that I am offering to others. The lotus offers us a lesson in a form that can be experienced with the five senses. The phoenix, on the other hand, is offering us a lesson in an esoteric formula. The actual bird known as a phoenix does not exist in the tangible realm. In accordance with esoteric tradition, something that is considered to be mythical is used to represent the spirit. We cannot see the spirit or soul, but we know it exists in some energetic manner. These stories of spiritual transformation are a powerful way to describe the progression.

The process of Expansion Mastery refers to a sense of balanced personal growth, which results in a fully actualized and consciously aware human being. Let's first address the *Expansion* aspect. As we have now come to understand, the universe itself is expanding at an incredible rate, much faster than scientists first anticipated. We are a part of the universe and it is natural for human beings to expand as well. Our spirits yearn for this sort of growth. It is not the idea of having and consuming more, it is the idea of becoming more, of "being" more. The balanced or harmonic growth associated with this type of training means that the individual is expanding in three ways. They become more sensitive and tuned into the subtle Divine forces around them, and they realize they are a deeply interrelated part of Nature, not above or separate from it. They also become hypersensitive to a deep connection to their own Higher Self and to all other human beings through their open-heart centers.

Expansion requires us to grow, and growth requires change. The charming bonsai tree stays small due to being kept in a small pot and constantly being trimmed. This small tree has the potential to grow into a large one if given the freedom. The goldfish too, remains small for its entire life when kept in a tiny fishbowl. But, place that same goldfish in a large pond and watch it grow. We are not separate from the tree or the fish. In order to expand, we too must be willing to leave the tiny box in which we place ourselves in the name of comfort to pacify the ego. We must be ready, willing and able to leave the unconscious life as a member of the herd and strike out on our own to explore the world, finding the truth for ourselves. Stepping outside of the box of commonality is the only way to expand. It's your choice. Are you content with living life as a tiny tree confined to a little world, or are you longing to grow into the beautiful, flowing willow, swaying high in the gentle breeze, expanding in all directions? This is Expansion.

The second aspect is that of *Mastery*. The journey towards mastery begins with a single focused effort. I feel that it's time that the "experts" were also true masters of what they share with others. It is the responsibility of those leading the way to not only be experts in their field, but to be masters of it as well; not by artificial ranks or titles, but through long years of consistent practice in order to acquire substantial results for themselves. True masters embody their practices. It is not simply something they *do,* it is something they *are.* Along with the fast-paced society of the information age came the "I want it all and I want it now" generation; then came the "I already know it because I read it online" generation. The main problem with both of these views is that they are built on faulty beliefs and impatience and have helped bring about a decline in true mastery.

It is time that we reclaimed our senses and realize that true mastery requires deep dedication, continuous study and practice and takes time. The need for patience is another strong indicator that what you're studying is worthwhile. There is no way to shortcut this; previous masters always pointed out this fact quite clearly. I am challenging all of you to abandon the illusion of the "quick fix" mentality and reclaim your right to become a master of yourself, your life and whatever else you choose. Do not accept the life of one of the mindless herd. Think for yourself, feel your own heart and get to know your own mind. Begin to subdue your ego in order to live and share with others from a place of authenticity within your heart. You must get out of your head to facilitate the awakening of your sensitivity to all things, uniting your Lower Self with your Higher Self to live the conscious, powerful life you were meant to live.

My intention is to state the information I am sharing with you in language that is as simple and clear as possible. Do not be fooled by the simplicity of the words, for it is within this paradox that you will discover the depth of their meaning. I am also extracting the essence of ancient teachings, presenting them without all of the mystical jargon typically associated with such wisdom, and without watering them down to a state of ineffectiveness. I'm writing this as though I were speaking to you directly in order to transmit it from my heart to yours. In some instances I will be attempting to express things beyond verbal description that must be felt to truly be experienced and known. When you happen across these passages, do your best to feel my words instead of merely reading them. This is the core essence of esoteric teachings that is passed on through stories and personal experiences more than through written texts. The grand idea is not for you to mimic my experience precisely, but to have your own unique experience. This way you will come to know its truth as your own, the transmission will be complete and your Expansion will be set in motion.

CHAPTER ONE

AWAKENING TO OUR PLACE IN THE UNIVERSE

*A new world is emerging right before our eyes. At the same time, the unsustainable world of the past struggles to continue. Both worlds reflect the beliefs that made them possible. Both worlds still exist—**but only for now**.*
— Gregg Braden —
(Deep Truth)

W hen setting out on a life journey, I have found that it is useful to not only know where you're going, but also where you are right now in the present moment. Let's begin our journey together by re-awakening to the fundamental understanding of humankind's place in the universe, of living between Heaven and Earth. This will help point the way for you to expand your sense of Self on your own personal life journey. You must also become aware of your position not only in space, but in time. This will help you to better grasp the current shifting era of climate change and of humanity's building desire to participate in tremendous transformation.

We are encountering the "shift" period of the legendary 2012 and we cannot deny that these are exceptionally interesting times. We all know dramatic situations are taking place that are far from the status quo, things that we read about and see for ourselves every day. The Earth's magnetic poles have been gradually shifting for years; this is an ongoing event that relatively few people acknowledge, but has been recognized by the scientific community. Is it a coincidence that this is happening in alignment with the teachings of multiple ancient traditions, from every corner of the world, referring to this period in time? I for one do not believe in coincidences. Likewise, I do not believe this astonishing moment in time will bring about the end of the world. It's believed the Earth has been through these events in the past with its obvious survival; I suspect it will do so again. Human beings, on the other hand, may be facing a time of challenge.

It appears the shift taking place is part of the usual 26,000 year cycle that has happened many times before. This subtle shift, due to the wobble in the Earth's rotation, causes a realignment of the axis; this has been happening for years and will continue for years to come before completion. Earth has already left its alignment with Polaris (the North Star or Pole Star) and is on its way to acquiring alignment with Vega, resulting in Vega becoming our new North Star. This is an axis shift of 23.5 degrees, respectively. During this period we are faced with what seems to us as time speeding up.

With this shift we can expect massive changes to ourselves, our environment and our ways of life. Change is a normal part of all things in nature; our breathtakingly beautiful water planet is not outside of the realm of change. From the research I have assimilated, the Earth's magnetic field is changing continually and the magnetic poles are capable of completely reversing at times. This is scientific fact as we see through articles from NASA and environmental scientists from a variety of countries. In an article published by NASA in 2003, Dr. Tony Phillips shared that scientists had found the magnetic field of the planet had weakened by 10 percent at that time. He also stated, "Sometimes the field completely flips. The north and south poles swap places. Such reversals, recorded in the magnetism of ancient rocks, are unpredictable. They come at irregular intervals averaging about 300,000–400,000 years; the last one however was 780,000 years ago. Are we long overdue for another? No one knows."

It stands to reason that if we are directly and substantially connected to this planet—and we all are—and the planet should go through massive change, so will the human race. This is where we as human beings are right now, in a process of great transformation. Dynamic changes to the global climate, to weather patterns and to all living things on Earth can be expected, but to what degree is unknown. What is even less understood are the changes we human beings will experience during this period of time and beyond. During this unusual period we will have an enormous opportunity – an opportunity to become greater than humanity may have ever been, through a spiritual transformation process that will reshape people physically, mentally, emotionally and spiritually. The result of your personal Expansion, as well as the Expansion of the collective consciousness, will be a unified sense of Self and a joyful, mindful experience of living a life of "Heaven on Earth."

Imagine walking through your normal day with a big smile on your face and a song in your heart, just because you feel happier and healthier. Imagine laughing with a new sense of freedom and spontaneity that comes from somewhere deep within. Imagine being able to hold on to this sense of happiness and open-heartedness no matter what else is taking place in your life. I am sure there are people in existence who cannot fathom having this as their normal disposition. This is not without good reason, and it is not their fault, but it can be changed. We all see the turmoil present in the world; much of it may seem disheartening, but it is still our choice to rise above these circumstances and discover a way to live the life we desire.

Many people have forgotten their truth and set aside their personal power. They've lost their connection to themselves and others, to their environment and to the truth of the Divine. People have become so busy trying to make a living and support their families that they have lost their sense of respect and compassion for others, oftentimes replacing these with a false sense of entitlement and superiority. Today, the average person spends their entire lifetime without much mindfulness for the fact that they are both spirit *and* body! Let's face it; many people walk through life in a state of unconscious numbness, stemming from a closed mind. This comes from a reluctance to leave or acknowledge anything outside of their comfort zone, especially if it has the potential to challenge their beliefs.

A state of imbalance is very evident among society; this causes a weak or nonexistent connection to Heaven and Earth. Few remember this is the rightful place of a human being in the universe, acting as a mid-point conduit for the forces that flow between Heaven and Earth. Using various metaphors, many spiritual and religious systems teach us that we are the result of the mixture of Heavenly and Earthly energies and elements. The Earth is our mother and the Heavens are our father. This is not exactly news, but is a truth many people have lost sight of as they become consumed by the demands of their fast-paced daily lives. This is one example of the esoteric meanings of the statement contained within various spiritual, religious and even martial traditions, which plainly states "honor thy mother and father." There are actually three layers of meaning to this statement. The first is to honor the mother and father who are your parents in this physical form; this is the generally accepted meaning that encourages appreciation for the people who brought you into this world and took care of you when you were too small and fragile to do it yourself.

The esoteric meaning of the statement refers to honoring the Earth and the Heavens. To acknowledge the Earth as your mother and the Heavens as your father in a larger cosmic sense is important. It is a well-established fact that human beings are connected to the Earth through the electromagnetic fields. It is also acknowledged that human beings are connected and affected by cosmic forces such as the sun, moon, and stars. The rhythm of our heart beat, our brainwave patterns, our mental and emotional states and so on are all affected or even regulated to some degree by the forces of Heaven and Earth; not to mention that we are created physically from not only the same energy as the Heavens and Earth, but the same elemental bases. Lastly, it is referring to honoring the one Universal Source that is both feminine (maternal) and masculine (paternal) energies. The Universe, God, Tao or whatever label you desire, is essentially gender neutral and without label. When you honor or love the Divine Universal Source, you are honoring the ultimate parent, the source of your creation and a part of who you truly are. Look back into the original teachings of most spiritual and religious systems before dissent and manipulation; you will find references to the Universal Source as both masculine and feminine energy. These ancient cultures and languages were not as ignorant or primitive as we are lead to believe; they have a very rich feeling and beauty associated with them when spoken and written. This feeling carries the expressive vibrational essence of the words, which has become lost to us in the west.

THE TRINITY

The ultimate expression of the trinity is that of Heaven, Earth and Being (humanity). An extremely significant factor in achieving success with your Expansion is the ability to perceive the world around you in a more enlightened and truthful way. Most people tend to view the world through the vision of duality, just like the Taoist Tai Chi symbol. In addition to the contrast and harmony of yin and yang, the symbol shows there is no total yin or total yang; this is what the small circles are representing. While this is indeed in accordance with the basic laws of polarity and attraction, it should be noted there is actually a third element contained within that famous symbol. The third element is represented by the curved line that seems to separate the two halves, which indicates interactive movement. When we awaken, we see through piercing eyes that the *two* is actually *three* and duality becomes the vision of the trinity. We are not merely our physical self or just our Spiritual Self; we are a combination of the two, at the same time and in the same place. The trinity is the concept of unity and completeness. It is this concept of three that unites opposites and offers wholeness. Please be aware that duality and trinity are not opposing concepts; the trinity includes and expands upon duality. It is this type of vision that will allow you to see with "esoteric eyes."

Duality offers us a basic understanding of contrast and balance in life; it is the basis of our existence, but things begin to transform once you learn to view the world through the lens of the trinity. After all, do we live in a two-dimensional world or a three-dimensional world? Yet most people view this 3-D world through a 2-D lens. When you become open to viewing reality through the lens of the trinity, your world greatly expands.

Here are some examples of viewing life through the trinity lens and the reasoning behind the power of the number three. We know from the sage advice of Lao Tzu that from the three comes all beings. When we learn to see things through the viewpoint of Heaven, Earth and Being (the "three"), we open our eyes, mind and heart to see everything. From the perspective of the three, we understand that the past, present and future are all the same, as the only real time that exists is the present and all things exist in the now. The power and influence of the trinity view can be seen as a part of nearly every religion and spiritual system, as well as in various aspects of society throughout time. There are religions that use this trinity or triad to symbolize Heaven, Earth and Hell, but more correctly it symbolizes Heaven, Earth and Being (humankind), as hell is a religious myth. It shows up again in Christianity as the Father, Son and Holy Spirit, and in the three-fold principles of the Emerald Tablet in Western Alchemy. The ancient Egyptian symbol of the Winged Solar Disc that adorns many entrance-ways of Egyptian temples serves as a symbol of the trinity. The three main branches of Buddhism—Mahayana, Theravada and Vajrayana—contain many three-fold philosophies, such as the Buddha, the Dharma and the Sangha. Mikkyo systems apply the *San Rai* (three prostrations) and the *Sanki Sankyo* (three refuges and three devotions) into its daily practices. Taoism and Chinese Medicine apply the concepts of *Jing* (essence), *Chi* (life force), and *Shen* (spirit), as well as focus on the three dantien, or internal centers of awareness. These are but a few of a multitude of examples that appear throughout the cultures of the world.

All of these representations of the trinity help us to understand our rightful place in the Universe. The energies of Heaven flow down through us into the Earth and likewise, the energies of the Earth flow upward through us into the Heavens. Human beings are conduits for the harmonious transfer of this subtle energy. There are also many activities that are designed to assist the practitioner in becoming more sensitive to their connection to Heaven and Earth. The Chinese art of Qigong (Chi Kung) allows us to open and work with the internal "energy" channels of the body to allow the free flow of Heavenly and Earthly energy through the body. The forces of Heaven and Earth can also be harmonized within the human body to be used for health, vitality and longevity, or stored within the body to be used at some later time. This is a clear example of the three-fold concept and trinity view of Heaven, Earth and Being.

GOD/UNIVERSAL SOURCE/TAO

It would be wise to define what I mean by Universal Source or God within the chapters to follow. Try your best to avoid the mental trap of relating back to what you already know or believe; see it with a fresh perspective in order to open your mind and step outside of your current comfort zone. This does not mean that you have to dispose of or immediately change your core beliefs; I am simply encouraging you to take back your personal sense of empowerment so you may begin to think, feel and experience things for yourself in order to know their truth. I am not attempting to offer you a new definition of God, but I am presenting a chance to expand your sense of knowing through a direct personal connection to this Source. Then you will know the truth as it is understood through your own perspective, allowing you to live as an authentic human being.

I feel that the largest mistake is to anthropomorphize the Universal Source. I know this may not please many male egos, especially those who insist that God must be a *Him*, but think about it objectively; read some ancient texts in the manner in which they were written instead of taking everything you read at face value. They make *Him* angry, judgmental, vengeful and petty. Take a moment and apply your own common sense—do you really think and believe that God, an all-potentiated, all-knowing, eternal entity would embody all the negative traits of a human being who is spiritually lost? These petty human attributes associated with God are the same fear-based emotions that keep people from experiencing the Universal Source directly for themselves by lowering their vibration and firmly fixing them within their ego.

What if God was really only pure love, joy, compassion, appreciation and non-judgmental, unconditional acceptance? Wouldn't that be the ultimate? If the Universal Source is pure love, then this entity cannot also be fear. When you think about that, how does it make you *feel*? What feelings do you experience in your abdomen, in your solar plexus and in your heart? Place your mind in these areas of your body and try to connect to the feeling. Stop ignoring what your body and heart are telling you for what you rationalize in your mind.

For the purposes of this book, I will frequently refer to the concept of God as *Universal Source, Divine* or simply *Universe*. The actual word(s) you choose have very little value. However, there is value in understanding that almost all religions and spiritual systems throughout the world use a word for God that contains an "ah" seed syllable. The vibration caused by this seed syllable, along with the emotion you associate with it, is very important. What is the typical sound across the globe uttered when we exhale and relax on a comfortable sofa, or when we sit back in a hot tub? The soothing and unconsciously produced "aahhhh" sound of relief as we exhale. When you feel this good, your vibrational frequency begins to rise. It is no coincidence that this is also the sound of ecstasy. If you know the Universal Source as the true spring of pure love, joy and goodness, this vibration will help you resonate closer to it by opening your heart.

If you associate the word for God with wrathfulness, guilt, vengeance and other negative emotions, then when you speak the name of the Universe it will take you away from connecting to it by lowering your vibration. For example, say the name of someone you perceive has wronged you in some way. How good do you feel afterwards? Don't think about it, *feel* it. You may get a painful feeling in the pit of your stomach or an accelerated heartbeat, your chest may tighten up or your mouth may get dry. How connected to the Universe do you feel in that moment? In contrast, now say the name of someone you adore; maybe the name of your loving spouse, caring parent or someone who has positively impacted your life. How do you feel now? Maybe this time you get a warm feeling in your stomach, tears of love and happiness in your eyes, or you feel your heart open even further. Now you see how the emotions associated with words can be so influential.

THE OLD WORLD REALITY — NEW WORLD REALITY

While human beings live in accordance with various natural cycles and patterns, it is well known and accepted that we are facing uncharted territory. Some of these patterns are aligning with each other for the first time in known history. Everyone from scientists to spiritualists agree that we are living in a world of rapid change. Just look at some of the events taking place as I write this book. Unemployment is out of control in the United States and throughout most of the world. Our school systems have failed, suffering massive funding cuts. Powerful governments are closing down and going bankrupt, failing in a multitude of ways and futilely attempting to hold things together. The economy has collapsed and threatens to drop even further, only this time far more seriously as we watch currency debasement wars on a global level. The health care system is severely broken, the housing market has collapsed, and the stock market remains extremely unstable and volatile. There are tremendous amounts of social unrest throughout the globe and multiple wars being fought around the world. Natural disasters such as tsunami, volcano eruptions, droughts, earthquakes, floods, mudslides and tornadoes are frequent occurrences.

These examples just cover the largest and most noticeable among the challenges of these changing times. I believe that all of the *symptoms*, whether on the personal, collective or planetary level are all easily discernable for those who are courageous enough to open their eyes and look around. Even marketing experts understand that people do not respond to the same stimuli they used to, and educators realize students of any age can no longer learn from the same educational models. Divorce rates are reaching all new highs while the number of new marriages is declining. Councilors know that the old models for structuring relationships are no longer serving couples. Things are simply not the same. We must acknowledge and accept that these changes are happening so we can move on to survive and thrive in a world that is transforming from masculine to feminine.

It is not uncommon these days for people to experience symptoms of feeling lost, empty, hopeless and unfulfilled. People tell me things just feel off or different and they can't put their finger on it. They are unable to figure out why things are this way, due to living fixed in their head and their lack of sensitivity for the world around them. Anyone exhibiting these symptoms should always still seek medical attention from their health care professional, but it is not uncommon to hear that they cannot find anything wrong. The dilemma most people end up facing is that they don't understand what to do about the way they feel. I was experiencing the same peculiar symptoms and I felt the same things you are feeling now. I know how unsettling it is when many of your core beliefs are called into question and you feel this mind-boggling, prevailing urge to make enormous changes in your life. I know how difficult it is to be honest with yourself. I hope I can clarify things for you, offer you a somewhat reasonable explanation, and also provide you with some great ways to turn those feelings into positive ones.

Whether you acknowledge that the Earth is undergoing a planetary polar shift, the change from the yang (masculine) to yin (feminine) cycle, or even simply that the geomagnetic field generated from the core of planet Earth is changing at a faster rate—we are certainly living in an increasingly different world. I am not going to provide you with doomsday predictions of where the world is headed or offer you a New Age conjecture of fluff or religious prophecy. I don't believe that anyone knows what's going to happen for sure at this point. However, there are overwhelming amounts of scientific research that shows the Earth's axis is indeed shifting. The largest indicators of these planetary transformations are the extreme weather and climate changes we are facing such as global warming and increased natural disasters in unusual places. Scientists have even openly stated that the four directions of north, south, east and west are no longer where they used to be. This is seen by airports having to change their altitude settings and even entire runways because they no longer coincide with the desired direction.

It is also worthy to note the additional shift of the Earth's masculine (yang) cycle changing to a feminine (yin) cycle. Depending upon the school of thought, these types of masculine and feminine cycle shifts happen about every 750 years to a few thousand years. This makes good sense when you consider that the energy of the North Star (Polaris) is considered to be masculine in nature, and the energy of Vega (the soon to be North Star) is considered to be feminine in nature. As large corporations and governments are constructed and run on a masculine model, we are witnessing their struggle to maintain control as they inevitably decline. Eventually they will have to accept the transition and restructure themselves to embody the softer feminine principles. As a result, we are currently seeing the rights of women under attack in a variety of ways, but this will pass as the feminine energy gains strength and women rise to become more powerful and influential in all areas of social order. The male dominated culture has run its course; it's now time for the remarkable women of the planet to stand up and accept their new roles as leaders in all aspects of life. The world will be counting on them!

Let me share some of the things that have changed within the new paradigm. We graduated from the industrial age to enter the information age, and now we are transforming into the intuition age. This is the transition from thinking to feeling; from the ego-ruled state of the mind to the spiritual state of the heart. As people currently remain so severely stuck in their heads, they suffer from overexertion in their brain and nervous system, resulting in symptoms such as being easily overwhelmed, mental fatigue and even mental illness.

Just look at the increase of mental instability in the world. According to recent studies, there has been a substantial increase in mental illness noted worldwide, and it is postulated that half of all Americans will suffer from some form of mental illness in their lifetime. Many attribute this to the calamities of natural disasters, the decline of global economies and increased psychological stress. I believe that these *reasons* are not the root cause; rather it is the changes in the geomagnetic (electromagnetic) field, resulting in energetic changes in the human body.

The geomagnetic field of the Earth is connected to our own personal electromagnetic field, which radiates from our hearts around our physical body. According to the studies by the Global Coherence Monitoring System, there is a direct connection between the energetic resonance of the Earth's magnetic field and the rhythms of the human heart and brain activity. When traveling into space, astronauts are equipped with a special apparatus known as the Schumann Resonance Device to simulate the frequency of the Earth's magnetosphere of 7.83 Hertz. This has a dramatic healing effect, as without it they become seriously ill. There is also evidence of the connection between Earth's field and that of the human collective behavior. Beyond the Earth, we know there is a direct correlation between the rhythmic pulse of our hearts and the pulsing of the Pole Star. Russian and American scientists have also shown that the sun directly interacts with the Earth's magnetic field, which in turn causes changes in human being's perspectives, emotions, behavioral patterns and brain activity. These are just a few ways that illustrate the deep interaction between human beings, the Earth and the cosmic bodies.

As we move into a feeling-based existence instead of constantly over-thinking with our analytical minds, we will blend the processes of mind with those of the heart. This will allow you to drop your mental awareness from your head down into your heart. This is the way human beings were meant to be. As you begin to succeed in doing this, it will help to alleviate much of the resistance of the nervous system and allow the mind to calm. Most Westerners are still so trapped within the dualistic mentality that they haven't yet grasped how thinking and feeling do not have to be completely separate things. Some still insist the thinking process of the mind is the highest level of intelligence, yet the refinement of relying on feeling and knowing in your heart is far more sophisticated and every bit as "intelligent." The final result is to not be stuck or confined to one way, but instead to know how to naturally and effortlessly flow between and balance these human systems, allowing whichever area is best suited to the particular situation you may be facing. In the beginning, this will most likely require conscious effort, but over time it will become as automatic as breathing.

The fully actualized human being is one who is capable of activating any of the three centers of awareness or brains that is desired in the moment. This same fully actualized being is able to naturally and instinctively activate and allow whichever "mind" is necessary and fitting for the moment. This means if you are working or in school, you allow the upper brain (in the head–upper mind) to analyze, problem solve and contemplate the correct answers to various problems and tasks. When it comes to movement-based activities, you allow the lower brain (in the abdomen, or intestines – the lower mind) to govern your movements from a sense of kinesthetic awareness and then refine that movement to be born of divine inspiration instead of conscious thought. The primary intelligence will be seated in the heart center (the middle mind), where you make all your life choices based on a sense of feeling-intelligence. Once developed, it is a simple and instantaneous process that does not require complex rituals, special membership cards or any other elitist trappings; it simply happens through your will and intent as the entire body and mind works together as a single harmonious unit. This is what true intelligence is all about; many cultures refer to it as the "heart-mind." Moving our base state of consciousness back to the heart-mind is a major component of the human evolutionary process we have already entered.

Here are a few helpful points to understand about the changes so that you may successfully navigate in the world. (Please refer to Table 1-1) The "Old Paradigm" column is meant to give you the mindset and philosophies that used to apply to our world. The "New Paradigm" column is to show you the transition in thinking and believing that we must embrace. This is not meant to be a complete list, but instead offers you enough of the contrast in order to see the difference for yourself. As you begin to awaken and observe, you will be better equipped to see the myriad of ways these changes show up in your own life.

Old World Reality	New World Reality
I can just push through it, it will be fine.	I have to know the root cause and change it.
The stuffy traditional business model is the only way.	The new idiosyncratic business model is how people relate.
My job takes hard work and is not meant to be enjoyable.	I should enjoy my job, otherwise I am not in line with my real purpose.
I will put my health in the hands of my physician and rely on medication. My health isn't my responsibility.	I will take responsibility for my health and follow a healthy lifestyle. When I need a doctor I will be involved and engaged in all decisions.
I can treat people poorly and still demand respect.	I treat others with compassion and respect for a mutually beneficial interaction.
That's just the way things are; I can't do anything about it.	If things are not serving me, I make the necessary changes.
I'll stay in the town I was born, get a job and keep it until I retire, and stay in my relationship no matter what. Then I have security.	I can allow for movement and change in my life when things no longer serve me. There is little job security left.
I do whatever I can to profit, even if I have to mistreat employees and customers or contaminate the environment. I put people at risk.	I want to serve my customers in the best way possible and treat all employees with respect. My business is sustainable and environmentally friendly.

I am not responsible for my life or actions. It's someone else's fault, I am a victim. I am entitled to have others take care of me and financially support me.	I take 100% responsibility for every aspect of my life. I am never a victim. I take action to support myself and live my own life experience.
I must have a traditional wedding and do what is expected by my family. My marriage must fit into the outdated social convention.	I have a creative, celebratory wedding. My marriage is a true partnership filled with joy and mutual respect.
I must have children no matter how I feel, because that's what's expected of me.	I should make a conscious, informed decision on whether I have children or not. It is my choice to make.
I see the world through only Duality.	I experience the world through the Trinity.

Table 1-1

Take a moment to make your own list to see what other ideas you can come up with. As you perform this simple act, your eyes will open even further to these amazing times of change. Maybe some components of your daily life just aren't effective anymore, requiring you to change your approach. As you can see, we are all headed in a positive direction, filled with growth and transformation. I feel that if the human race can band together and make the transition from a head-centered existence to a heart-centered way of living, we will have the ability to reach our full potential as a species. We could live a life that for all intents and purposes would be Heaven on Earth. Can you imagine, even for a moment, what the planet could be like if we were able to achieve such a thing? Can you imagine all people the world over living in harmony, helping each other to enjoy life, looking out for one another without petty judgments? I truly hope so, because that's the only way it can be manifested into reality.

NEW THOUGHT OR ANCIENT WISDOM?

There was a movement that came to fruition in the latter half of the 19ᵗʰ century that became known as New Thought, sometimes looked upon as a "New Age" type of movement. The school of New Thought suggests that human beings are actually divine entities or pieces of God, that God is infinite and thereby in all things, and that the highest spiritual principle is found in unconditional love. However, these concepts have been around and actively taught for thousands of years. The core of these concepts is contained within the very early religions throughout the world. Many of these teachings have been removed from the texts in order to keep them from the masses. Numerous ancient religions kept them shrouded in mystery to keep them safe, as well as to pass them on to only those they deemed worthy.

They had to be very careful to pass these treasured teachings onto only the most trusted of disciples in order to preserve and protect them. This sort of secrecy existed until just recently when this wisdom began to make its way into the light. While some may argue this endangers the teachings, I feel it is necessary at this point in time to give them back to the people, ensuring the survival of both the practices and of humanity. Not doing so is to risk the chance that they will fade into the shadows of the past and be lost forever. I further feel that right now is when people need to apply this knowledge the most. I will share some of these ideas with you from the areas of study that I am acquainted with, and from there you can look for them within your own religion or spiritual system.

Let us first look at the idea of the present moment that Eckhart Tolle has made so famous with his incredible book *The Power of Now*. For many this concept of "now" was an amazing new insight, though in reality it too has been in practice for thousands of years. It is a well-known practice within the original native religion of Japan, known as Shinto. This shaman-based religion refers to the teaching of the present moment as *tadaima* which means "only now," and *nakaima*, which literary means "the middle of now." According to my teacher, Grandmaster Masaaki Hatsumi, this concept was known and applied by the ninja or shadow warriors of ancient Japan, which he writes about in *The Essence of Budo: The Secret Teachings of the Grandmaster*. The samurai warriors of Japan were likewise very well educated in this concept of being in the moment.

Even more recently, people are figuring out that manifestation takes more than simply wishing, using positive thoughts or meditations. They have learned that it requires self-mastery of your thoughts and feelings, the things you say, and the things you do. These things are the very keys to creating your experience of reality. This concept is taught at the very core of Shingon and Tendai Mikkyo esoteric Buddhism where it is called *sanmitsu* (three secrets) and applies thought, word and action. Both systems came into Japan from China back in the 8th and 9th centuries. This idea is also brought into play through the esoteric Buddhist method of a *goma* (fire ceremony). This can have various applications, but a basic example includes sending your foremost desire off on the winds to be received by the Heavens. It has been my experience, as well as that of my students, that this is a very effective practice.

We have the idea of clearing one's mind in order to receive divine insights and guidance. This concept is very old and applies a level of "no-mind" that is typical of someone who has undergone a spiritual awakening. This idea has existed for thousands of years within Taoism where it is usually referred to as stillness; it is known in Japan through Zen and various martial arts systems as *mushin* (no mind). These high-level skills are becoming lost as the proficiency of practitioners diminishes, and as masters no longer desire to teach these things to students. They are then believed to be only myth or legend. Once you accept something as legend or myth, you cut yourself off as being able to attain it. This ancient knowledge and skill must survive and we must use it in order to survive as well.

It is once again time to open your eyes to the reality of these concepts and make the effort required to attain their knowledge and skill. These things are no longer going to be shared with a select few, they will be openly available to all who step up to reclaim them. However, only a select few may be ready to receive them and apply the necessary effort required for mastery. Now is the time; be one of the few and hopefully you will lead others to become one of the many as we reclaim our power as human beings.

EXOTERIC AND ESOTERIC

Nearly every system of religion, spirituality, martial arts and healing has teachings that are considered to be exoteric and esoteric, although the esoteric are seldom spoken of in a setting of mass instruction or guidance. This is partially to keep them secret to protect their existence and their integrity from those who would misuse them, and partially because those listening would most likely not understand what they were hearing anyway. Exoteric, according to the Merriam-Webster Dictionary, means "suitable to be imparted to the public, belonging to the outer or less initiate circle and relating to the outside, external." Esoteric, according to the same source, refers to the "designed for or understood by the specially initiated alone, requiring exhibited knowledge that is restricted to a small group, difficult to understand, of special, rare or unusual interest."

Esotericism deliberately conceals the truth from those who are not ready to receive the teachings or are not privileged to receive them. This is mistakenly viewed by some as elitism, but in truth it originates from a defense mechanism put in place long ago to keep these teachings from being eradicated by rulers and religions that did not want the common person to have this knowledge. Esoteric material is often viewed as being untrue or even outright hokum. This is generally due to the limited viewpoint of most Westerners, who tend to take everything at face value due to the linear thinking patterns prevalent in Western culture. Without the esoteric knowledge of a system, it becomes an over-simplified, diluted system with very little real value. Take the knowledge of the esoteric shared with you here and apply it to your own scriptures or texts; they will come alive with deep, rich value that enhances your life. However, also keep in mind that esotericism is, by its very nature, unable to be solely explained through the conventional means of the written word, which is analytically based. Esotericism is passed on as oral traditions and requires one to experience it in order to know its truth through feeling.

I will be offering the Expansion Mastery program by both exoteric and esoteric means in order to assist in your awakening by providing you both the inner and outer lessons. The first stages of the challenges will be considered exoteric, or an outer lesson, and will represent those exercises that can be easily observed and felt by the practitioner. I use the term exoteric to refer to ideas and concepts that are easily digestible by society and essentially easier for you to understand and practice. The main challenge with this material will be to remember to do them consistently. They will be represented by mindfulness practices.

The second type of challenge will be considered to be esoteric, or an inner lesson, and will represent those exercises which cannot be seen (without psychic vision) but must be felt and experienced. I use the term esoteric to mean an idea or concept that is known and understood by few and has multiple layers of meaning, all of which are correct. In addition, esoteric teachings are usually passed on through stories of personal experience which hold the essence of the lesson at their heart. It has always been in our nature to tell stories, and as the esoteric teachings are about living consciously and naturally, I will provide stories explaining the core essence of the exercise. These will be represented by connection practices. The esoteric challenges may be a bit more demanding for you at first. They are designed to offer a higher level, deeper sense of knowing to the topic at hand and they may be of great value to spiritually advanced readers. Together, the exoteric and esoteric practices form a complete and practical system of deep knowledge.

MANAGE YOUR THOUGHTS, WORDS AND ACTIONS: THE FUNDAMENTAL TOOLS OF CREATION FOR PHYSICAL BEINGS

The concept of sanmitsu (three secrets) that I discussed earlier is primarily found in the Japanese systems of Tendai Buddhism and

Shingon Buddhism, collectively known as Mikkyo. The three secrets they teach are thought, word and deed. If we look at this remarkable teaching through an esoteric lens, we can see that it is a key to unlocking your potential as a human being, helping you gain the ability to have an active role in creating or your own life experience. I feel it is extremely important to stress here that reading about these "secrets" is not the same as actually knowing them. It takes time and effort to develop the capability to effectively apply this concept and achieve real results in your life; mastery takes diligent practice. However, I assure you that they do work as my fiancé and I apply them consistently, along with many of my teachers and students alike.

Many people attempt to study and practice this concept, yet they cannot get it to actually manifest in their life. The problem is few can trigger the power of sanmitsu, quickly discarding it as a false teaching when nothing could be further from the truth. The secret to activation lies in developing mental, emotional, physical and spiritual discipline. Of primary importance is the catalyst of emotion that must be interjected into all three steps, along with vibrational alignment. These two components are significant for the success of manifestation.

Human beings, especially in the West, must once again develop a strong sense of discipline. We have lost our way. Ask yourself a simple question in order to determine how disciplined of a person you are at this very moment: "What practices do I have in place that I perform every single day?" By "practices," I am referring to daily physical activities. Do you practice Tai Chi, martial arts, yoga or stretching? Do you run or workout at the gym? What mental practices do you perform daily? Do you meditate, pray, read or declare positive affirmations? You can ask yourself the same thing regarding emotional practices and spiritual practices. Checking your email, Twitter account or Facebook page simple do not count. I found as a martial arts instructor that the attention span of the average adult in the early 1990's was around 45 minutes long. By 2010, I found that time had lessened to be between 15-25 minutes at best. I have also found that it is very difficult to get anyone to perform a daily activity for a full month; most do not make it through the week.

I know you are busy; believe me, I am busy too, as is everyone else. But I have also found, even when I was putting in 20-hour work-days, that I could still make time for what I needed to do. I know that you can too. I encourage you to reclaim your self-disciple, self-motivation and your ability to focus. Start small and make the practice short and easy; if you keep it enjoyable you will have a greater chance of succeeding. I have found that the toughest part is not in actually doing it, but in *remembering* to do it. Many people have not lost their ability to focus on something like this; they simply become distracted by all the necessities of the day ahead. Write yourself a reminder and place it where you will see it in order to spark your memory.

As you practice the challenges and exercises in this book, you will begin to develop a three-fold view the world. You will learn to relate to any situation with a sense of mindfulness toward Divinity, Nature and human connection. You will also begin to awaken to your place in the universe between Heaven and Earth. Expansion Mastery is about your own personal journey to become who you want to be. The challenges presented in the pages to come are not about fitting into anyone's perspective of who they think you should be; it's about being true to yourself to live an authentic, inspired and fully engaged life.

THE EXPANSION MASTERY SYSTEM CHALLENGES: A PRACTICAL PROGRAM OF COMPLETE PERSONAL EXPANSION

I define "Personal Expansion" as a transformation that goes beyond growth or change. It is a method which facilitates your personal evolution in all areas of self through the active application of ancient techniques. I have extracted the essence of these techniques and created a system to master yourself and your life that fits the new paradigm and the shift we are experiencing. Now that you better understand what is happening within you and all around you, it is easier to realize that you have to change some of your behavior patterns. You must get up and be active, taking full responsibility for yourself and your actions. You must have a good subtle energy practice in place as a way of helping you through the electric, magnetic and vibrational changes that are happening to you. You should realize that these and other exercises have the potential to help you to not only survive these trying times, but to thrive during them and long after they've passed. As you begin the process of evolving into a fully actualized being, I will offer you some "challenges" to assist you along the way. I use the term "challenges" here for a number of good reasons.

First of all, recent studies show that human beings are moving 90 percent less than they did just a couple of decades ago, so moving and performing even light exertion can be challenging for some in the beginning. Technology, while being absolutely awe-inspiring, also has people sitting far too much. The human body was designed for movement. When the body is seated for extended periods, especially in a poor posture position, the circulatory system begins to weaken, the blood becomes stagnant and blood clots can develop. You also prohibit the sacral pump from moving cerebrospinal fluid through the spinal column to the brain. Your fascia, the connective tissue that wraps around the muscles in the body, settles into place and can cause poor posture to become your normal body position. It has been recommended that you take one to two breaks per hour to get up and move around. This does not only apply to air travel; it is the same for the office or sitting on the living room sofa. This is fundamental for health and for your success in personal Expansion.

Another reason I use "challenge" is because I am personally challenging every one of you to actually *do* what I am presenting here. Reading about it is not enough; you need to actually do the practices in order to reap the benefits. I am also presenting these exercises in the form of a challenge because they take time to be internalized. This requires consistent practice and patience. Please enjoy these exercises and the challenges they present, looking upon them as a way to celebrate your life instead of something you must work at.

As there are various layers of knowing and feeling to each exercise, make sure to read the exercises as many times as needed to really allow the depth of the challenge to sink in. Make sure to feel as though you have a firm grasp of the practice and are comfortable trying it before starting. Later you will learn how to create your own versions or extensions of the exercises, customizing them to fit your own personal growth and life purpose. There is no single system that fits everyone perfectly, as we all have our own unique life lessons to learn and our own purpose to live. I have drawn methods from many systems as a way to offer you a well-rounded program of substance. This is not a compilation of basic methods collected by jumping from one system to the next every few months; it is the best of the systems which I have spent decades studying and practicing to become intimately connected to Heaven, Earth and my own heart. I continue to practice these methods with the goal of complete mastery in mind.

The people in your life are great indicators of your progress. I had family, friends and co-workers all telling me that they noticed big changes in me at various stages in my own personal Expansion. Most of the time, I could not tell that anything had happened, yet their unsolicited feedback gave me the proof and encouragement I needed to keep going.

There are many great authors, speakers and experts today offering outstanding methods for self improvement. However, the approach I am presenting for you is meant to be a fully integrated system that will help you to develop all aspects of yourself and bring them into a unified whole. I fully believe that once you can live in harmony with the complete unification of your physical, mental, emotional and spiritual selves as well as your environment, both seen and hidden, then you are living as a fully actualized human being.

Use the Expansion Mastery System in harmony with your own system of beliefs in order to activate the potential of your being. To believe there is only one true way and that all others therefore must be wrong is the epitome of a closed mind. If you are travelling along the path of Expansion and feel that a particular religious or spiritual view doesn't feel right to you anymore, you will most likely need to open your mind, summon your courage to alter the belief to whatever extent necessary and continue on your way. This process may seem frightening at first, but it actually becomes exhilarating and enjoyable. Remember that part of true mastery is being able to discover truths for yourself from within, not just believing what someone else is telling you.

CHAPTER TWO

HEAVEN

When Human Beings Interact With the Energy
Of Heaven, the Spiritual Realm Is Manifested.

We are born into the physical world from the realm of spirit, blessed to experience the wonder of both worlds. As young children we begin to explore our new environment with curiosity and delight in each new experience, while still maintaining an unbroken connection to the Universal Source. A child does not seek to understand the spiritual through external sources as adults do, for they still possess a unity with the Universal Source, not falsely viewing themselves as separate. This connection remains present until the development of the ego, which solidly grounds them in physical reality. It is at this time we begin to forget our Divine heritage and lose our effortless access to spirit. We sacrifice our relationship with the Source, seduced by our inaccurate perception of an exclusively tangible reality. The demanding voice of the ego gains volume, convincing us of our separation and drowning out the sacred whisper of our Higher Self.

Should you have any doubts that your spirit or soul exists simply because you cannot see it, I would point out that you cannot see your thoughts, but they still exist; you cannot see pain but you sure feel it, and you cannot see your actual emotions, but you definitely experience them. This invisible realm exists; it's as real as anything else in the dimension of time and space. The dimension of spirituality is important for balance in our lives.

We live our lives positioned between the two different realities of the physical world and the non-physical world. Let's begin our adventure with the non-physical or Heaven phase as the ancients have prescribed. The first steps on the path of Heaven, Earth and Being are to develop a sense of mindfulness for "Heavenly" things and to establish your connection to the many aspects of Heaven. Heaven is referring to the celestial bodies and grand energy field, as well as the divine nature of the Universal Source. I am not referring to an actual place in the sky, but a place that can be experienced while you are living. The Heaven stage of your growth is learning to know Heaven for yourself and within yourself. It is about re-establishing a real, honest connection to your Higher Self. Once you do this, you will develop the ability to navigate your spiritual path with the direct voice of the Universe to guide you.

Life is meant to be a conscious and joyous celebration, not something to suffer through in order to gain rewards in an afterlife. It is time to awaken your inner awareness to reclaim what is rightfully yours. Develop the ability to know from your own heart what serves you best, without allowing others to dictate your actions or decisions. Many people have fallen into complacency, content to hand over their engagement with life to mindlessly sit on the couch with a beer in hand, staring at the television with eyes glazed over, their body and mind rotting away. Turn off the TV and start living your life! Actively participate in the divine magnificent adventure you are here to experience!

Within the Heaven chapter your focus is to come to know yourself as a Spiritual Being, and to re-establish your direct connection to the Universal Source. It is to initiate a true relationship to your Higher Self, awakening to the magic and wonder that life offers you every single day.

The challenges I am providing here are simple, natural and enjoyable in their implementation, but astonishing in their results. As you begin to undertake the challenges, you will come to know your eternal, divine spiritual nature.

OBSERVATIONAL MIND & THE EGO

"There is no other hell than to live in the ego. And there is no other Heaven than to come out of the ego. Bliss is the absence of ego. When there is no ego, what remains is blissfulness."
— OSHO —

There are various attributes associated with Heaven as the first phase of progression. The mental state of Heaven is to be used as the observational mind. By engaging the observational mind, you separate from the random ego-driven thoughts and reactions of an undisciplined mind, observing your own mental conditions without judgment. This is necessary to realize that your ego is not the real you. Once you are able to observe your ego separately from your consciousness, you quickly come to understand that those sporadic thoughts running around in your head like hyperactive children are not your thoughts at all. The ego hides within the shadowy recesses of your mind, responsible for all the mental clutter you struggle with every day. By observing the ego as something separate from yourself, you expose it and begin to control it. Once the ego can be called out in the open, it already begins to lose its hold on you. When this happens you must be strong and stand firm in your practices because it will fight back, and the ego fights dirty.

I always inform my students that the ego is the toughest opponent you will ever face; this is where the heart of a warrior is valuable. This is not to say that overcoming the ego is difficult for everyone, as it is an individualized experience. Those who successfully subdue their ego go on to achieve great things in their lives with sincerity and humility, while those who succumb to the ego remain stuck in repetitive cycles, unable to free themselves from the chains of their own life lessons.

People controlled by their ego usually gravitate towards competition. Competitive sports in general usually cause an inflation of the ego and distract from spiritual evolution. The standpoint of "my team is better than your team" sets the stage for the ego to take control through the illusion of superiority.

The ego is the most substantial obstacle separating us from a heart-centered, fully conscious life as a balanced being of the physical and spirit. Spiritual progress is unattainable while strengthening the ego. By their very nature, these two things are opposing forces that cannot coexist. Subduing the ego is one of the initial steps required for true spiritual growth. As you progress with your spiritual Expansion, you will begin to experience the benefits of inner peace and tranquility that are not present in an ego-centered life.

The first time you achieve success with the observational mind, you may feel the strange sensation of having two thoughts in your mind at the same time, and you may even wonder how *your* thoughts can be continuing when *you* are not controlling them. These things are completely normal; just relax and keep observing. It is very important not to judge your thoughts, as judgment will snap you out of this frame of mind and ground you back into the dominance of the ego. The Universal Source does not judge, regardless of what some may preach. Abandoning self-judgment will allow you the freedom to step outside the continuous spiral of ego-driven thoughts and see things from a clearer perspective. I came across a clever t-shirt that stated it very simply: "Your ego is not your amigo."

VIBRATION & ENERGY

Through the science of quantum physics we understand that absolutely everything is made of energy. We also comprehend that energy cannot be created or destroyed. External sources can generate energy, but energy itself originates from the Universal Source. Yet so many Westerners have a problem believing in the concept of energy. Your thoughts are energy, your words are energy, your physical body is energy; everything is energy. When matter is reduced to its most basic form, there is no form;

all that exists is vibrating energy. The Earth's energy frequency vibrates at around 7.83 Hertz, and according to science and ancient mystics, the universe itself vibrates. Ancient mystics believe that the universe vibrates with the sound of "OM." Of course, you and I are vibrating, as is everything else in existence. This is why movement is so important to human beings. Moving spiritual practices such as the circle walking of Bagua and others will offer you greater results than non-moving forms. However, once you are able to combine the moving and non-moving, you have the recipe for great Expansion.

The universe is filled with energy. The so-called "empty" space is not really empty at all, but filled with the potential of limitless creation and energy. Buddhists know this concept very well, referring to it as the Void, and Taoists refer to it as Primordial Energy. Today scientists refer to it as dark matter or dark energy. In the Bible, in Genesis 1:2 and 1:3 it talks about how there was darkness and God said, "Let there be light and there was light." God and darkness existed before the light. I think this gives us something to seriously consider when understanding dark matter and the Universal Source. Energy is at the heart of everything; it composes everything in existence. Our physical form vibrates at a slower frequency than our spirit, giving it solidarity; our spirit vibrates at such a high frequency that we cannot usually perceive it with our eyes in the realm of time and space.

> *"Concerning matter, we have all been wrong. What we have called matter is energy, whose vibration has been so lowered as to be perceptible to the senses. There is no matter."*
> — **Albert Einstein** —

Here we are presented with another Universal truth; the Law of Vibration. Nearly everyone on the planet has heard of the "OM" sound used in some meditations. Not as widely known is that it is actually performed in three stages, not just as one. First you make the "Oh" sound with the mouth open. Then you transform into the "Mm" sound by lightly closing your mouth without allowing your upper and lower teeth to make contact; you should feel your lips vibrating. Then gently bring the upper and lower teeth together while you continue the "Mm" sound; you should feel the vibration in your lips, teeth and skull. This should be practiced in a smooth, fluid manner within the span of one breath.

Of course the universe is vibrating at a much greater frequency than we are capable of hearing with our human ears. When scientists slow down the frequency, the never ending hum of the "OM" vibration can be heard. The "OM" sound has been used by Tibetan religions, Hinduism and others for thousands of years as a method of *mantra* to connect to the universe. They knew that by performing this particular sound, we could vibrate our form in harmony with the formlessness of the Universe.

The "OM" is also the vocal vibration that resonates with the upper energy center in the head. Most spiritual and religious systems have some way to raise their energetic vibration, knowing this activates the Spirit and gets us closer to Universal Source. There are bells, gongs, chimes, seed syllable sounds, songs, music, shaking and words that are all designed to raise our vibration to a more Divine level. Sometimes the seed syllable "AUM" is practiced, comprised of three syllables but often taught in a four stage sequence. You begin with the open-mouthed "Ah" sound, merging into the "Oh" sound by changing the shape of your lips with the mouth still open, then into the "Mm" sound with the lips closed but the teeth not touching, and finally into the "Mm" sound with the upper and lower teeth touching. This should be practiced in one single smooth breath as it was with the "OM."

Ancient swordsmen knew the secret of vibration very well. They trained relentlessly with their swords and extended their vibration into the blade. This is one reason why the sword is considered to be the soul of the samurai. Later, when they needed to return to the high vibration attained while training, they merely had to grip the sword to reset their vibration to that which was left in the sword. This is a similar effect in returning home after a vacation. Vacations are always great, but there is nothing like sleeping in your own bed. There is a vibration within the space of your home, created by those who live there and the activities that transpire inside. If you have a comforting home environment, you will reset your vibration to that frequency upon returning to it.

Actors should be aware of this "vibrational resetting method" and have it in place to reset their vibration after every role. Anyone working in a negative environment should make sure to vibrationally realign themselves when they clock out for the day. I found it very challenging to keep a higher vibration when I was a factory worker. I eventually had no choice but to leave this type of atmosphere, allowing my own personal Expansion to unfold to the vibrational heights I knew was possible. Yet, by practicing the challenges in this book, you will be able to maintain and even elevate your vibrational level regardless of what type of environment you work in. That which you resonate with on a vibrational level, you attract into your experience. Once you vibrate with the frequency of joy and appreciation, you will attract a life that allows you to experience more joy and appreciation as your life becomes increasingly more magical.

> *"Everything is energy and that's all there is to it. Match the frequency of the reality you want and you cannot help but get that reality. It can be no other way. This is not philosophy. This is physics."*
> **— Albert Einstein —**

The work being done by Masaru Emoto and others on the effects of emotional vibration on water crystals are extremely well known, and accurate, with good reason. The interesting factor is that they aren't just using sound as a way to carry the vibration into the water, but some tests are accomplished simply by writing a word on a piece of paper or tape and placing it on the container. They find it still affects the vibrational frequency of the water, making the crystals look either distorted and misshapen or brilliantly beautiful. Our words are truly powerful, whether spoken, written or thought. Now, consider that we humans are made of 70-80% water. It's amazing to consider how our vibration is affected by the things people say to us and what we say to others. It is also affected by the things we read or write, as well as the things we think or even what others near us think. That's because all of these forms of means of communication and mental processes have emotional attachments associated to them.

If the molecules of water can be changed in color and shape to be jagged and dirty looking by saying a word like "hate," imagine what happens inside of you. Likewise, if we say something positive like "joy" and the molecules change into a beautiful and elegant crystal snowflake, then again you see what may happen inside of you. The question is, what do you want your cells to resemble? Once I fully grasped the implications of these water studies I made some changes in my life. I became very mindful of the quality of things I surrounded myself with; no more TV, no more newspapers, no more senseless internet browsing. It made a tremendous difference in the way I felt and acted. Then I limited how often I was around people who had negative attitudes and the places I went that felt low in vibration, such as fast food restaurants. These things impact who you are in a substantial way. I am a believer of "every little bit helps."

Here are some fun bonus exercises. Find a place that you feel safe and secure that is relatively quiet and either sit or stand. Say aloud the word "joy," feeling the vibration inside you during and after. If you need to repeat it a few times to pick up on the vibration that's fine. Once you can do it with the word "joy", now try it with the word "sorrow." Listen to the tonal quality of your voice and notice any changes. Feel its effects on your body as it resonates within your physical form. You may notice that there is an amazing difference between the feelings of these two words. Play with others if you like; test the process and get tuned into your own body. Make sure you end this type of exercise with a positive word in order to keep your vibration resonating higher.

Now try to apply the same level of sensitivity to music; how does it make you feel? Really listen to the music and lyrics to understand how they affect your vibration. Once you get used to living in a higher vibrational state, you will desire to only listen to that which raises your vibration. Don't be alarmed if you notice your tastes starting to change! Now, do the same thing with television programs and movies. Watch a "feel good" movie or a comedy and place your awareness on your vibration; feel what emotions it invokes in you. Then watch a drama or horror movie and see what happens to your vibration. Many are addicted to the lower vibrational realms of the physical world and often are too numb to realize something better exists.

Now you are able to discern for yourself and decide on your entertainment choices accordingly. Try to feel the vibration of gossiping, getting angry, putting someone down, receiving a gift, telling someone you love them, or whatever else you feel the need to test out. Just make sure to try the exercises more with positive things; you will appreciate it in the long run.

THE LAW OF ATTRACTION: APPLIED THOUGHT, WORD, EMOTION AND ACTION

By now everyone has heard of the Law of Attraction, the idea that like attracts like. Whether you ascribe to it or not is up to you, but I can state with certainty that you wouldn't be reading this book if it didn't work. The Law of Attraction is the application of sanmitsu, or the three secrets of thought, word and action. The secret to activating sanmitsu can be found in your emotional and vibrational alignment.

Thoughts and emotions are the first secret of the equation. You have to become mindful of your own thoughts, learn to control negative, self-defeating mental behavior and gain control of your ego. The second part of this area is to become aware of your emotions. Most people are controlled by their emotions, as they react to life events instead of responding to them. Through developing a sense of mindfulness for your emotions, you can learn to transform your negative emotions into positive ones. You must learn to use your emotions as a guide, as in listening to your heart. The third part is to make the situation a win-win-win, as in the outcome being beneficial to all involved. You then need to *allow* the Universe to decide what and when is right for your greater good. These are three important key factors for success. Meditation and the ability to still your mind are very crucial to developing the mental discipline needed for success in this area. As I applied my sense of mindfulness to my thoughts and emotions, I stopped mindlessly reacting and began to respond mindfully instead. This took a substantial amount of effort on my part, but it became easier with diligence. I practiced this in meditation as well in actual circumstances. When I caught myself engaged in a thought or emotional response that I knew was reactionary, I would stop and decide upon a better, more positive response. Over time I stopped reacting and began to respond when and how I consciously chose.

Words and writing are the second secret of the Law of Attraction. You must develop a sense of mindfulness for the words you use, making a conscious choice to keep them positive. Vision boards and affirmations are very helpful tools for success. Writing down your desires and goals adds substantial power to your words. My fiancé and I wrote affirmations on a vision board of some pretty lofty goals, and we observed every one of them come into reality in the exact order and way we had written them on the board. This is another area where I applied a sense of mindfulness to circumstances in order to choose my words more carefully and constructively. When I was speaking and became aware that I had used a word or phrase that could have been stated more positively, I would stop what I was saying and take a moment to rephrase it. I had my fiancé help me with this. If I was speaking and she caught something I missed, she would point out that there was a better way to state it. Likewise if I caught it, I would point out that I wanted to find a higher vibrational phrase and then state it in that manner. Over time, this trained me to hold awareness for the things I said and wrote.

Here is another exercise to try that I find very helpful. Take a piece of paper and write down a goal or something you would like to experience. Write it in present tense as though you are already experiencing it. This trains your mind to know that it is possible. Then either put the piece of paper up where it's always visible or fold it up and keep it with you. Wait and see how long it takes before you start to hear about things similar to what you wrote; maybe some strange "coincidence" that you hear on TV, overhear someone in the supermarket or even see it on a billboard. These are all signs that it is coming into your reality, and it will not be long for that particular situation to unfold within your experience.

Action and doing is the third secret to the equation. You must take action in some way to facilitate the manifestation process. Some people believe all you have to do is think it, say it or meditate on it and it will happen. I don't think so. Remember that all energy vibrates and everything is made of energy. We are living in a time-space physical reality that requires physical motion of anything in existence; as such, you need to move toward your goal or desire in some way. How much or how little action you take may depend on what you are attempting to manifest into your life experience. Causing and reveling in drama is not going to help you succeed; getting rid of the drama is part of the key to successful action.

FIND A SYSTEM THAT FITS

If you already have a spiritual system in place for yourself, even if it's undefined, that's great. You need to have something as a base, something that offers you direction, knowledge and skill. If you do not have a formal system of some kind, then I encourage you to investigate a number of systems and come to know which ones resonate with you. There are an incredible amount of systems out there that offer tremendous value to the spiritual seeker, and you do not have to limit yourself to just one. There is no one single right way. I would caution you in regards to religion, as many of them are not interested in spiritual development, but there are some individuals who are honestly trying to help you find what you seek. Investigate thoroughly and make sure that whatever you choose feels right to you in your heart.

It is pertinent to choose with your heart instead of your head, because the head (ego) will direct you to select the most convenient option, or the one that won't challenge you to expand. Be true to yourself and live your authentic path regardless of what friends or family members are doing. I recommend tracing the system to its roots to discover its original teachings and from where it originated. This will also allow you to make sure the system is intact, or at least has the knowledge and methods that interest you. For instance, Chan Buddhism was taken to Japan and became Zen, but Zen Buddhism does not contain all of the original components of Chan Buddhism. Zen received the mental and spiritual methods required for enlightenment, but it did not inherit the formal energetic body practices that Chan has in order to keep its practitioners healthy. This is important because many systems of spirituality and religion build mental and spiritual growth, yet neglect the physical body. Make sure the system offers balance in mental/emotional, physical/energetic, and spiritual practices. If the system requires blind faith, it is most likely not very functional and will not provide balanced teachings.

NON-RESISTANCE: GOING WITH THE FLOW

In order to experience your Divine nature and inherent power as a human being, you must learn to become non-resistant. You must learn to move with the natural flow of the universal energy, to ride the waves of the Divine, instead of swimming against the current. Non-resistance refers to remaining relaxed and avoiding tension or worry. It suggests the ability to let go of negative emotions that lower your vibration and prevent you from expanding. It also refers to letting go of the ego, allowing yourself to be guided by your Higher Self. There is an amazing current of energy to life, flowing all around you in the empty space. When you develop the ability to sense it, feel it and connect to it, you receive Divine guidance in all you do. In the beginning you will question it, but over time you will be able to feel when you are connected and moving with its gentle supervision. This is the goal of non-resistance.

Begin practicing this by noticing your level of flexibility and observe your willingness to be open to new experiences. Reluctance to embrace new ideas may be caused by resistance in your nervous system or mind. Your mind closes out of a response to fear, which is associated with the ego. You must come from a place of non-resistance without allowing others to manipulate your life. It is not about always doing what you are told by others; rather, it's about being comfortable in relinquishing a controlling grip on life. You must learn to feel what is best for you, which requires supreme relaxation. Non-resistance teaches us to let go of trying so hard, living from a place of ego, and helps us to regain our harmony with the Universe.

If I am at a restaurant and my order comes out a little different than expected, I don't get upset. I open my mind to the experience and think about the chance to expand by trying it. In this case, it may not be an accident, but a divine reward. If it turns out I don't enjoy it, then I address the situation with compassion, not anger. This approach will help you keep your vibration up. When you begin to glimpse life through the eyes of the Divine, you will notice that events initially seeming like misfortunes are often there to help you in some way. You may lack the vantage point to see it in the beginning, but it will become more noticeable over time. Once you surrender your resistant behaviors, life gets far easier and presents you with many unexpected gifts. I suppose some might call it luck, but it's actually just the natural flow of the universal energy without your resistance.

SYNCHRONICITY

Synchronicity is a term coined by the famous Swiss psychologist, Carl Jung. It generally refers to two or more events that are coincidently happening together, although seemingly unrelated. In my experience, synchronicity is a way to know that you are on the right track, walking with a strong personal connection to the Universe. Synchronicity happens when you are acting in the best interest of your higher purpose; Divine influences converge with your actions in the same moment.

This occurrence helps you to know that you are tuned in and living a mindful, spiritually centered life. Notice seemingly coincidental occurrences, but know them for what they truly are – forms of communication and manifestation from your Higher Self and the Universal Source. I often refer to synchronistic events as "sign posts" along the path, letting you know that you are on track. I encourage you to learn to feel when these types of events occur. In some cases, I can feel them building to a point where they are about to manifest into the physical reality before they do.

Some frequent occurrences of synchronicity I experience include looking at the clock when it is 11:11 or 3:33. There are other numeral consistencies of course, but these are the ones that present themselves to me most often. They are considered to be power numbers, especially the 11:11. This occurrence is a bridge between the physical and non-physical worlds. If you notice that you are randomly checking a clock only to have it reflect 11:11, quite often it is a good sign that you are awakening to the union of your physical self and your spiritual Self through this awareness. As I was sitting at my desk typing this very paragraph, I decided to check my cell-phone to see if my fiancé had sent me a text message as she always does on her lunch break. The time on the phone was 11:11 AM. I see that as a reflection that I am doing what I am meant to be doing at this very moment. As you travel on the spiritual path and generate lasting progress, you will notice this happening time and again.

Another phenomenon I experience is that I will be typing something on the computer and will hear someone say a word or phrase as I am typing it. It may be someone walking by outdoors, a movie line or song lyric, but they will say what I am typing at the exact moment I am typing it. When I am really open and the words are flowing freely through my fingertips, this may happen four to six times! Sometimes my fiancé and I will be enjoying a quiet evening of reading, and as she begins to read aloud something particularly interesting, the word she says will be the exact word I just finished reading in my own book.

Living an integrated life of harmony with Heaven, Earth and Being, synchronistic acts will become commonplace. They are continuously provided for you; the more sensitive and mindful you become, the more you will cultivate an awareness of them. Eventually you will see how nearly everything that shows up in your life has deeper meaning—such as an unexpected event that puts you in the right place and time to meet someone important. I have even experienced a synchronistic event within another synchronistic event! It's like synchronicity's version of double vision.

KNOW YOUR COSMIC ESSENCE

Connecting with the sun, moon and stars is important to the human species. These celestial bodies impact the conditions of Earth to support and sustain life. Likewise, they affect our own personal human condition. Those who have evolved and shifted into the new center of being usually have some sort of practice in place that consciously connects them to these galactic bodies. While this sort of connection can be effectively made through meditation, it is my advice to follow a more active approach at this point in time, such as Qigong or circle walking. Both of these practices are feminine in nature and will be supported by the changing energy field of Earth.

Connecting to the Big Dipper or North Star may be more advanced techniques, but by simply going outdoors and finding them in the night sky you are getting a certain degree of benefit. Here is a simple exercise to help get you started. Find somewhere quiet and safe to stand. You can sit if it's easier for you in the beginning so you do not get dizzy and fall. It is best to be outdoors when you do this, but it can also be performed indoors if that is not a viable option. Begin to settle into your position, getting balanced and comfortable. You are going to focus deep into the Heavens, so it's important to get a solid connection to the Earth prior to performing it. The further out into the cosmos or Heavens you go, the better connected to the Earth you want to be. Close your eyes and begin breathing deeply to form a bridge to your Inner Self. Begin to focus on your lower dantien, the lower abdominal center. A good way to do this is to visualize (and later feel) a sphere of glowing energy in your lower abdomen. Allow your awareness to travel down through your legs into the Earth. Don't stop at the bottom of your feet; keep going right into the ground at least three times the length of your physical body.

Visualize your awareness going through the soil and deeper through the layers of Earth. If possible, extend your mind to the planet's core. See its iron center rotating, generating the magnetic field that rises up to the Earth's surface. Feel this electromagnetic connection in your body. Allow all your negative emotions to drain down from your body into the ground where the planet can recycle them. Allow the planet to turn your negative baggage into positive energy, which it then sends back to you as healing energy. Once you feel grounded you are ready to proceed.

Have a certain star or constellation in mind to connect with before beginning, or you can simply get started and notice through your sense of awareness which comes to you. In the beginning, I recommend starting with one in mind so you can have a clear direction. Later on, just go with the flow and see what presents itself in your field of awareness. Know where it is located in the sky and try to align the top of your head with it. In Hindu yoga systems it is the crown chakra, in Taoist practice it is the *bai hui* point.

For this example, let's focus on the seven stars that comprise the Big Dipper, also known as Ursa Major, the Seven Great Sages or the Big Bear, depending on which part of the world you are in. According to the Universal Tao System founded by Grandmaster Mantak Chia, the Big Dipper emanates an infrared light that is believed to effect or even control the four seasons on Earth; it is also a major source of Heavenly energy for all living things. The Big Dipper relates to the third eye center of the human energy body. Begin visualizing (or even just think about, if you have a hard time visualizing) all seven stars shining down to a single point of focus to your third eye at the center of your forehead. Feel the coolness of the starlight as you are bathed inside and out with the intense infrared light. Feel yourself vibrating at a higher frequency as you glow brighter and brighter on the outside of your body, allowing the light to run down your central channel. It begins at the upper center of awareness, cascading down to the middle and then the lower center of awareness. Envision all three centers glowing brighter and brighter. Take a moment to bathe in this beautiful, powerful light.

Notice it activating the cells of your body, as they are made of the same elements as the stars themselves. Many scientists believe that everything is made of stardust, including you and I. This is your cosmic essence. Feel the interaction between your cells and the Big Dipper as it rejuvenates your entire being. Condense all the glowing light into a small sphere in your lower abdominal center in order to store it there.

Take a moment to appreciate the Big Dipper. Focus your awareness back upon your breathing and reconnect to your sense of being grounded in the Earth. Then become aware of your body once again while you gently open your eyes. You should feel a sense of inner peace and rejuvenation at the same time. This provides us with a greater reason to intimately connect with the stars, instead of only looking up at them occasionally when we are outdoors in the evening.

The level of consciousness associated with the Heaven concept is the "Cosmic Consciousness," that sense of consciousness that is Divine and expansive, correlated with our Spiritual Self. In the beginning of your Expansion, you will come to know your relationship with the sky, the cosmos, your own Spirit and the Universal Source. Once you succeed in separating yourself from the ego through the use of the observational mind, you will become open to the incredible, ecstatic nature of life. You will begin to feel as though you are living in Heaven on Earth.

THE HUMAN CENTER OF HEAVEN

The human center of Heaven is referring to one of the three centers of awareness within the body, the upper center. This is located in the very center of your head. Some may know this as the upper dantien. The upper center has intelligence, yet it is also our connection to our Higher Self and to the realms of the Divine. This is a great place to begin, as so many people are currently stuck in their head. It is also a fitting place to begin our inner observation, as we will be separating the observational mind from the ego, a sensation that most people naturally perceive as happening in their head. It is here we address the observational mind and mindfulness.

This upper center of awareness is sometimes referred to as the Jade Palace. The upper center is not designed for "energy" storage, as this leads to over-heating of the brain and should be avoided. The lower center of awareness awakened in the Earth segment is the body's bio-battery and this is where energy storage and distribution takes place. The brain and its parts, including the pineal gland, the pituitary gland, the thalamus and hypothalamus are all associated with this upper center and will be addressed directly or indirectly within this set of challenges. All three points of the third eye will be focused upon; between the physical eyes at the eye bridge, in the center of the forehead and in the center of the upper forehead at the hairline. The three points of the crown will also be affected, located in the very center of the top of the head, and both slightly in front of and behind this center point. The function of activating these areas is to balance the brain and give it relief from over-stimulation. This will allow the brain to "cool" and help resist damage from blocked and excess energy in the head. We will work with the physical and non-physical upper center, connecting to our Higher Self and the Universal Source.

THE HEAVEN CHALLENGES

The primary function of the Heaven exercises, called *challenges* in this program, is to assist you in re-connecting to Heaven and the depths of what Heaven represents. It is the Divine nature of your Higher Self, the cosmos and the Universal Source. If followed with dedication, the challenges will help you stimulate your subtle energy system, while strengthening and balancing the upper center of awareness.

The challenges are designed to begin with things that seem rather easy or even simple. Don't be fooled by this, as it takes discipline in order to perform them consistently. It is a paradoxical truth that the simplest has the most depth and is therefore often the most difficult. The Heaven phase of the program will occasionally allude to the areas of Earth and Being, as all three are all intertwined and cannot be completely isolated from each other. There is no need to feel overwhelmed by the detail; it is provided for you so you may have solid instruction, but in the beginning it is most important to relax and focus on one step at a time.

The exoteric exercises are where you practice to relax mind and body to achieve inner awareness. The exercises in the esoteric set are designed to create a greater sense of mindfulness and help attune you to the subtle forces of the universe. The exoteric and esoteric come together to release the resistance that lies deep inside you. Mental relaxation is extremely important if you understand that your reality is created by the power of your mind. Once you become aware of the resistance within yourself, you can begin to liberate yourself from it.

HEAVEN CHALLENGES
EXOTERIC CHALLENGES: AWARENESS

CHALLENGE ONE
Night Sky Observation/Standing Silver Strand Posture

THE IDEA
The first part of the Heaven set is to simply make the time every night to go outside and look up at the stars. As you do this, observe the thoughts that run through your mind; do not attempt to affect them, but simply observe without judgment. This will help you begin reclaiming control of how you use your time, as well as to develop the willpower to participate in practices that facilitate change in your life. It will also help you to slow down, relax and begin to calm your mind, decompressing from the stresses of the day. This is extremely valuable due to all the information and mental over-stimulation in our society. If the weather does not permit you to see the stars, then simply look upward and realize the stars are still there shining brightly behind the clouds whether they are visible or not.

You most likely remember doing this when you were a child, lying on the grass with your arms folded behind your head, gazing upward at the twinkling light, entranced at the sheer expansiveness and mysteries of space. This is a natural compulsion, as children maintain a connection to Universal Source; unfortunately, due to the changes in our culture, even they are trading in this experience for evenings spent inside playing video games. Embrace that feeling of wonder again and encourage your children to do the same; sit in a love seat on your front porch or relax on the deck. Better yet, grab a blanket to spread on the grass or lay on the grass itself, whatever feels the best to you at the time.

The next step is to get familiar with the sky again. Human beings have disconnected from the Universe and from Nature; we must reestablish this connection in order to become complete. Reacquaint yourself with the constellations and learn to read the weather by looking at the moon. Most people don't know the location of their internal organs anymore, let alone where the constellations are. We need to get back to Nature and once again know our vehicle (body) and environment (sky and planet).

Remember the old saying, "Red sky at night, sailor's delight. Red sky at morning, sailor take warning." My grandpa was a Navy cook during World War II and a hunting/fishing guide in Upper Michigan. He recited this saying many times; he knew how to read the weather, the time and more by looking to the sky. We have lost touch with Nature; most are unaware that a red sky in the evening indicates good weather for the following day, while a red sky in the morning indicates moisture is in the air with the likelihood of an approaching storm system. How about rings around the moon? This is usually an indication that bad weather is on its way. These methods are far more accurate than the evening weather report you most likely watch.

The second part of this exercise addresses the issue of your body posture and your connection to Heaven and Earth, with the emphasis primarily placed upon the connection to Heaven. This is the Silver Stand. This posture and exercise is very powerful, having the ability to raise your vibration. The first thing I will address with the posture is that it's about standing up; we sit far too much and it is terrible for us. Simply standing has tremendous health benefits over sitting, and standing with correct posture multiplies the benefits. If, for serious medical reasons you cannot stand, then it is okay to sit. Our spines are abused by the compression of walking on concrete and by the poor posture we apply by sitting for extended periods of time.

Sometimes this exercise is called the "Golden Cord of Kuan Yin," incorporating the Goddess of Compassion gently tugging on the cord as you are gently suspended by it. I prefer the "Silver Strand" version described below, as I connect better to the cosmic nature of the practice with the color silver. I do not resist when the strand occasionally appears to me as gold, as you must learn to trust that you are being given what you need. This is why we don't force our desires upon these types of practices; we accept what is given to us with appreciation. The silver stand is a single cord of "energetic consciousness" that is extended upward through the Central Channel of the body. This strand is initially felt as a type of cord, but as you advance, you should feel this become a spiral-strand. This stand then extends upward into the Heavens where it is directed to align with and connect to the North Star.

THE FORMAL PRACTICE

- Set aside 5-10 minutes each night before you go to bed or whenever is convenient for you. You can go longer if you like.
- Turn off the TV, videogames and computer and walk outdoors onto your deck or into your yard. Barefoot in the grass or sand is best; try to get off the pavement. Take a moment and look up, taking in all the Heavenly beauty.
- Remember to keep quiet during this time. If someone else comes outdoors with you, wait to talk about the experience until it is finished. Talking about it as its happening actives your mind, and thinking and talking are just the opposite of staying quiet and stilling your mind of thoughts.
- Once you've quieted down and have connected to the Heavens, what do you discern from it? Does it look or feel like rain is coming? Does it look clear and bright? Try to get an idea about the weather for the evening and tomorrow from what you see.
- Take a moment at some point to learn the placement of some basic constellations, and then find them when you are outdoors. Is there one or more that you feel a personal connection with? Maybe there is just one that sticks in your mind or that you personally use to guide you. Take a moment to locate it in the night sky and enjoy its presence and beauty.
- Begin the formal exercise by finding a flat, even place to stand, where where you feel safe and relaxed. Outdoors and barefoot is greatly preferred, but if you cannot do that, then anywhere

is fine. Stand with your feet parallel to one another and a few inches apart. Make sure that the entire bottoms of your feet are in contact with the ground, your knees are unlocked and your hips are aligned over your ankles.

- Relax your abdomen and your lower back while making sure your back is straight. Allow your chest to relax and slightly sink inward with your back slightly rounded. Do not stick your chest out as done in the military; this causes the energy to leave your center, activates the ego and weakens the mind to be more susceptible to the influence of others.

- Make absolutely sure that your neck is straight. You can do this by gently pushing your chin back and lowering the head slightly. Practice this in front of a mirror a few times to get the hang of it.

- Let your shoulders hang naturally, keeping your arms by your sides with your fingertips pointed down toward the ground.

- Take a moment and inhale as you gently rock forward to the balls of your feet (but don't leave the ground with your heels) and then gently rock back onto your heels as you exhale. This should be subtle. Be careful not to lose your balance. Feel yourself rooting to the ground, establishing a deep connection to the core of the Earth. Do this three to nine times.

- Come to settle in the center of your feet and breathe normally. Tuck your tailbone slightly by sliding the sacrum forward. This will help ground you and steady your balance. Relax your muscles and then relax your spine and your breath. Close your eyes half way; closing them completely can cause you to lose your balance while standing.

- Try to envision or feel (whichever sensory function is more natural to you) as though your spine is a cord from the tip of your tailbone to the top of your head, and feel what it would be like if Universal Source were to gently tug on that cord from the Heavens in order to slightly separate each vertebra.

Then, focus your awareness on the center core of your body, the Central Channel (*Chong Mai*), going from the top of your head to your perineum. It's all right to imagine it at first, but you need to make the effort to feel this Central Channel instead of imagining it.

- Rolling your eyes upward, look to the North Star. Feel the Silver Strand as it radiates down from the star and into you through the crown of your head. Envision the Central Channel glowing with bright silver light and that light expanding out through your entire body, while it remains concentrated in the center. Feel your heart beat with the same pulsating rhythm of the star. If the light should glow gold or white, just allow it; don't force it to be any other color. Feel it gently stretching you upright. You may feel each vertebra separate from the others. Feel yourself get slightly taller. You may even hear a mild crack or pop from the skeletal system; this is natural, as things are going back where they belong.
- Now slowly raise your arms upward so that your arms are stretched above your head with all fingertips pointing toward the sky. Hold this and breathe for three or nine breathes, or as long as you can without creating tension in the body.
- Slowly lower your arms back down to your sides and rest in a natural standing position.
- Now just relax and see how good it feels!

PERSONAL EXPERIENCE

When I was young, my grandpa would explain the sky, how to read the weather, and how to know the directions by way of the stars (as well as the sun). He used short rhymes as a way to help me remember and I am sure that's how they were passed on to him. The practice of preserving esoteric knowledge in the forms of poem and song is extremely common and effective. I always enjoyed lying in the yard looking up at the stars, knowing that they held so many mysteries and experiencing awe at the pure vastness of space. I still enjoy taking a leisurely evening walk with my fiancé and looking up at the moon and stars. I find this to be very therapeutic on many different levels; it helps me to connect with Nature and to the stars and planets, as well as feel a deep sense of peace.

I learned the silver strand for the first time nearly two decades ago, and it keeps appearing within my martial and meditative practices for good reason. This has very profound mental and emotional effects. Like many people, my head tended to lean forward and I needed this exercise to help correct that. As my posture improved, so did the amount of energy I had to make it through day-to-day demands. My spiritual connection also improved substantially. I was more open and able to receive direct communication with my Higher Self as well as through Divine inspiration. My footwork became much lighter, not only in martial arts training but in daily movement. Remember that these exercises are not something you do and then put on a shelf; they need to be an intimate part of who you are.

CHALLENGE TWO
Stretch The Body & Jump For Joy

THE IDEA
Perform a simple stretching routine. Stretching and relaxation go hand in hand. In the Bujinkan organization there is a wonderful set of ancient stretching exercises called *Ryutai Undo* (Dragon Body Exercises). The Bujinkan teachings contain a two-volume manual referred to as the *Tenchijin Ryaku no Maki* (Book of Heaven, Earth and Man). The Ryutai Undo offers great flexibility in the lower body and spine, stimulates the natural healing processes, and provides gentle organ massage if combined with proper breath work. They promote freedom of movement, control and awareness of one's body. They also utilize the use of the Dragon Body, which refers to specific waist movement that ultimately turns in three directions at once. This also refers to having a supple, flexible spine. If you practice a solid routine for stretching that you enjoy it, then by all means use that one. Do

not bounce or force the body into a stretch; instead you want to relax deeper into it. This helps the body, mind and nervous system to relax and adapt to the movement properly. The way I have always taught is that stretching should feel good, like the first stretch of the morning when you awaken. If it hurts you will stop doing it after a very short time anyway, making no progress. Consistency is again a key factor; you should be stretching every day, either in the morning, in the evening, or both.

The next area of this exercise is designed to get you a little more active. Perform this one only if you are physically healthy enough to do so and you have performed the light stretching routine as stated above. There will be some alternative versions offered here and on my website if you are unable to do the usual set. Find a place you enjoy; somewhere outdoors in the grass is preferred, but avoid concrete if possible. Wear a comfortable pair of shoes for support or go barefoot if you like. Now begin to jump! Make sure to land softly, bending your knees every time you land; never jump and land with your knees straight. This has some surprising effects; it allows you to disengage the direct connection with the Earth for a brief moment and helps decompress the joints. Try to develop a sense of self-awareness while you are momentarily suspended in the air at the apex of the jump. The jumping motion will also massage your internal organs, and loosen the muscle tissue to prevent atrophy. Jumping around will also help to keep your ankle, knee and hips joints strong and supple.

There are many ancient shamanic healing methods that center on movement, dance, shaking and jumping. You may find that you even start feeling younger by doing this. Have you observed how children jump up and down when they are excited? It really is okay to act like a child once in a while! According to Taoist thought, the legs grow old before the person grows old; in other words, the legs are often the first area to show the effects of aging or even indicate premature aging. As people age they resist bending over, the care of their feet suffers and they begin disconnecting from their bodies from the ground up. Jumping and stretching will help keep your legs healthy and young.

THE FORMAL PRACTICE

- Stand up straight and take a few deep breaths to relax your mind and body. Raise your hands up in front of you like a boxer covering during a fight. Make sure to keep your hands in loose fists and your elbows down. Get a firm footing and then bend your knees slightly, making sure it's comfortable and there is no strain on your knees.

- Slowly begin to turn from the waist, first to the right and then to the left, gently stretching your body from side to side. Do this three times to each side and then return to center and relax.

- Slowly allow your body to bend forward and go down as far as possible without straining. Exhale as you bend and relax. Just hang there for a moment; do not bounce or force yourself to go lower, let it happen naturally and easily. This may take longer to accomplish, but it's much healthier for your system and you lessen the possibility of injury. Inhale as you straighten yourself back up and repeat the first stretch a couple times on each side.

- Find a secure and comfortable place to sit to prepare for the Dragon Body Exercises. Once seated, begin by performing a few simple exercises to increase strength, virility, and balance the nervous system. Massage the bottoms of your feet with your thumbs or knuckles. Hold your leg slightly above the ankle and rotate the foot to cause the ankle to rotate, nine times in each direction. Then take either the big toe or first three toes and gently rotate them as well. Perform all of these on the left and right.

- Begin the first stretch of the Dragon Body Exercises. Sit with your knees out to the sides and the bottoms of your feet together on your centerline. If your feet cannot touch, then get them as close as you can without stressing your body. Gently push your knees down toward the floor. While this exercise is sometimes called the *butterfly*, avoid the bouncing motion of the legs that is sometimes taught, as this is actually detrimental to the progress of the stretch and increases the risk of injury. Just relax into it and breathe deeply. Once you can do this, exhale and lean forward as though you are going to touch your chest to the floor or your feet. Do not focus on leaning forward from the head, lean forward from the chest. Go easy and relax into it. Inhale deeply as you raise your body to the upright position.

- Begin the second stretch of the Dragon Body Exercises. Remain seated and extend your legs out straight in front of you. Twist your body from the waist, slowly and gently from side to side. Inhale when you turn to face center and exhale when you turn to either side. You should notice that as you twist to one side, one leg extends and the other retracts. Afterward, they should be the same length. Do this three times to each side. Then stretch forward as though you are trying to touch your toes and try to place your face on your legs. Hold the position and relax and breathe.

- Begin the third stretch of the Dragon Body Exercises. Put your legs out to the sides like you are doing a "splits" stretch as far as they can comfortably go and massage the inside of your thighs to loosen the muscles and connective tissue. You can place your hands behind your hips and gently push yourself forward, allowing your hips to roll slightly. This should offer you an even greater stretch. Lean toward each leg and gently reach for your toes. Exhale each time you lean forward and inhale when you raise your body. Think of lowering your chest to your thigh, not your head. Come to center and reach out to the front; if this is easy for you, then strive to put your chest on the floor. Exhale as you go down. Hold the position, relax and breathe.

- Begin the fourth and final stretch of the Dragon Body Exercises. This stretch is yoga-like in nature; these exercises have even been lovingly referred to as "ninja-yoga." Slowly and gently go into a kneeling position, sitting back on your heels if you can. If that's comfortable, then you are going to gently and slowly reach your hands around to rest your palms on the soles of your feet. Align the Pericardium 8 points (as in acupuncture) in the center of the palms with the Kidney 1 points in the center of the balls of the feet. From here you are going to exhale and push your abdomen forward on an upward 45-degree angle as far as possible without straining. Allow your head and neck to relax so you are looking above or behind you, depending on your level of flexibility. Hold, relax and breathe deeply. Inhale as you return to the kneeling position. If that movement is comfortable, return to the neutral kneeling position and bring your feet out beside the hips just enough to allow your buttocks to go to the floor. If this is too difficult at first, then just practice the first part for awhile until it becomes easier. Exhale and lower your body back to the floor. In the beginning it is helpful to keep your hands on the ground where they can offer you support. Later, you will rely more on the abdominal muscles to lower you to the ground. Lie back and breathe deeply; stretch you arms above your head if it's comfortable to do so. Bring your elbows to your sides and use your forearms and hands to rise back up. Always raise your body straight up; avoid rolling to the side to get up, as this can cause injuries to your joints, spine and muscles. When you are comfortable, use your abdominal muscles to lift you back up into the kneeling position. The exercise is not complete when you are on the floor, it is complete once you have come back up into a kneeling position.

- If done correctly, this will not put stress on the knees as is commonly believed. It will stretch the quadriceps muscles of the thighs and the lower back. Your lower back may be curved at first; the idea is to get it flat on the ground. The same goes for the space behind your neck. You want to be completely flat. Caution should be taken to keep your lower back safe and healthy. Do not force it. When you get to the maximum position your body allows, you should relax and breathe.

- Use these stretches as a base, but please feel free to add to them with any other type of stretching that you personally enjoy.

- Stand up slowly. Freely move around and shake your body a little bit; the Taoists call this "shaking the tree." Now, gently, start to jump. The idea here is to break contact with the ground. Just loosen up, relax, breathe and leap around, or just up and down, whatever you feel. Jump three to nine times. This is a great way to awaken your nervous system and loosen up your body. It also helps to counteract some of the affects of gravity on our bodies.

PERSONAL EXPERIENCE

I have personally been doing this stretching set for over 23 years and it is outstanding. I have had a great amount of abuse on my body between martial arts training, factory work and other wear and tear. I am now 47-years-old and still get up every morning pain free. My knees do not ache, and I have never experienced any back problems. I feel that the healing effects of this exercise have been exceptionally beneficial for me. The stretches also help to relax your mind and nervous system, which is extremely valuable in itself. The jumping is a natural healing movement and one that allows you to deal with excess energy in the body so it doesn't end up becoming a form of blockage later on. I still do both, usually daily. I have also learned how to stimulate certain pressure points during the stretching to enhance the performance of the exercise and promote the well-being of my body. I do offer these refinements in my personal training courses (available on my website) and people love learning how to increase their performance with basic exercises.

CHALLENGE THREE
Sacred Art, Respect For All Divine Representations

THE IDEA

Develop a sense of respect and appreciation for sacred art. This may seem simple at first; however, I am going to challenge you with this one. I would like you to begin by spending some time looking at sacred art that appeals to you through your chosen belief system. If you don't have a particular belief system, then look around for spiritually-based art that you find attractive or that resonates with you at this time. If you have the financial means to purchase some of these pieces of art and have them in your home, I recommend it. Place them where you will prominently see them to gain their full benefit. Surrounding yourself with sacred imagery is a powerful way to energize your living environment and yourself.

Then start to look into scared art of those systems other than your own, holding a respectful mind and open heart. As you look into these things and expand your mind, you will learn how most systems are very similar; they just have different cultural methods of expression. Sitting in judgment of another will lower your vibration and thereby separate you from the Universal Source. I have artwork from sacred temples in China, Japan, Egypt and some of these are one-of-a-kind, original pieces. However, you can get things out of books and magazines, or go to online sources for great posters or prints that you can easily afford. There are certain forms of art that do not seem to resonate with me, but I acknowledge, appreciate, and respect them and what they symbolize.

THE FORMAL PRACTICE

- Go to your local bookseller or an art museum and look at some books and artistic pieces that contain sacred art of various religions and spiritual systems. In the beginning, look at the systems that you resonate with the most. There is usually a lot of symbolism hidden within the artwork by the artist. Examine them closely and find what types of sacred art you enjoy the most. Get to know this part of yourself.

- Acquire some sacred art to have displayed in your home. It can be in whatever price range you can comfortably afford. There should be symbols of your spiritual or religious system in your living environment in order to serve as a constant reminder to yourself to be mindful of your Divine nature. Decide on the particular art with a sense of mindfulness and purpose, making sure you can feel it.

- Now let's stretch your mind and beliefs. Observe spiritual or religious-based art that does not come from your foundation of spiritual practice. You do not have to purchase it or display it in your home, but you should spend some time studying it. Develop a level of appreciation and understanding for different works of sacred art. You may find it helps you to add depth to the understanding of the art you enjoy.
- Expand yourself to be capable of offering unconditional acceptance and appreciation for sacred art of all systems. This form of unconditional respect is much more in alignment with the Divine than to think that your way is the only "right" way. This does not mean that you have to practice the system of another, or change what you are practicing; it is a matter of personal Expansion.

PERSONAL EXPERIENCE

I have always enjoyed most types of art. There are still forms of art that I am really attracted to over others. Those preferences are not based on someone or some religious system telling me what to prefer and what not to look at; it is based on my own personal feeling. Do your best to curb your judgments of things you don't understand or resonate with at the time. Judgments are not a divine form of thought, and being judgmental will lower your personal vibration. Understand that the form of art that you do not enjoy is found to be completely inspiring to someone else. I learned to be accepting of others beliefs and their right to live as they wish; that can begin with allowing and accepting the sacred art of others.

When we moved into our apartment in California we decorated it with a heightened sense of mindfulness. We display the works of art that inspire us the most. Shortly after moving in, we invited the young couple next door over for introductions and a glass of wine. Upon entering our new home, one of the first things the young man stated was, "This is a very spiritual place; it feels so good in here." He went on to ask how I received my spiritual teachings, to which I explained my experiences to him. He looked at me with tears welling in his eyes and professed with a quivering voice that he wanted to be more spiritual and exclaimed how much he needed that in his life. I felt his heart open just a bit. I also had the opportunity to visit the home of musician Jah Levi. He was allowing Grandmaster Mantak Chia to teach there, and this stunning home was filled with fantastic spiritual art.

CHALLENGE FOUR
Breathing Method (Abdomen Breathing & Breath Bridge)

THE IDEA

Breathing exercises are an important part of this level. The Latin word for "breath" or "to breathe" is *spiritus* and clearly shows us the connection between the breath and the spirit. You will use the breath as a bridge into your Self so you may establish communication with your Divine nature and ultimately the Divine Universal Source. People walk through life holding their breath; this instantly separates them from the Divine. People hold their breath out of fear, pain, physical exertion and mental tension. Breathing methods are taught to pregnant women to assist in childbirth; they are taught during physical workouts. Martial artists coordinate the breath with their movement; they use the breath to develop power, unwind their nervous system, and control their emotions. Professional singers and speakers are proficient in breathing methods, as are healers, who use breathing to energize themselves and help guide the internal energy through their body to the patient. While abdominal breathing will serve to awaken your sense of awareness in the lower center, it is the breath itself that is the primary focus here.

Begin by maintaining mindfulness for times when you catch yourself holding your breath. Holding the breath is unnatural, as it breaks the rhythm of the breathing process. Work to correct this with a natural even flow in your breathing. After you correct the act of holding your breath, you can begin to perform a healthy and natural method of breathing, known as *abdominal breathing*. Have you ever watched a baby sleeping? You should notice the baby's belly is rising and falling, not the chest. That's how we should be breathing too. Breathing from the upper chest is considered to be shallow, labored breathing and only utilizes the top two thirds of lung capacity. This is forced breathing due to the ego's need to control everything, including the breathing process. Heath care professionals are taught that a child will breathe from their abdomen up until age seven or eight; at that time, the breathe will switch and come from the chest, and it is considered an abnormal assessment finding if this is not the case. This is the age when we begin to lose our connection to the Universal Source and fall under the spell of the ego. This process begins at around age three, when a child begins to identify themselves as a separate entity upon viewing their reflection in a mirror. Prior to that time, they will not associate the image in a mirror with themselves, as they have no concept of "I." Reestablishing abdominal breathing is one more step you can take to reconnect with the Divine as you did as a child.

You are going to learn how to drop your breathing down into your abdomen and breathe in a more relaxed, healthy manner. Test yourself—does your chest or abdomen move as you inhale and exhale? If you are breathing from your abdomen and your breath cycle is only a few breathes per minute, you are doing it right. Once you have this down really well, begin to slow down the number of breaths you take in a one-minute period of time. Most people gulp and choke air like a fish that jumped out of the aquarium, lying on the floor. Slow down, relax and just breathe deep slow breaths. When you can get your breaths down to three to nine per minute you are doing great. This can help with blood pressure problems, relieve stress and anxiety, increase internal energy flow and facilitate longevity.

The second part of this exercise is dealing with the breath in a way that will help you to gain fast and easy access to your Inner Self. In the beginning it usually takes around 21 breaths to turn inward; the breathing process acts as a bridge from your outer realm reality to your inner realm reality. Over time and with practice you will get so you can do this in less than one full breath. The point is to eventually be able to drop right in to immediate, deep meditation. Many spiritual and religious systems like to tell you that you need a bunch of special ceremonies, rituals and instruments while doing this for such meditations. While some people may find these things helpful, they more often serve as expensive distractions that help the ego more than anything. Basically, all you need is your breath, nothing else.

THE FORMAL PRACTICE

- **Abdominal Breathing:** First find somewhere comfortable to sit. It doesn't have to be a quiet sacred space, but that may help in the beginning. Sitting on a couch, chair, the floor or a *zafu* (cushion) is all fine—wherever you are comfortable and capable of sitting upright with a straight back. You can sit with your back against a wall if you need the stability.

- Gently place your left hand on your abdomen and your right hand on your chest. If this feels completely unnatural, then change your hands, but you want the extra sensory feedback in the beginning.

- Take three deep breaths and feel what part of you is moving under your hands. Is it your chest or your abdomen? Unless you have been trained to breath otherwise, chances are your chest is moving and the breath cycles are short.

- Take three to nine slow, easy breaths and focus on purposefully moving your abdomen out when you inhale and then drawing it in slightly when you exhale. Inhale and the abdomen moves out. Exhale and the abdomen moves in. When you are breathing in this fashion you provide a gentle massage to the internal organs. This is a bit exaggerated, but it will help in the beginning because it is so dynamic. Once you can do this and feel your abdomen moving without much difficulty, you can place both hands on your abdomen to feel it rise and fall with your breath. You may even find this very comforting.

- Now, sit, relax and breathe without thinking about it. When you can get your breaths down to three to nine per minute, you're doing great.

- **Breathing As A Bridge:** First find somewhere comfortable and quiet to sit. Make sure your back is straight and loosen any tight fitting clothes, such as belts, tight jeans or any other binding articles of clothing.

- Place your eyes in one of two positions: either completely closed or closed half-way. Then just relax and take three deep breaths, making sure that they are coming from your abdomen, not your chest.

- Focus on your five physical senses, one at a time: your sight, hearing, taste, smell, and touch. Really place your focus on each one individually to make it hyper-sensitive, sensing all that is around you, and then let it go, removing your awareness of it.

- Simply focus on the breath, think quietly to yourself, "I am breathing in (as you breathe in), I am breathing out (as you breathe out)." Then let this thought fade and remain aware of the breathing process, in and out. If this is too difficult to begin with, you can simply count your breaths for awhile. An inhalation and exhalation equals one full breath.

- Try to get to where you can count 21 breaths without your mind becoming distracted, which is completely natural in the beginning. Try not to become frustrated or angry, as this will considerably impede any further progress.

- Once you can count to 21 without being distracted, it's time to leave that method and return to observing the breath. Counting is a lower level version of the exercise, as it distracts the mind enough to keep you from effectively turning inward; the counting will ground you in the outer external realm by using the analytical mind, which is exactly what we need to turn off for meditation.

- Relax, breath slowly and deeply and observe your breaths come in and go out, naturally and easily.

- To cross the "bridge" back to the physical world, you are going to just reverse the process. Allow your focus to go to each of the five senses and reconnect to each of them again. Slowly begin to move your body to reconnect to your physical form and slowly open your eyes, evading any direct light. Take a moment to relax before standing up.

- **Note:** The Taoist Qigong version of this last step is to rub your hands together vigorously 36 times and then rub them slowly over your face before you open your eyes. I recommend trying both versions and see which one feels better for you.

PERSONAL EXPERIENCE

I have been working on these breathing methods for over three decades. Not only do they keep me health, but they have also served to keep me feeling young and filled with energy. According to my heart surgeon, they are also responsible for helping save my life and make the healing process so much quicker, easier and less painful. Ever since my near death experience from the inability to breathe by choking on the jawbreaker, I was fascinated with breathing techniques. I studied everything I could find from every system I could find. When I had access to a teacher, I would learn the breathing methods directly from them. When I didn't, I would learn them from books or audio instruction. Back in 1998, I had an article entitled *Learning To Breathe* published in *The Source*, a newsletter that was put out through a martial arts instructor in Santa Cruz, California. Upon attending a training camp in the Santa Cruz Mountains, I had a young man approach me and ask if I was the author. He told me the article affected him deeply; he had been experiencing difficulties in his life that left him with thoughts of suicide. After reading my article he learned to value every breath he gets to take as a special gift, and he kept it taped to the wall above his bed to read every morning and night.

These breathing methods helped ease my recovery after the heart surgery. The surgeon told me I scared the hell out of him while I was recovering, because he saw no movement in my chest after he started my heart. He said he began to panic and was getting ready to take additional drastic measures when the anesthesiologist noticed that my stomach was raising and lowering. He breathed a sigh of relief, and later told me he'd never seen that in the thousands of heart surgeries he has performed. He inquired how I'd attained that as my normal breathing pattern. The way is the same one I shared with you above. You can understand how it helped with recovery, right? Think about it: my chest had just been cracked open and then wired shut. Imagine how it feels to have your broken sternum moving with every breath you take. Ouch! I didn't need to use morphine or even Tylenol to help with pain, because my chest was able to lay still while my stomach did all the moving, giving the sternum time to heal. I have to admit that I never planned on that application, but I was happy I had it.

Remember to finish performing all of the Exoteric Exercises above before beginning the Esoteric Exercises. If you have not gotten control of yourself enough to accomplish the exoteric studies then you will not have the foundation necessary to succeed in the esoteric studies. If you are able to perform every exercise in the exoteric section and you are gaining the benefits they offer, then step right up and get started in the amazing world of the subtle and unseen.

ESOTERIC CHALLENGES: MINDFULNESS

CHALLENGE ONE
Unification Of Thought, Word & Action
(The Three Secrets)

THE IDEA

Let us approach the topic and study of sanmitsu (the three secrets), which are also in reality the core teachings of the Law of Attraction or tools of creation. We discussed this topic earlier and now it's time to put it into action. Coordinating one's thoughts, words and actions is a challenging process that requires great mental discipline. I have trained with various instructors of the esoteric systems of *Mikkyo*, gathered numerous out-of-print texts on these systems and have applied it to my life for many years. We will be drawing from its roots as well as modern interpretations in order to grasp it more completely. The esoteric exercises can be challenging, as by their very nature they defy verbal, written or any other conventional analytical explanation. Much of Mikkyo is passed on by telling stories that help generate certain feeling-based responses and special exercises to transmit knowledge and personal experience. It is a balance of knowledge and experience that you are striving for. I will do my best in these sections to share what cannot be shared so that you may come to know what cannot be known.

The first phase of creating harmony within our thoughts, words and actions is to establish the ability to observe our thought processes and make the necessary changes to support a higher vibration. Meditation is a wonderful and enjoyable way to learn to observe your thought, at least in the beginning. I do recommend being able to apply the "catch and correct" method which I developed as I was performing daily activities. While engaged in various tasks, I would hold a sense of mindfulness for my thoughts. Whenever I noticed that my thoughts were leaning toward the negative, I would gently stop myself and correct that thought to one that was far more positive. I reached a level where as soon as a thought began to enter my head that was not as positive as I wanted, I could smile and halt the thought. I would investigate what sparked the thought or consider if it was simply ego-driven, and then change it to a positive thought or a blessing. I began to observe that many of the thoughts were random negativity sparked by the ego. As I made the effort to catch and correct my thoughts, I engaged the ego and began to subdue it through this process.

The next phase of unifying one's thoughts, words and actions is to address the words that escape our mouths. Grandmaster Masaaki Hatsumi shares that his teacher, Toshitsugu Takamatsu, warned of speaking too much, as it can deplete ones Spirit. This is another lesson taught within various religions and spiritual systems, as well as authentic martial arts. I have become very careful with my words and thoughts. I am blessed enough to have both martial and spiritual teachers guide me in this area, pointing out that if I say negative things, the vibration will cause harm within myself. Many martial artists may know that if you strike someone and do not know what to do with your body and mind at that point, the vibration of your intentions and the energy of the physical strike bounces back into your body, traveling back to your heart to cause you harm as well. This is another reason why you hear the great masters say that to kill another is to kill a little of yourself.

The third phase is addressing your actions. Are the things you do right and just? Look around you to see all the drama, manipulation, control and games that people play with others. This is truly heartbreaking and evidence of how far from our spiritual nature we have gotten as human beings. How much hugging, touching, kissing, back-patting, high-fiving and hand-holding do you see go on? When you coordinate a sense of mindfulness between your thoughts, your words and your actions, you will begin to unlock the extraordinary power of a human being.

THE FORMAL PRACTICE

- First, we will address the *Thought* area of this practice. Apply the observational mind you learned earlier to become mindful of the thoughts you think. It is important not to judge them; simply watch them flow in and out of your mind unimpeded. It has been said that we have over 60,000 thoughts go through our mind on any given day; don't worry about catching them all, just do this when you are able. Once you can observe your thoughts, the next step is to quiet the mind in order to lessen the number of thoughts you have. Remember that stilling the mind is also working to overcome the ego. Just as the silence between the notes of the Japanese *shakuhachi* flute offers a beauty even more potent than the music, so too is the value of the silence between your thoughts. This is called "supreme tranquility," and it is within that silence that you can hear Universal Source. Once you are able to limit how many thoughts you have, your next step is to correct any of the thoughts considered as negative or unproductive chatter. This is addressed in all spiritual and religious systems, which the Buddhists refer to in the *Eightfold Path* as "right thought." It is also called skillful thought or pure thought. The goal at this point is to have some amount of control over your thoughts so you are thinking positive things more often, and thinking far fewer unnecessary thoughts than that of the average human being. This also makes the mind still and quiet, giving you inner peace and the ability to hear the whispers of the Divine.

- Second, we will focus on the *Word* area of the practice. Begin paying attention to how much you talk, the topics of conversation, the value of your words and the effects that your words have on others. Then begin to choose your conversations more carefully, evading the desire to always jump in to appease the ego's need to be the center of attention. Instead, increase your listening skills and just hear what others have to say. Then begin to notice (again applying the observational mind) the effects your words have on the ones to whom you are speaking. Did a certain word or the tone of your voice hurt them when that was not your intention? Begin to recognize these reactions that others have to your words so that you may come to fully understand the power words have. Words are very potent, as they carry the vibrations of thoughts out into the reality of time and space. When you choose to speak, do so mindfully to inspire and help others, and cause good feelings (vibrations) within yourself at the same time. This is seen in religious and spiritual wisdom as, "If you can't say something good, don't say anything at all." Buddhists referring to the Eightfold Path would call this right speech, pure speech, or skillful speech. How often do you tell those close to you that you love them? If you are like most people, it is not nearly often enough. Take every opportunity to share your love with them and pay attention to how it feels inside yourself to do so. Love is one of the most powerful and positive words we have in any language.

- Third, we will focus on the *Action* area of the practice. Begin to monitor your actions; are they the actions of a spiritually enlightened person? Are you helping others freely? Observe your actions as well as non-actions—are you doing nothing when you should be springing into action to make a difference or assist someone who needs your support? When it comes to actions—they seem easier to address than dealing with one's mind. However, actions do speak louder than words. This means your actions are exceptionally powerful. This is because your actions are the physical manifestation of your words. Start to *do* things that are more positive, spiritually-based actions. Wave and acknowledge someone you have never met, say "good morning" to your neighbor and offer them a smile. Start to do more positive, constructive things with your time. Sitting on the couch or in your favorite chair watching TV certainly does not count as skillful action. Exercise, prayer or meditation, getting out into Nature and respecting where you live are all right action. Rescuing animals and protecting the environment are right actions. There is a great and simple way to practice righteous action with the old saying, "Commit a random act of kindness daily." Why limit yourself to one? When the actions you take in the world reflect the higher vibrations of your thoughts and words, you will harmonize these three secrets and greatly empower yourself as the co-creator of your life experience.

PERSONAL EXPERIENCE

When I began to go through this area of study in Mikkyo, I went over two weeks without speaking – not intentionally, it was just the side-effect of the exercise the way I experienced it. Old co-workers still talk about the time they thought I was mad at everyone because I stopped talking to them, and others thought I was too conceited to speak to them. Funny how we perceive things isn't it? Therein lies a lesson in perception, but that's another exercise entirely. The mastery of your thoughts, words and actions is crucial in your personal evolution. To accomplish this gave me far more control (mastery) over myself, over my own thought processes, my own dialog and my actions. It only took a second for me to realize that I needed to take 100 percent responsibility for every single thing I thought, said and did. Wow, was that ever an eye opener! This was mind-blowing and a little frightening at the same time.

I reached a point through this exercise where I really didn't like much about myself, which is a normal part of the process. I realized how many of my thoughts, words and actions were less than positive, and I started to wonder how I had become a person that was so far from who I wanted to be. What an amazing thing to realize! It was then I became very motivated to change who I was, and I set out to become someone better, thereby growing, changing and evolving in the process. I learned how my thoughts become actual things in my field of reality, and how my words, which are vibratory in Nature, effected not only those they were aimed at, but also myself and others who may have heard them. That's a lot of power! I also learned how important my actions were, when to take action and when to take non-action, which was an essential lesson for me personally.

CHALLENGE TWO
Prayer & Blessing

THE IDEA

Prayer and blessing are not only used by major religions; every system offers its own unique form of Divine communication through praying. Most systems use some type of *mudra* (hand posture) that involves bringing the hands and fingers together in various combinations. Even martial arts movement incorporates this technique. This symbolizes the coming together of your physical self and the Universe. One should be mindful when bringing the hands together, as physically touching the palms will ground you in your physical self, but does offer mental strength. Bringing the hands together without touching the palms and only lightly touching the fingertips allows you to stay more clearly connected, both energetically and to the Divine. Be mindful of your intentions and goals, and place your hands in the correct position for the desired task. Apply prayer far more often than just when you are in trouble or want to ask for something. Begin to use prayer in whatever way works for you; you can even create your own unique method, as prayer is about your personal connection to Universal Source and does not concern anyone else. Prayer is about you attuning your vibration to a higher, more Divine level and communicating with the Universal Source. Prayer is your time to ask and receive guidance, offer your gratitude, and feel the Divine nature inside yourself.

Blessings are a beautiful thing; they help you apply a higher sense of mindfulness. When you damn something, the negative vibration is put out into reality; but if you bless it that positive energy is offered and also resonates within you. Blessing something or someone shows that you are in a state of non-resistance and going with the flow of a situation. I recommend daily prayer; it doesn't have to be long, just a moment or two. I also recommend blessing someone or something as often as you can; you can do it out loud if you choose, but it isn't required. When I first started this practice, it was through clenched teeth that I would bless the driver who would cut me off just to cause some drama and satisfy their own ego. But it was a start. It's much more effective to simply experience the situation and bless that individual and their superb driving skills. In this way you are sending forth the energy to help them to develop better driving skills. This will prevent you from sinking to their level; you do not allow the actions of someone else to lower your vibration and match that of the one they are displaying.

THE FORMAL PRACTICE

- **Prayer.** Begin by instituting some form of prayer into your daily or weekly routine. I recommend that it be a daily practice, but start small and work your way up if you need to do so. Your prayers should be directed as a form of communication, not for what you want or to enter into a bargaining agreement. It's an opportunity to connect with your Higher Self and to the Universal Source; it should be viewed as a very honest connection. Make sure that you place your hands together lightly or just apart for the best results. Do not squeeze the palms together, as it grounds you in your physical form; you are trying to make contact with the Divine energies, so align the center of your palms but do not physically touch them together. You can lightly touch your fingertips if you wish. Hold your hands in front of your heart during the process; this is a type of portal that you need to use to generate the connection.

- **Blessing.** Begin this part of the exercise by having a willingness to bless others. Offer a blessing to someone in a way that would connect with them positively. In other words, if you run into someone who tells you they are going through a program to stop drinking, instead of judging them, stay neutral to the situation and then bless them either out loud or silently. Your blessing may be as simple as saying to yourself, "Bless them for making such an attempt to change their life for the better, and bless their ability to overcome their addiction." The important thing is to feel it come from your heart; this makes all the difference. Remember that judging another is a weakness of your mind. The enlightened person knows the addiction is part of a life lesson that is a necessary part of their experience.

PERSONAL EXPERIENCE

I utilize the act of prayer every morning as part of my normal routine. I place my hands close together in front of my heart without allowing them to touch, I focus on opening my heart and I connect to the divine. I offer a prayer, putting my intention out into the Universe for the health and well-being of others in my life, such as family and friends. I also include someone who I feel may have wronged me in some way. I direct my thoughts and feelings to those of appreciation and send those vibrations out into the universe. There are times when I feel so filled with love, joy and appreciation as I perform my morning prayers that my chest aches and my eyes well with tears. I can recall praying when something bad was happening in the past and feeling as though there was no connection, that I was not being heard. I hadn't learned how to pray by making an actual connection to the Divine at that time. Now, I feel completely "plugged-in" and able to connect intimately with the Universal Source; it's an entirely different experience.

As I practiced the art of blessing others, I realized the positive energy I sent out helped the other person no matter what the circumstances. It helped me by raising my vibration as well, even in perceived negative situations, avoiding anger and keeping my thoughts and emotions level and calm. I began to feel much more conscious of myself and less controlled by other people, circumstances and my own untrained reactions. I can recall being around ten years old and hearing my grandma bless things that went wrong. If she were in the kitchen and dropped a slice of cinnamon-sugar toast on the floor, she would not yell "Dammit!" She would exclaim "Oh, God bless it!" I did not understand it at the time, and it seemed mildly humorous that she chose not to say a bad word – but in a way that kept the situation light. I found it pretty cool and not always easy to do; I give my grandma a great deal of credit for this ability. Not to mention introducing my brother and I to the tastiness of cinnamon-sugar toast.

CHALLENGE THREE
Qigong Energy Exercise Number One

THE IDEA
This exercise is designed to help activate all three dantien centers of awareness in your body. An important factor in practicing Qigong is to find a pleasant area where you won't be interrupted and can maintain a positive state of mind. Wait about one hour after eating, or drinking anything cold to perform the practice. With Qigong and meditation, the idea is not to isolate yourself in a little soundproof world, but to learn to practice these things with noises around you without agitation or disruption. It is helpful to have a safe, positive place that feels good to you. I like to practice in places I particularly enjoy, such as by the pond in my local park or on my deck in the morning with a fresh ocean breeze in the air.

Western science acknowledges that there are three brains in the human body. The first brain is obviously in your head, the second brain is in your lower abdomen – specifically in your small intestine – and the third brain is in your heart. There are actually neural cells in your small intestine and in your heart. The heart is considered to be an intelligent organ and has the capacity to remember. All three "brains" are connected by the vagus nerve, which facilitates communication between them. You can focus on these three centers by keeping an open mind, an open heart and by listening to your gut instincts. Please see the work performed by the Heartmath Institute for more specifics on this, as they have excellent technical literature on the subject.

The exact location of the three centers varies slightly from person to person, as everyone is built differently. The basic locations and areas of focus will be included in the exercises in order to assist you. You want to become sensitive enough to feel the blood flowing in your body; once you can do this, you should be sensitive enough to feel the energy as well. It is usually a very subtle feeling in the beginning, but will become much more noticeable once you've been practicing for awhile. You can derive the energy from the sun, moon, stars, constellations, or even planets and solar systems. It is believed that you draw vital life force in from the air you breathe and the food you eat as well. The three energy centers are not the same as the physical organs in the body. They are small hollow areas in the middle of the brain in the head, in the center of the intestines and in the center of the chest, not the heart organ itself.

If you studied any spiritual art as presented in a previous exercise, did you notice the halo effect around the heads of Jesus, Buddha and other enlightened figures? That is symbolic of the upper center being activated and shining brightly. Notice how many paintings and statues of religious icons there are with the heart shining out in all directions. This symbolizes the middle center being activated. Then we see the extended lower abdomen in the very old paintings of Jesus, Mary, Buddha and so many others, which symbolize the lower center being "full" and powerful. These centers of a human being have been an important part of our religious and spiritual belief systems, and they are symbolized in its various imagery.

The lower center of awareness is of primary focus in many martial arts. Lessons tell us to move from this area of the lower center, referred to in the Japanese martial arts as the *hara*. The middle center is focused on in religious and spiritual teachings when opening the heart to develop compassion and healing. The upper center is focused on in spiritual teachings to connect to our Higher Self or the Divine Source.

THE FORMAL PRACTICE

- Find a safe, quiet and comfortable place to sit. You can stand if you really want to, but be careful as it becomes easy to lose your balance during such practices.
- Close your eyes or leave them half-way open. Begin by taking three deep breaths, settling into your position and relaxing mentally and physically.
- Now apply the Breath-Bridge technique to go inside yourself.
- Allow your focus to be directed to your abdomen, right around the naval. The lower center, or dantien, is located around two inches below the naval and about an inch and a half behind it in the very center of your body. Over time you will develop the ability to feel these areas within yourself.
- See this area in your mind and visualize it glowing bright gold. If another color appears, that's fine, use it. Offer no resistance to the process; assume that the process itself is Divine and probably knows what it needs better than your ego.
- Envision energy from the Earth's center rising up through the ground, through your perineum (located between your genitals and anus) and up into the lower center. See it glowing bright gold, shimmering and getting more intense with every breath. See it pulsing and growing as you breathe, shining outward all around you.

- Begin to condense the golden light into a sphere as you continue to breathe. Take a moment to feel your connection to the Earth. You feel centered and calm, yet alive and alert. Maintain this glowing sphere as you move on in the exercise.

- Move your awareness through your body to your head—to the forehead area and then into the middle of your head where the upper center is located.

- See this area in your mind and visualize it glowing bright gold. If another color appears, that's fine. Offer no resistance to the process.

- Now, see the light of the sun, moon and stars coming down into your crown (top of your head) into your upper center, glowing bright gold, shimmering and getting more intense with every breath. See it pulsing and growing as you breathe and shining outward all around you.

- Begin to condense the golden light into a sphere as you continue to breathe. Take a moment to feel your connection to the Heavens, to your Higher Self and to Universal Source. Maintain this glowing sphere as you move on in the exercise.

- Allow your focus to be directed to your heart center, right around the center of your chest.

- See this area in your mind and visualize it glowing bright gold. If another color appears, that's fine use it. Offer no resistance to the process.

- Now, see the golden energy spheres of the upper center and lower center coming to mix the energy of Heaven and Earth in the middle center. The middle center of the heart is glowing bright gold, shimmering and getting more intense with every breath. See it pulsing and growing as you breathe and shining outward, enveloping you and radiating in all directions.

- Take a moment to feel your connection to the heart center and to all other living things. Feel a sense of unconditional compassion and oneness. Experience the nurturing energy of the Earth and the healing energy of Heaven as they converge in your heart.

- Begin to condense the golden light into a sphere as you continue to breathe. Take a moment to feel your connection to the heart center, love for yourself and for all humanity.

- Now, simply relax your mind and feel the inside of your body. Expand your awareness to your entire body. See the energy from all three golden spheres glowing and pulsing inside you. Place your attention on the sphere in the upper center and guide it softly down to merge with the sphere in your heart center; then allow that combined sphere to softly sink down to merge with the sphere in the lower center. The three become one – see the brightness and feel the power. Condense it to the size of a large marble and store it here in the lower energy center.

- Slowly relax and breathe to reverse the Bridge process and return to an external state of awareness. Very slowly begin to connect to your five senses and then gently start to move. Slowly and cautiously open your eyes. Sit for a moment before getting up.

- **BONUS:** Want to turbo burst your performance with this exercise? When you finish the visualization portion of the exercise, rise into a standing position. Stand with your feet a few inches apart and the toes pointed forward. The knees are relaxed and slightly bent. The spine is straight, but the sacrum is slightly tucked forward (or under you depending how you view it). Align your head with your spine. Now, bring your hands together in front of your body near your torso. Clasp them very loosely without the palms making actual contact with one another. Keep them on your centerline. Your hands can be at a height that is between your heart level and throat level, whichever is most comfortable. Now slowly and gently extend your arms, stopping when you feel the point where tension begins to occur. It will most likely happen quicker than you thought. Hold it there for three to nine breaths, depending on your comfort zone. Relax the positioning and move your body around to shake it out. This really helps connect all three centers of awareness in the body.

PERSONAL EXPERIENCE

I have been studying movement through the methods of the inner and outer worlds for decades. After teaching thousands of students over the past thirty years, I have found that many who cannot feel energy are limited due to either not believing in it or simply being too young in their inner sensory evolution to notice it. It took some very serious and dedicated study to learn to relax my mind and nervous system enough to become sensitive of my inner body. Some of the sensations that initially arise from opening these centers and clearing energy blockages may be slightly uncomfortable; try your best to work through it. It has been my experience that activating these three energy centers is not a subtle occurrence. If they do not pass shortly, then simply stop for a bit and allow the energy to calm down. I like to practice Qigong in any location that I find to be beautiful or powerful, from the Great Wall of China, to sacred mountains, to my own home.

CHALLENGE FOUR
Qigong Energy Exercise Number Two

THE IDEA

This set of Qigong movements is meant to bring the forces of Heaven and Earth together and harmonize them within you. I get a sensation of "bringing Heaven to Earth" as I perform this set. This version will include some internal alchemy, so it may be different from other versions of it you may have seen or learned in the past. This version of the exercise was taught to me by Qigong Master Michael Winn, and is used to assist in opening the microcosmic and macrocosmic orbits; both are very important practices for handling the energy field changes that are affecting human beings.

The goal of this exercise is to open the energetic pathways of your body to allow the forces of Heaven and Earth to flow through you and interact with your own energy. Bringing Heaven to Earth is more than merely a mental visualization or desire; it describes what will be happening on an energetic level. This is another great way to begin experiencing Heaven on Earth.

THE FORMAL PRACTICE

- Begin standing in a natural position, feet shoulder width apart, hands by your sides, and back straight. Take a few deep breaths and relax. Make sure you are in good spirits and excited to perform this practice.

- Bring the hands in front of the lower abdominal center (below the bellybutton) with the palms facing your body. This directs energy back toward you.

- As you inhale, raise the hands slowly as if they were floating up on their own. The hands rise up to a position as though you were hugging a ball. The fingertips point towards each other and slightly down, while the palms should be facing the heart. Keep the shoulders relaxed and down; raising the shoulders too much can drain your body of internal energy and activates the ego. As the hands come up you are raising the Earth's energy through your body.

- The hands continue their movement all the way up over the head to the base of the skull where it meets the spine. Avoid locking the elbows when the arms straighten as the hands pass over the head. Hold your hands about an inch from the head with your fingertips pointing towards each other and aligned with the Gallbladder 20 points at the base of the skull. The palms face the skull. Arch your back slightly. Internally, the energy is being drawn up the spine through the use of the hands.

- Take the energy and bring it over the head and back down the front as you bring the hands over your head and down your face. Cross the hands as they come over the head so that the centers of the palms are aligned, and allow the elbows to come together. As the hands come down, you are bringing Heaven's energy down and through you.
- Bend over slightly forward to tuck both your chin and tailbone as the hands come down over the face, and then straighten up back into an upright posture as the hands continue down the front of the body, keeping the palms in line the entire time. Allow the elbows to life to keep the shoulders relaxed as you straighten the body, releasing the energy down the center of your body. Allow the hands to continue travelling to come to rest at the lower center. Let the Heavenly energy continue to go down through the legs into the Earth.
- Repeat the movement three to nine times. To give a simplified overview, raise the hands over the head and behind the back of the head while straightening the body to stand erect. Slightly arch the body, then bring the hands over the head as you draw the elbows in and curve the spine, tucking the neck and tailbone slightly. Stand upright as you allow the hands to travel back down to the lower center. Repeat.
- Now simply relax and observe the feeling in your body and your place in the universe in between Heaven and Earth.

PERSONAL EXPERIENCE

When I learned this exercise years ago, it really helped me to connect to and feel the forces of Heaven and Earth as they flowed through my body. I was able to achieve a much greater sense of awareness and feeling for both forces through this simple process. This really helps the process of connecting to Heaven and Earth and then expanding into a state of Being. The most powerful aspect of this for me was in feeling the nurturing energy of the Earth interact with my own and the wonderfully warm and comforting sensation that resulted. Likewise, to have the Divine energy of Heaven intermingle with my own energy was exhilarating, and I experienced the phenomenon of a vastly expanded sense of consciousness and well-being. This created the feeling of internal balance that brought a sense of peace.

CHALLENGE FIVE
The Tibetan Mind Seal

THE IDEA
Forming the hand posture of the Tibetan Mind Seal is a very easy and effective way to help balance and steady the mind. I have personally used this *mudra* (hand posture) with a few students to assist them with sleeping difficulties and other instances where the brain forgets to turn off and rest. I have also had effective results applying this as a *flying needles* technique where it is utilized on someone at a great distance. Sometimes the brain can become stuck in "survival mode" where the right and left hemispheres of the brain simply continue to tag team each other, never allowing both halves the opportunity to rest and rejuvenate. This simple finger weaving technique that I learned from Sifu Matsuo can help you greatly with a variety of issues with the mind. It is easier to make and maintain positive changes in yourself when you have reset your brain to accept and hold those changes. This serves well for balancing the upper center of awareness and the brain itself.

While a mudra or "hand posture" may seem unusual to you at first, you are actually performing them unknowingly on a regular basis. The *okay* hand sign is a mudra, as is the *thumbs up* signal, and bringing the hands lightly together for prayer is one of the oldest hand postures. All of these hand postures include focused mental intent, feeling and a particular vibration. The body postures of yoga and the martial arts are simply full-body representations of hand postures. If you look at ancient works of art, you will notice that the hands are usually in some form of posture within nearly every religious and spiritual system.

THE FORMAL PRACTICE

- The Tibetan Mind Seal can be performed by taking each hand and bringing them together with both palms facing upward.
- Then cross your little fingers and bring both thumbs over to gently press on the tips of the little fingers you just crossed. The feeling is that you are holding and slightly stretching the little fingers in place with your thumbs.
- Allow the ring fingers to come together and stick straight up.
- The middle fingers will come together and cross in a similar fashion to that of the little fingers.
- Now, lightly hook the middle fingers with the index fingers. Once again the feeling is that of holding and slightly stretching the middle fingers in place with the index fingers.
- Finally, bend both wrists slightly so that your ring fingers point straight up and your hands are basically in front of your heart.
- Place the focus of your eyes on the tips of the extended ring fingers. Hold this position for nine to twenty-seven breaths, and then slowly unweave the hands.

PERSONAL EXPERIENCE

This exercise has helped me during times when my brain would just not shut down and allow me to sleep. In times of great stress your mind can slip into the flight or fight of survival mode; the hemispheres of the brain bounce back and forth instead of turning off and allowing for proper rest functions to take place. This hand posture can help for various misfiring of the brain, such as those I experienced after open-heart surgery. I've used this on students with insomnia and those with trouble focusing. I saw significant to drastic improvements in every case. This can be used by yourself or along with a healer who either does it for you or has you perform the hand posture while they work on your crown and third eye areas.

In one case, I had a student who professed that he could not sleep more than an hour at a time without waking up and having difficulty going back to sleep. He said he had not slept for more than two hours at a time since he was a child. I had him perform the Tibetan Mind Seal and explained the process, after which he left for a weekend in Chicago. When he returned, he told me he had slept for 13 hours that night without waking up a single time and was now resting regularly. He appeared to be more rested and his energy was much more even. This exercise works primarily with the upper energy center of the crown and third eye centers and balances the hemispheres of the brain. With this area cleared and balanced, you will have improved physical and mental health.

CHAPTER THREE

EARTH

When Human Beings Interact With the Energy
Of the Earth, the Physical Realm is Manifested.

I n this chapter you will begin the second phase of the unification and Expansion process. Here you will create a deep connection to the Earth (Nature) while also re-establishing and deepening a connection with your own physical body. Humanity is abundantly more understanding that we must be more mindful of how we treat the Earth; however, most still do not take it to heart that we must also be mindful of how we treat our bodies. Many religious systems refer to the body as a "temple," yet physical neglect is all too common. Neither spirituality nor religion should deter you from caring for and connecting to your physical self. Your body is a gift from God, meant to be appreciated and treated as sacred. I used the phrase "The Kingdom of Heaven is within," in earlier chapters; combine that with the idea of "The body is a temple," and you start to get the picture.

The physical body is the temple that houses the Divine Spirit. While I understand the value of creating holy structures on sacred energy locations, the importance of your own inner wisdom and physical temple cannot be overlooked. Humanity has lost the connection to itself, the result of which is easily seen in all of the external creations we develop that mimic the human being and our processes. It is time for us to come back to ourselves and care for our temples. Mindfulness of healthy eating habits, proper exercise and rest are great ways to begin. We have allowed our senses to become dull and have sacrificed our health. The small percentage of our senses and brain-power that we actually use is frightening. It's distressing to read the studies that show how human beings typically only use two percent of their optical intake ability and filter out ninety-eight percent of what we actually observe. Prepare to be awakened by practicing the challenges in this phase of the program, as you heighten the use of your senses and learn to listen to and feel your body.

The Earth is over 70 percent water, just as are human beings. We understand that emotions cause the water molecules to vibrate at various frequencies. We must comprehend that the water of the Earth and the water inside our bodies is connected; through this we begin to understand how our emotional states influence not only the well-being of our bodies, but the entire Earth as well. Systems such as Feng Shui, Taoism and Shinto aid us in staying in tune with the energies of Nature. When you are sensitive enough to feel the space around you through the application of these methods, you can feel how amazing it is to move in the same current as Nature.

Human beings are not separate from the Earth; they are not separate from Nature. The human ego has created the collective illusion that we are better than Nature, when nothing could be further from the truth. Humans are intimately connected to the Earth and an intricate part of Nature. This is fundamental to the student of the martial arts. An important principle is to study Nature and the nature of things. Coming to know the laws of Nature and their processes apply not only to fighting, but to our daily lives. Human beings originate as Heavenly energy and are manifested into the material reality through the same physical elements that make up the Earth (and stars). The electromagnetic energy of the Earth is interacting with us every moment of every day. Re-establishing our close connection to the Earth will have mutually beneficial healing effects on both human beings and the planet. A sense of daily mindfulness for this is how ancient, indigenous people lived, and what we have presently forgotten. Humanity must regain a sense of respect for Nature and realize it is only because of the delicate balance of conditions of this planet that we survive. By mindlessly destroying Nature, we in turn destroy ourselves. As spiritual seekers, we must not neglect the physical form; we must care for our temples and the sacred ground they walk upon. Through the trinity vision of wholeness, when I address the Earth, I am referring to the planet itself, all of Nature and the physical body of the human being.

THE DUALITY OF THE THIRD DIMENSION

"Under heaven everyone knows that the existence of beauty depends on the existence of ugliness. Everyone knows that the capacity of kindness depends on the existence of the unkind. Existence and nothingness are mutually born. Difficulty and easy complete each other. Long and short shape each other. Tall and short rest upon each other. Sound and music harmonize each other. Before and after follow one another."

— Lao Tzu / Solala Towler —
Tao Te Ching / Chapter Two

Duality is a profound Law of Nature that offers marvelous promises of balance and universal harmony. Whenever there is a poisonous plant in Nature, there is usually another plant nearby that contains the cure. It is not just the poisonous (bad) plant that exists, but right there next to it is a healing (good) plant. Nature always provides a balance. This is the concept of duality through Nature. The trinity vision would include what we human beings do with those plants. We could use them as medicine or as reverse medicine; either way this interaction offers a sense of wholeness. Reverse medicine is a term associated with the martial arts and its use of healing methods when applied for the purpose of harming. This is employed through internal energy techniques, bone manipulation, and external herbs and medications, to offer a few examples. It is vital to grasp the dualistic nature of the world and comprehend how intentional human interaction with it creates the trinity effect. This is part of the wonder and joy of living in the third dimensional reality of Earth.

Duality gives us a fundamental idea of how balance and harmony are held in the universe. It helps us to understand the paradox that while opposites exist, they are not at odds with each other, but must act as harmonious complements. The perspective of duality also offers us the ability to know what we *do* desire through the experience of understanding what we *do not* desire. It is from knowing the things we don't want that we are able to better understand the things we do want; in this way, the things we don't want actually serve us and should not be labeled as "bad." The trinity makes room for the in between or something better, which is a more complete approach.

Human beings live in this dualistic reality without always being completely aware of it. Look at the inventions of humankind. Most of these things are merely external representations of our own internal systems or the processes of the cosmos. In a nutshell, our technology mimics Nature. However, technology is missing crucial factors that Nature always provides; this is a reason for the de-humanizing effects of the information age. The features missing are spirit and emotional connection. While we should acknowledge the important contributions of technology, we must avoid being so heavily dependent upon it, as it is detracting from the connection we have to one another and the Earth. Here are some examples to illustrate my point and help you to more clearly and accurately see the world around you.

- Pumps simulate the action of the human heart and circulatory system.
- The computer imitates the human brain.

- Electrical systems simulate the human nervous system.
- Prosthetic devices and artificial joints act as human extremities and skeletal systems.
- The automobile took the place of riding a horse.
- The idea of flight was born from watching birds.
- GPS is a substitute for reading the sky and knowing the directions.
- Synthetic medication parallels natural herbal cures and body hormones/enzymes/processes.
- Cell phones and teleconferences replace human face-to-face conversation and energy exchange.
- The battery acts like the human internal "bio-battery" of the lower dantien.
- Clocks and calendars parallel the Earths orbital cycles.

You can clearly see the benefits that technology offers to humankind. However, when used excessively, technology can create a sense of laziness that results in the loss of emotional connection with the heart and to the Divine. We get wrapped up in creating synthetic versions of the natural world, but the technological replacements will never be better than the originals. We have come to use technology as a short-cut and an alternative to taking care of the natural equipment of our own bodies. Imagine if we were to place the same degree of thought and effort to mastering our own minds and bodies that we apply to discovering the next technological breakthrough. The enlightened masters of the past diligently cultivated their spiritual essence with this level of dedication. I believe we need to emulate Nature by balancing our technology use with mastery of ourselves. I feel confident that the intuition age we are moving toward will provide the opportunity to bring us back into our natural alignment with Nature.

Through the Law of Duality, we then understand the world around us. We know that when there is day, there will be night. We know that because there is an inhalation, there will be an exhalation. We know that because there is activity, there must also be rest. Duality helps us to make sense out of the world through this predictability. It is when things become balanced that you are taken closer to the natural way and the truth.

THE FOUR SEASONS

The seasons are incredible times of the year that we all enjoy, but the changing of the seasons is the most enjoyable aspect of them. Those times of change, between the seasons, are the moments of excitement and anticipation. We enjoy the changes in climate and scenery. Our bodies naturally regulate their internal processes to act in accordance with the changing seasons; this allows us to see our deep connection with Nature. It is extremely important for us to maintain a relationship with the Earth as it passes through the seasonal cycles. You should be able to feel when the next season is approaching without relying on a calendar. It is then ideal to immerse yourself into the present season and experience it to the fullest. The seasons offer us an excellent window to view the natural concepts of fluid beliefs and a fluid mind, as discussed in Chapter Six. The seasonal cycles offer us a glimpse of nonresistance, as we must accept the impermanence of the seasons as they rise and fall and appreciate what each has to offer in the moment.

The importance of living naturally within the seasons is taught within many spiritual systems, especially exemplified within the Taoism of China and Shinto of Japan. Let's begin our exploration of the seasonal cycles with spring. I realize the weather and environment differs geographically, so adapt this appropriately to where you live. I will provide you with dynamic examples for the most complete illustration, drawing from my experience living in lower and upper Michigan as a young man.

Spring is the season of renewal, rebirth and new growth. The energy that was drawn deep into the Earth for the winter begins to expand outward into the world. This renewed life force of the planet causes the seeds and bulbs to stir from their slumber, the flowers to expose their beauty and fragrance, and the leaves to once again claim their rightful place on the trees. Imagine the amount of energy it takes for a tiny sprout to work its way out of a seed, thrust through the soil and emerge into the world. The melting ice allows the rivers and lakes to flow as warmth begins to spread across the land. There is a feeling of freshness in the air, a permeation of revitalizing energy. Due to the transitory nature of the spring, the air remains cool at times; do not resist this coolness, but instead, allow yourself to feel it. Do not run indoors and turn up the artificial heat in order to hide from the spring. This gives your body the signal that it is summer, confusing your internal energy. The use of artificial temperature control is unhealthy for your body and explains why our systems do not work correctly anymore.

Eating foods that grow naturally in the spring is important for optimum health. We need to eat what is locally grown in our immediate environment, as Nature is providing food with the essential qualities we need for the current cycle. This is an important time to eat fresh, raw, whole foods and avoid anything processed, artificial or shipped to where you live. If it doesn't grow in your area at this time, don't eat it; if you do eat something out of season, minimize your intake. If you don't like the food that is grown in your area, perhaps it's time to move somewhere that offers the foods you need and enjoy. Pay attention to the sun and moon instead of the time zone and clock to know when you should sleep, especially as we manipulate the clock with Daylight Savings Time. You may notice your body and mind want to stay up slightly later in the evening and get up slightly earlier than you are used to in the winter. Spring and summer also offer us the most advantageous time to engage in lovemaking, as we are filled with renewed desire and energy. There is a reason spring is known as a time of love.

Summer is the season of growth, passion and vigor. Summer is when the energy of the Earth is radiating outward at its strongest. This is the time to participate in activities requiring the use of more energy. This is why vacations, sports activities and new adventures traditionally take place throughout the summer. You utilize the additional energy you receive from the Earth to perform these activities and preserve your life force energy. As the summer brings the intensity of heat, allow your body to experience the increased warmth when the temperature rises.

Air conditioning is detrimental to your health and once again sends the body an opposing signal, causing a variety of ailments such as sinus problems and headaches. Perspiring is a form of natural detoxification and is beneficial to the body, although you must in turn pay attention to your hydration status. Those who do not exercise regularly and hide from the summer heat with air conditioning are not allowing the body to regulate naturally. When the sun is blazing and you choose to hibernate indoors with the air conditioning cranked up, it sends a signal to your body that it is winter, causing the body to draw your internal energy deeper inward instead of letting it expand outward with the summer. The moment you step outside, your body gets a different signal and tries to readapt to the environment. See the problem here? This confusion creates turmoil in your energy system that can manifest into physical ailments.

Eating foods that are grown naturally in the summer around where you live is a wise and healthy idea. Avoid routinely slamming ice-cold beverages or frozen treats, as this is harmful to the body. Drink room temperature or slightly chilled beverages if you need relief; but it's healthier to drink things that are closer to your core body temperature.

I have been practicing the sword with my teacher in Japan when it is in the mid-nineties and humid; I am dripping wet with sweat and the air is so heavy that it becomes difficult to even breathe. When I am allowed to take a break, I am served hot green tea. While it may not seem refreshing to Westerners, it is the healthy approach that avoids shocking the system with something that is cold. Ice cold drinks shock the spleen and digestive system, as well as the body's ability to regulate the internal temperature. As long as you are not shocking your system with cold beverages or too much sugar, you can eat more meats as your digestive system should be optimally functioning during this season. The summer is the time to stay up later and awaken earlier, following the pattern of the sun. It is typical for healthy individuals to require less sleep during the summer with the expansion of energy coming from the Earth's core (heart). It is also a great time to increase your energy cultivation practices.

Autumn is the season of harvest and relaxation. It is a time when the air feels comforting and there is a quality of pervading contentment. The leaves turn into a brilliant palette of golds, reds and oranges before they quietly fall from the trees, drawn back into the Earth, recycled to create more life in the spring. This poetic depiction is a central concept in one of the samurai short sword lineages, where one must cut with the unpredictability of a falling leaf. This process is an example of the Earth pulling its energy inward. During this period, you should begin to cool your body down and slow your activities. This is when you begin taking it a little easier to conserve and gather your energy. Enjoy this time of year to relax and feel the comfort of your environment, your home and the love of those closest to you. This is a great time for family and friends to be near and spend time together.

Eat those foods that are available in your area. Healthy and natural comfort foods are meant for this time of year. This is the time to begin cutting back on how much meat you consume and focus more on hearty vegetables, such as are prevalent during the traditional time of harvest. Reduce your intake of red meats and pork while turning your attention to poultry and fish. This is a great time to increase your internal energy storing practices. You will begin to require more rest in this season, going to bed earlier and sleeping in slightly later.

Winter is the season to stay close to home, hibernate and draw your energy inward, just as the Earth draws its energy inward to its core. This is why the leaves wither and die, the grass loses its vibrant green color and the plants wither or at least diminish, depending upon where you live. Winter is a way for the Earth to recharge its planetary battery; all of the heat and warmth is drawn back into the core of the planet so it can gather its strength, and we should follow suit. In many places the snow begins to softly fall, cloaking the ground in a shimmering white veil. The air feels lifeless, with a frosty chill that can be frigid enough to make your lungs ache as though ice crystals are forming with every breath. While the kidneys enjoy this time of year, it is to your advantage to warm them up through vigorous rubbing if you must be involved in heavy activity. Do your best to avoid activities, which will cause you to overheat during the winter. While it may be unpopular, lovemaking should be reduced in the winter, as it is hard on the kidneys and sexual organs. Avoid cranking up the heat as a way to resist the cold; allow yourself to experience it.

Eat those foods that you find in your area during this time. You may have to store certain foods to carry you through, depending on where you live. While I do not recommend freezing or microwaving your food, as both of these methods kill the energy of the food, you may have little choice but to implement freezing certain foods to last through the winter. Your digestive system slows down during the winter, making it a good time to eat less meat. This is the season of hibernation for us as well as for animals, so it is valuable to get more sleep by going to bed earlier and rising later. Energy usage should be kept to a minimum throughout winter as well. Remember, it's about drawing your energy back into your core and working to rejuvenate it. It's a great time to increase internal energy cultivation and storage practices while minimizing strenuous physical exercises.

There is also a fifth season, which is referred to as Indian summer or late summer that occurs between summer and autumn. Some systems of study apply this time of year as an actual season and it warrants being noted. With the planetary shifts we are experiencing, the familiar seasons are presently in a state of instability. I feel it is vitally important at this time to flow as naturally as possible with the seasons, feeling them from day to day in order to move harmoniously with them.

THE FIVE ELEMENTS

The five elements are said to be the building blocks of all matter. Ultimately they are all energy, but here they are examined in their physical form with a portrayal of how to live in harmony with them. There are different schools of thought on the five elements. The Western schools focus on the Hellenic physics version of only four elements: Earth, Water, Fire, and Wind. The Eastern schools focus on five elements: Earth, Water, Fire, Wood and Metal (Gold). I will be utilizing the Eastern version for this system, as the Western school addresses duality but neglects the completeness that is inherent in the five element systems. It is said that everything in the universe is made of the same energy, outwardly manifested in the form of the five base elements. This is one example of how we are all one; we are all connected because we are all made of the same matter. All of our energy (spirit) comes from the same Universal Source in the non-physical reality and is transformed into the same base elements in physical reality.

These elements are not independent of one another; they interact with each other constantly. In developing an understanding for each element as its own individual entity, it is also beneficial to grasp the concept of their interaction with one another. This offers you a glimpse of the natural cycles of the world around you and illustrates how you are an integral part of them within the grander scheme of Nature. As you begin to grasp the interaction of these cycles, it is easy to see the viewpoint of the trinity come through.

The first and second cycles are existence cycles of natural harmony. The first is the Creative or Productive Cycle. This cycle helps shed light on how one element plays a role in the production or support of the next in the sequence. In this cycle, water creates wood, wood creates fire, fire creates earth, earth creates metal, and metal creates water. The next is the Destructive or Control Cycle where we see the opposite happening. This cycle shows how one element plays a role in the destruction of or overcomes another. Here, water destroys fire, fire destroys metal, metal destroys wood, wood destroys earth and earth destroys water. This cycle illustrates how one element regulates the other.

The third and fourth cycles represent the first and second cycles when they are in a state of disharmony. The third is the Over-Acting Cycle and here water overacts on fire, fire overacts on metal, metal overacts on wood, wood overacts on earth, and earth overacts on water. The fourth and final cycle is the Insulting Cycle, where water insults earth, earth insults wood, wood insults metal, metal insults fire, and fire insults water. These cycles allow us to notice when the elements are out of balance. When the Productive Cycle becomes unbalanced, the result is that one element is depleted by another that takes from it. When the Regulating Cycle is out of balance, it causes the element that is normally regulated to become excessive, thereby gaining control over the element that would balance it under normal conditions. The third and fourth cycles do not act in a circular manner, but move in more of a star or pentagram pattern.

Living in harmonious union with these elements allows us to understand our deep connection to Heaven, Earth and Nature. We come to know that just as these elements are happening in Nature, they are also happening within us. The elements provide us with an excellent example of how we are not only made of the same physical elements as the Earth, but the processes of their interactions are same within us as they are for the Earth. For example, our internal organs (physical) and emotions (mind) correlate with these same elements. The fire element corresponds to the heart and the dualistic emotions of passion and anger. The fire element can also be connected to the summer. These cycles are represented in the Earth as a macrocosm and reflected in the human being as a microcosm.

THE NATURE OF NATURE

The nature of Nature is change. Human beings have a wonderful opportunity to learn to accept change through the constant lessons that nature provides. The seasons come and go, with no way to cling to a single season forever. The elements rise and fall through the cycles of creation, destruction and interactive balance. Despite these rather evident examples, it has become human nature to resist change and seek a way around it. It wasn't always this way; people of the past lived in harmony with Nature. They understood the ways of Nature and knew they needed to respect it in order to survive. Being in tune with Nature offers a stress-releasing, healing effect; this is why we intuitively create parks, campgrounds and engage in so many outdoor activities. In recent years, children have largely stopped going outdoors to play and people act as though they fear the sunshine. As a result of this, people are suffering from Vitamin D deficiencies and other ailments. Having a strong relationship with Nature during these times of great change will help you to adjust to them as they arise.

Human beings are interacting with Nature at all times. The human electromagnetic field is sending, receiving, and interacting with the same electromagnetic fields produced by all living things – plants and animals alike. These fields are relatively subtle and can be difficult to feel, but it is very possible when you develop a higher level of sensitivity. The very nature of Nature is to nurture, to provide and sustain the conditions for life. At times Nature can seem harsh by taking lives, and at other times it provides everything we need for enjoyment and prosperity. It is within the rhythm of Nature to act in cycles; these patterns allow Nature the opportunity to regenerate and continue on. In modern times we have separated ourselves from Nature to the extent of losing our sensitivity and connection to it. Reconnecting to Nature and holding a sense of appreciation for it will rekindle your sensitivity to your environment.

In the past, human beings could still feel the powerful energy vortexes and ley lines of the Earth; it was in these places they constructed temples and churches. This is what makes these places so special, powerful and spiritually charged. They were made of very specific material and constructed in ways that allowed for the natural flow of energy, just as in the ancient philosophy of Feng Shui. It is evident how much of this sensitivity we have lost today; we erect these supposedly sacred buildings on any plot of land that can be afforded or where it seems to be most commercially advantageous. The majority of the modern sites of temples and churches have no sacred connection to the power of Nature. This is one reason we enjoy visiting sacred sites throughout the world and why they are so incredibly special. The amazing temples of Egypt (the ones that haven't been moved), the mountain temples of Japan and China, the ancient churches of Europe and other sites all over the world attract tourists and pilgrims.

These powerful places offer an energetic charge that on some deep level still draws us to them. Energy lines (ley lines) and vortexes cover the globe and we interact with them whether we is feel it or not. This may shed some light upon why certain areas attract happier, more successful people and other areas end up poverty-stricken or overrun with crime. A wonderful example of this can be seen right here in California with Mt. Tamalpais and Mt. Diablo. Both mountains offer breathtaking views of the San Francisco Bay area and wonderful hiking opportunities. The powerful energy of Mt. Tamalpais however, has long been regarded as highly spiritual and positive. This has attracted many spiritual leaders over the years, including the Dalai Lama. Mt. Diablo, on the other hand, received its name for more reasons than merely the red hue it gives off at sunset; the native people avoided this area and referred to it in their native tongue by a name only translatable as "devil." While mountains are widely known for their spiritual attributes, some contain more positive energy vortexes than others.

Moving in harmony with Nature and recognizing our deep connection to it is crucial to our spiritual development, physical health and mental stability. I travel the world to visit energetically charged sacred sites and offer my sincere appreciation for the beauty of the Earth. I practice methods that continue to develop my levels of sensitivity to the energy of my environment and allow me to be closer to Nature. Getting back to Nature allows us to regain our power as human beings and once again walk harmoniously with the natural forces. Nature is where we get to witness the manifested Universal Source.

THE HUMAN CENTER OF EARTH

The human center of Earth is the lower center of awareness in the abdomen, or lower dantien. This is also generally known as the *seika tanden* or *hara* (belly) in Japanese terminology, famous within the martial arts throughout the world. However, it should be noted here for the sake of detail that the seika tanden refers to the lower dantien (center of awareness below the navel), while the hara generally refers to the entire abdominal area and occasionally to a specific point in front of the lower dantien (seika tanden). In Chinese culture this area is known as the "false dantien." This does not mean false in a sense of being untrue; in this case it simply means "lesser." This area is able to store only small amounts of bio-energy, whereas the actual lower dantien, located deeper in the center of the lower body, is able to store incredible amounts of bio-energy. For those who study energetic anatomy, the true lower dantien is located midway between the naval center and the door of life (*ming men*). The door of life is the energy gate located between the second and third lumbar vertebrae. The term hara also refers to a sense of strength and presence that comes from developing a connection of awareness to this area of the body.

The lower abdominal center is the center of doing. It is the internal bio-battery and once developed allows you to harmonize, collect and store the energies of Heaven and Earth for greater vitality and longevity. Let's be truthful; we could all use a little more energy! When people move with grace and power, they move from this lower center. The lower center is the center of awareness. This is where the consciousness is located that allows you to move with a sense of kinesthetic awareness, allowing you to have a feeling or sense for where every part of your body is in space. We develop this further by allowing ourselves to move with the guidance of the Divine.

There are some simple physical triggers that help the activation of the lower center. Slightly bending the knees helps activate it, whereas standing with your knees locked will disconnect you from it. Opening the *kua* or hips slightly will also help to activate this abdominal center, as will gently tucking the sacrum. Perhaps one of the most important ways to do this is through the use of the vagus nerve. This nerve is extremely important to martial arts, Qigong and any full body presence activation practice. Not only is the vagus nerve responsible for controlling the immune system, but it also serves to allow communication between all three energy centers of the body.

The vagus nerve comes from the brain down through the body into the lower abdomen, where it connects to every major organ. This nerve is paramount to getting your consciousness to drop down from your head into your heart and lower abdomen center. Once you have established clear communication between the three centers by way of the vagus nerve, you will begin to awaken the awareness and intelligence within every cell of your body. The vagus nerve is an important part of most ancient and esoteric teachings. It is activated through various meditation methods, relaxed stretching, Qigong forms, Taijutsu, Tai Chi and many other martial arts that rely on relaxed body movements. Basically, any activity that helps you to relax mentally and physically will stimulate the activation of the vagus nerve.

> *"By activating the vagus nerve, you can control your immune cells, reduce inflammation, and even prevent disease and aging! It's true. By creating positive brain states—as meditation masters have done for centuries—you can switch on the vagus nerve and control inflammation. So relaxation—a state of calm, peace, and stillness— can activate the vagus nerve. And the vagus nerve, in turn, activates your stem cells to regenerate and renew your tissue and organs."*
> **— Dr. Mark Hyman —**
> (*How the Dalai Lama Can Help You Live to 120*)

The research I have gathered clearly shows that while a fetus begins to develop brain matter in the head, at a certain point that matter moves down to the abdomen and becomes the intestines. The process continues by creating more brain matter that is to remain in the head and become the brain itself. The organs of the brain and intestines, especially the small intestine, are basically the same and there is evidence of intelligence in this tissue. This should be no surprise, as science has confirmed that there is intelligence in every single individual cell in our body. It is this lower center that allows us to firmly connect to the Earth, to move naturally and effortlessly. Through practices that engage the vagus nerve, we can begin to drop our mind from our head to our lower abdomen and activate this lower center. This is the desired purpose behind many martial arts exercises. The challenges of this stage will be designed to help you in activating this lower center and dropping your consciousness down to this area. Through such activities, you will begin to establish a deep and meaningful connection to the Earth, to Nature and to your own physical body.

The primary function of the Earth challenges is to assist you in re-connecting to the Earth and the depths of what the Earth represents. It is the nature of your physical self, the elements that compose the physical you and the physical world around you. It is all of Nature and the Earth itself as a living, conscious entity in a celestial body. If followed with dedication, the challenges will help you stimulate your physical system to strengthen and balance your lower center of awareness. Once these exercises become part of who you are, you will begin more consciously aligning with the subtle forces of Nature.

EARTH CHALLENGES
EXOTERIC CHALLENGES: AWARENESS

CHALLENGE ONE
Physical Kneeling Posture – Physical Grounding

THE IDEA

Seiza (pronounced "say-zah") is the Japanese term meaning "proper kneeling seat." This position grounds you and connects you to the Earth, and is performed by sitting on your knees with your feet underneath your buttocks. Your back is straight, your eyes are forward and you hold the feeling of being aware, alert and alive. This body posture also contains holding the attitude of strength or relaxed immovability. To slouch in this posture indicates a sloppy body and mind. When you slouch there is pressure on the heart and lungs, heaviness on the legs, and the mind feels "muddy." This posture alone offers very deep experiences of serenity, strength and awareness.

This posture is of great help if you feel an emotional disturbance, or if you are scattered and having difficulty focusing. If you kneel into seiza with "live toes" where the toes are folded under the feet, pay particular attention to your big toes. Should there be discomfort there, you may have a weak lower back and be subject to injury or back pain unless you begin to strengthen it. To assume seiza, simply lower yourself into this posture in a place where you feel safe and secure; relax, and Nature will do the rest. This posture allows your energy to sink and settle into your lower center. This is said to be the seat of your Being. Sitting and relaxing in this keeling seat position will also benefit you in your quest to activate the vagus nerve.

THE FORMAL PRACTICE

- Slowly lower yourself down first with the left leg going onto the knee. Allow the toes of the left foot to bend. Allow your right knee to point out to the right side. Try not to lean your head or torso forward. Be mindful as you enter this posture. It is not uncommon to feel mild discomfort in the beginning. If you experience this, take your time and move into it slowly.
- Then lower the right leg down onto the knee. Unfold your toes and allow the tops of the feet to slide into place on the floor. Sit back onto your feet and relax into the posture.
- Keep your gaze gently focused forward; do not look down, as this can sacrifice your balance. Keep your spine erect with your hips under your shoulders, relax the chest and allow the shoulder joints to hang naturally. Your lower center should gently push forward. Your hands are placed on the folds of the legs on the upper thighs. The feet should be straight back behind you, but they can also be folded one over the other, creating a small seat.
- You may desire to place some artwork in front of you to hold your attention, or you could perform some simple meditation, visualization or prayer. The key here is to feel how you naturally connect to the Earth; you should also be able to feel your energy sink into your lower center.
- As an alternate version to try, sit in this kneeling posture but instead of with your toes outstretched behind you, tuck them under. This will raise your body.
- Do whichever version feels the best to you, but you should be able to perform the posture both ways.
- **BONUS:** If you really want to super-charge this exercise, you can add this in. Touch your little finger tips to your thumb

tips on either one or both hands. The other three fingers should be straight. Then lightly place your fingertips on the ground to touch the Earth. Breathe deeply and evenly. If you are somewhere in public and need to ground yourself, you can touch the little fingers to the thumbs as before and point the fingers toward the ground or interlace the two "rings" made by the thumbs and little fingers of the hands with the fingers pointing upward. This works well if you need to ground yourself mentally, emotionally or physically. The hand has great symbolic representation in every spiritual system, as it is the expression of the heart. This is a type of mudra or energy hand posture. Here the little finger represents the Earth and the thumb represents the void. Bringing them together is a powerful gesture of your intention to ground and become stable and calm.

PERSONAL EXPERIENCE

I have been sitting in the kneeling seat of seiza for decades. It has never been uncomfortable for me, but never force it or stay in this position if it is painful for you; this will not allow the mind to rest or the body to relax. This posture is used at the beginning of martial arts training as a way to help the students and teacher to center themselves, to get grounded and to be ready to focus on the training. The strength of the warrior can surely be felt in this position. The posture is then repeated at the end of the training session as a way for everyone to refocus and re-center themselves after the strain on their muscles, nervous system, and emotions. In addition, this posture is also used by meditation systems to help you become calm and focused in order to center your mind, body, and spirit.

I have had extensive experience with the various hand positions of esoteric spiritual systems, as well as ancient martial systems. This can have great influence over our mind, body and energy. These things are not magic; your desired manifestation is not instantly produced by simply placing your hands in a certain position. You need to train yourself to respond in a desired fashion with them. For this Earth Ring (Bonus), you can activate it by holding the hand position, breathing deeply and focusing on being calm. It helps to sit in the kneeling seat as taught in this section. After practicing with the hand position, you will be able to become calm and centered simply by placing your fingers in this position. The fingers do have specific elemental and energetic properties, so it is important to position them correctly. It is the unification of the mind, body and spirit that charges these hand positions and yields results.

CHALLENGE TWO
Beyond Going Green – Be The Greenness

THE IDEA
Going Green is a concept that is continuing to progress, as corporations and individuals alike pursue more Earth-friendly, sustainable practices. This is impressive and greatly warranted, but we want to go beyond to *become* the greenness. Here I will address the practice for the individual, but I do offer a version of this to businesses that will help them to reach the next level of best practices for the new economy and new environment; this includes the transition from "being green" only for the Earth to properly interacting with employees and customers. Common acts of mindfulness and respect for your living environment are a good place to begin; this can be anything that allows you to contribute to the health of the planet. The primary point in "being the greenness" is to interact with Nature. Plant some flowers, trim some trees, do some landscaping that requires you get your hands into the soil and get dirty. We are meant to interact with the soil, as there are bacteria and other components that are beneficial to human beings; too much sterility is harmful. Maybe plant some vegetables, herbs or whatever you would find enjoyable and beneficial to the environment and yourself. It is becoming increasingly difficult to trust any produce in a supermarket, so growing some of your own food is a concept that assists you in taking ownership of your own well-being.

Did you know that simply admiring the beauty of a tree or the fragrance of a rose bush sends positive vibrational energy to those things and to the Earth itself? We have a beautiful little park nearby where we enjoy practicing Tai Chi, Qigong and martial arts; we admire and appreciate it to share positive energy with our living environment and the planet. Do your best to share positive energy with the places you enjoy the most.

THE FORMAL PRACTICE

- I recommend finding some enjoyable ways that you can solidly interact with Nature and give respect to the planet. Any outdoor activities such as hiking, swimming, or noncompetitive sports are great options.
- Act! Plant some tree seedlings, clean up a beach or park or recycle your trash. Do something physical and tangible to make a difference. Find a way to make a contribution to saving the planet and safeguarding its well-being.
- Go to a park, a beach, a mountain trail, or wherever you enjoy going to be in direct contact with Nature. Stop and look around at the wonder and beauty in front of you, feeling a sense of appreciation for the Earth. Think of your heart opening with appreciation for everything the Earth offers and supplies. Feel that sense of appreciation mix with love and send it down through your feet into the ground. Think of that energy going right to the core of the planet, the Earth's heart.

PERSONAL EXPERIENCE

I do many things in an attempt to be sensitive to the well-being of the Earth. I always act in a respectful manner regarding trees, plants and other forms of natural life. I do not mindlessly carve trees with a pocket knife, break branches or destroy flowers or other plants. I recycle what I can and act with respect for my environment. However, I feel that what has the most impact is to perform Qigong outdoors.

Qigong helps you connect to the energies of Heaven and Earth and allows those forces to interact through you; by treating your body as a temple, you offer a clean conduit for the energies. Make an effort to do something that helps you create a bond with the Earth by caring for it. One of the most disturbing sights to me is an urban area where there are no trees, the grass is dead and all that remains are buildings and concrete with trash laden streets. This shows blatant disrespect for the environment and severe disconnection from Nature. We can no longer afford to take the Earth for granted and trample all over it. Our existence depends upon the well-being of the planet and its tolerance of us as a species.

CHALLENGE THREE
Your Body, The Temple

THE IDEA

We have heard the statement "the body is a temple" from nearly every religion and spiritual system in existence. There is good reason for that! While it is common knowledge this statement refers to keeping your body fit, clean and healthy, there is actually far more to consider. Treating your body as a temple holds the meaning that you should have respect for your physical self. Keeping your physical self or form in shape, clean and dressed comfortably and appropriately is essential; it shows that you have self-respect. Did you know that the ancient Egyptians built their temples in the shape of a human being? While visiting Egypt back in 2010, the well-respected Egyptologist who acted as our tour guide offered us a challenge: to see what the temple at Edfu was actually about in terms of its metaphysical representation. I accepted that challenge. I think he was very surprised when I described to him the shape of a human being's energetic anatomy, and recognized various rooms that allowed for starlight, moonlight or sunlight to shine upon the crown.

Native Americans also made their dwellings sacred, designing them in a layout that represented the universe and its workings.

Remember that your body is only the physical "you." It is a temporary temple that is home to your spirit. That divine essence is the *real* you; give it a good home! If this body is the home for the Divine energy that is the true essence of who you are, and it is part of Universal Source, doesn't it make sense to care for it properly? Allowing your temple to be neglected and run down shows mental weakness and offers little chance at a strong spiritual or Divine connection. As I stated above from my own experiences, Qigong is a great way to interact with the forces of Heaven and Earth, permitting you to feel how important it is to keep your body clean and healthy, inside and out. If you have energy blockages in your body, not only does it disrupt the energies of Heaven and Earth, but those blockages may lead to illness. When your body is clear of energy blockages, the energy flows freely, leaving you feeling enthusiastic and healthy.

THE FORMAL PRACTICE

- Begin your day with a stretching routine. One is provided in the Heaven Section; you can add to it if you desire.
- Do something physical to care for your outer temple: running, martial arts, weightlifting, yoga, walking, Pilates, or anything else you enjoy. Obviously, cleanliness factors in here as well. It doesn't hurt to do something to pamper the body; you can soak in a hot tub with candles lit and a glass of your favorite beverage, get a massage, or whatever makes you personally feel good.
- Now do something for your inner temple. Engage in breathing exercises, Qigong, Tai Chi, energy healing, acupuncture, eat something healthy, take nutritional supplements that serve your needs, meditate; be even more creative.
- Take just a few minutes to think about how your body is a temple for your spirit or soul, the Divine energy that is focused into physical reality. Get to know this relationship of

your physical and spiritual Selves, the expression of which is manifested through your heart center.

PERSONAL EXPERIENCE:
I have been stretching my body consistently for over three decades. I am constantly exercising and physically challenging myself. I am quite flexible for my age and I am able to move without any pain, even with a multitude of past injuries. In the past five years or so I have gotten far more conscientious about my dietary intact. For years I neglected my temple and beat the living heck out of it, with sixteen to twenty-two hour work days and going for three or four days at a time without more than a few hours of sleep. I consistently ate late at night due to my busy schedule. After the wake-up call of a heart attack, I got a lot smarter! Here I can encourage you in what to do by sharing my example of what not to do. I now have a daily regimen of stretching, an abdominal routine, and using my Bowflex or going to the gym. I then practice Tai Chi, Bagua and Qigong. I also may practice martial arts, do an intense cardio routine, take an evening walk, or hike mountain trails or redwood forests. I stay very active and love it! I also make sure to get proper rest now.

CHALLENGE FOUR
Love Where You Live

THE IDEA
We all have places we want to go and visit, that's only natural and healthy. Exploring the world is one of the pleasures of being here in this time-space reality; it's a playground filled with adventures. In the movie *The Wizard of Oz*, there's the saying "There's no place like home." That should be the case for us all. I love traveling the world, meeting fascinating people, and having incredible adventures. Now that I live in such an amazing place, I am not always in such a hurry to leave it, and I always appreciate it when I return. When I am in Japan, China,

Egypt or wherever I find myself, I am there completely and I enjoy every moment of the experience, but I am always ready to return home. Do you love where you live? Many people don't, but they should. I love the serenity of the location of my home. I love seeing the mountains, the ocean, the sunshine, the lack of humidity, and tremendous variety of plant life. I love that the outstanding city of San Francisco is merely minutes away, filled with opportunities and fun adventures, and I enjoy the iconic nature of the Golden Gate Bridge. How do you honestly feel about where you live?

I contend that you, as an awakened human being, should reside in an area that resonates with you and fills you with joy just to be there. Maybe you always wanted to live in a certain state, in the mountains or by a lake, or maybe where they have certain types of food. What's stopping you? Take a moment and think about this: If you could live anywhere in the world you wanted, where would it be and why? Set the excuses aside and think about what it would take for you to get there. I believe that loving where you live is an important and potent way to share positive energy with the Earth and constructively connect to Nature. I include my living location in my morning appreciation process, and my fiancé and I are both very open in sharing how neither of us would rather live anywhere else in the world. That's a remarkable statement to be able to make and one that allows us to appreciate the Earth on a very personal level.

Once you get a clear idea of where you desire to live, it's time to be brave enough to make the actual move. You must learn to transform thought into action in order to create the reality you desire. It may not be easy, and at first it may seem completely unfeasible, but you will discover an answer with perseverance in deed and trust in the universe. If you are not currently living in your ideal area, I would recommend finding things about your area that you do find pleasurable. By connecting to the things you do enjoy instead of only those things you don't, you will raise your personal vibration and better align with the location you would love to live in. Offer appreciation for the attributes of your current home while holding the desire to live in the place you'd truly appreciate.

THE FORMAL PRACTICE

- Look around you and list at least ten things that you truly cherish about where you live – the things that bring you enjoyment every single day.
- Take a moment and think about somewhere you always wanted to live – a place you'd rather make your home more than anywhere else in the world. List ten things about that place that give you such a strong desire to live there.
- Now, if you have not actually visited that place, then I suggest you do. Hop in your car or on a plane and embark on an adventure. Check into the place, absorbing the culture, the people, the food, the environment, the ways people make a living. Make sure it truly resonates with you and that your desire for it wasn't your imagination or a false perception.
- Move there. That's right, it's just that simple. If you could not come up with ten things that you absolutely love about where you live, then chances are you don't belong there; I recommend moving to the place you would love to be.
- No excuses. Plan out what it would take to make the move and begin implementing those things. I am not suggesting just dumping everything and moving away; you need to apply some common sense and do it responsibly. But why stay where you are not happy? Just because you were born there, or perceive you do not have the funds or courage, or feel you cannot move away from your family? These are usually false beliefs you possess due to the conditioning of others. Life is meant to be an adventure – live it like one!

PERSONAL EXPERIENCE

I did it. I left my family, my friends, my business, my full time job, nearly every facet of my life. It was not easy, but I knew what I needed to do to be happy and live my life purpose. I had obstacles in my way, yet I waded through them one by one and accomplished an incredible goal of moving to where I can see the Golden Gate Bridge. I left

Michigan behind to embark on an adventure in China before arriving in my personal dream location of Marin County, California. If I can do it, you can too. Now that I'm in California, I could write pages of reasons why I love it here. I literally created the opportunity to live anywhere in the world, and my choice was perfect... for me. Where is perfect for you?

ESOTERIC CHALLENGES: MINDFULNESS

CHALLENGE ONE
Connecting To The Earth

THE IDEA

This Qigong exercise is for connecting to the planet's core. It is a very effective way to ground your energy and establish a deep sense of connection to the Earth, even helping with jetlag. As you perform this exercise, try to allow the Earth's electromagnetic pulses set the rhythm naturally instead of attempting to control it yourself. The best way is to not think about it; let go and let yourself be guided. It is not unusual to experience feelings of self-healing, love and safety when connected to the Earth. Enjoy it; it's a beautiful way to get in touch with your Mother.

Here are a few other simple ideas that you could apply to connect to the Earth. Sleep on the floor; by this I am talking about a traditional futon or at least a lower bed frame. The closer you are to the ground, the more energy you draw into yourself during the night. Generally, the Earth's energy enters your body through the spaces between the vertebrae and at the point called ming-men (door of life) between your kidneys. If you awaken feeling filled with energy, you are effectively taking in the energy as you rest. If you are groggy and need a few cups of coffee before you can wake up, you are not absorbing the energy in the night as you should be. These exercises should help you with this. Walk on the grass or sand barefoot whenever you can; the thick rubber soles of shoes combined with all the concrete you walk on serves to dull your connection to the Earth. Direct contact to the ground with your bare feet will help establish a stronger connection to the Earth and bring the natural Earth energy up through your legs.

THE FORMAL PRACTICE

- Stand in the natural posture that you learned in the Heaven section of exercises for the "Silver Strand."
- Now, gently and easily begin to shift your body weight onto your right leg and slightly back onto the heel by pushing against the ground with your left foot. The left foot should rise onto the ball of the foot, putting pressure there. This pushes what is known as the Kidney One (K-1) point into the ground, also known as the "bubbling well." It is located between the 2nd and 3rd metatarsal bones of the foot. If you curl your toes down it will make a small depression in this area of the sole; you can use this to help locate the Kidney One point.
- Set the left foot down, transfer your weight lightly to the heel, and repeat the same process of pushing against the ground with the ball of the foot on the right side. Keep doing this until you form an easy, natural rhythm. Do not think about it; let go and allow yourself to be guided. Place your mental awareness under your feet until it feels like walking in taffy.
- Extend your mental awareness further into the ground until you can clearly visualize and feel yourself being connected to the Earth. Your mind should travel at least three body lengths into the ground, then go even deeper to connect to the very core of the Earth. Feel yourself exchange energy with the Earth's core. The nurturing energy from the Earth rises through your legs and into your lower energy center; you push the energy from your lower energy center back down into the Earth. Along with the energy, you can also send any negative emotions of which you'd like to dispose. The Earth will recycle these negative emotions into positive energy to be used by all living things.

- You can do this for as long as you like. Before you finish the exercise, keep your body moving and relax the mind. Allow any thoughts or feelings to gently arise and observe their contents.

PERSONAL EXPERIENCE

I really enjoy this exercise, as it helps so well with jetlag. I fly several times a year and most of those trips require eight to fifteen hour flights. The jetlag can be brutal, and when you are traveling for martial arts training, you have got to be ready to go the next day. This easy exercise will really help you connect deeply to the Earth and its core. It has helped me to stay grounded while going through some very mentally and emotionally challenging times, as well as offering healing energy to help me recover from physical issues such as heart surgery. As you perform this exercise, you should utilize the physical triggers for activating the vagus nerve and lower energy center; keep your knees slightly bent, open the hips, tuck the sacrum and relax.

CHALLENGE TWO
The Five Elements

THE IDEA

The *Tao Te Ching* states that "The One produces the Two, the Two produces the Three, the Three produces The 10,000 Beings." But there is another version that expands upon that, originating from the Taoist Internal Alchemy teachings. It states, "The One produces the Two, the Two produces the Three, the Three produces the Five, the Five produces the Eight and the Eight produces the 10,000 beings." The "five" is referring to the five elements of Earth, Water, Fire, Wood and Metal. The elements are considered to be the building blocks of all physical things in the universe. Understand these elements as the composition of the physical you and the world around you. Start a list with two columns. At the top of one write "Me," and at the top of the other write "The World." On the side write the names of the elements. I will provide you with some basic ideas that you can then expand upon. You can also apply the Earth, Water, Fire, Wind and Void model if you like.

THE FORMAL PRACTICE

- Make cross headings of Earth, Water, Fire, Wood and Metal. In each one of those, write as many things as you can think of relating yourself and the elements. Do the same for the things that make up the world (Earth). I have supplied you with examples to help you begin.
- Understand how the elements allow us to see the relationship between ourselves and the world around us. They help you know you are not separate from Nature, but made of the exact same stuff. This serves to validate that no one is more or less important than anyone else. We are all special for exactly the same reasons.
- The next part is easy and very enjoyable. Write another heading for each of the elements, and then list ten things you personally appreciate about the various aspects of each element. I have shared some of my own with you.
- Write a third list using the element headings and list their interactions and their alchemical states. For example, water becomes slush, and slush becomes ice. You can also go in the other direction to see that water becomes steam, and steam becomes vapor. The important thing is to internalize and recognize these interactions everywhere, as everything. (Please refer to Table 3-1).

ME	THE WORLD
Earth – bones, muscles, organs	Earth – soil, rocks, beaches, mountains
Water – blood, saliva, urine, body fluids	Water – oceans, lakes, rivers, rain, ice
Fire – electrical currents, metabolism	Fire – lightening

Wind – breath, cellular respiration	Wind – air, sky, clouds, smoke
Void - consciousness	Void – all the potential within the field

EARTH
1. Walking barefoot on the beach.
2. The smell of fresh cut grass in the summer.
3. Hiking on a mountain trail anywhere in the world.
4. Viewing all the amazing types of flowers.

WATER
1. The power of the ocean waves.
2. Swimming at night in a great pool in the moonlight.
3. Hearing the gentle pattering of rain on the roof.
4. Taking a long soothing shower or bath.

FIRE
1. A fire in the fireplace when it's cold outside or during the Christmas holiday.
2. The sunlight filtering through the windows in the morning.
3. The romance of candlelight during dinner.
4. The warmth of the sun shining on your face.

WIND
1. A cool breeze through the window at night as you drift off to sleep.
2. Watching a hawk play on the air currents.
3. The scent of the ocean in the air.
4. Watching leaves dance on the autumn wind as it blows.

VOID
1. The amazing potential for something great from what seems to be nothing at all.
2. The potential to see the universe in a grain of sand or a child's smile.
3. The creative potential of a human being.
4. The cycles of Nature.

Table 3-1

PERSONAL EXPERIENCE

Learning about the elements is one thing; it has been another thing entirely for me to really connect to and internalize them. I see how they create everything, including myself. It is amazing to view the world through this type of lens, as you see the connection of all things from their base elements. I have studied the elements from many perspectives and strive to see the correctness of them all. Once you have a sense of knowing for the elements, you will be more closely connected to all things in the Universe.

CHALLENGE THREE
The Four Seasons / Nature's Cycles

THE IDEA

By living in harmony with Nature, you will seamlessly flow with the seasons as they change from one to another. You may remember a time when the seasons were very distinct and the change of seasons was very discernable. These days, however, things are not quite so distinguishable. One day while living in Michigan, we had the rain of spring; it got hotter and we experienced summer; the air cooled off and an autumn breeze began to blow; by early evening it was snowing. We must become fluid and nonresistant in our ability to change and adapt with the cycles and attributes of Nature. My grandfather had knowledge of the local wildlife, lakes, forests, weather patterns, any aspect you can name; he was in touch with Nature and always prepared for sudden changes.

THE FORMAL PRACTICE

- Live in harmony with the four cycles. Enjoy and relax into each cycle instead of resisting it. As you get more sensitive to your own physical form, the energies inside you and all around you, you will become sensitive enough to feel the minute differences as the seasons change. I am not talking about looking on a calendar; those dates are merely suggestions of when the seasons are normally expected.

- Eat the foods that are "in season" from your area. This is an extension of loving where you live. Enjoy the local foods and eat organically grown, hormone-free foods; this is also related to treating your body as a temple. Remember that everything is interrelated, especially these natural practices.

- Participate in the seasons. During spring, go outdoors and enjoy the budding of the leaves on the trees; watch them as they pop out and cover the bare wood with lush green wind ornaments. In the summer, go to the beach and feel the sand between your toes, getting sun exposure. Everyone today is so afraid of the sun's rays that they have developed deficiencies. When autumn takes its place, enjoy the colors of the changing leaves and the crispness in the air. As winter helps pull your energy back into your body, do not resist it. Get outdoors and feel the snow or rain (depending where you live), take deep breaths of the cool air and enjoy the cozy warmth of being at home. Embrace each season, making sure you are offering total acceptance and enjoyment of them.

PERSONAL EXPERIENCE

Growing up in Michigan gave me the opportunity to experience the seasons in a dynamic way. As a child I loved seeing the flowers pop open in spring, swimming in the family pool in the summer, feeling the coolness of the autumn, and making snow forts in the winter. The seasons used to be very distinguishable; climate changes have caused the seasons to blur together. I enjoy each and every season for what it has to offer, from the quality of the air, the foods produced, the temperature variances, and the various holidays we celebrate.

CHALLENGE FOUR
Feng Shui: The Flow of Nature and Natural Energies

THE IDEA
Feng Shui offers great insights into the subject of energy flow within personal living and working spaces. The first time I traveled to China, we received a great lesson in how the principles of Feng Shui have been responsible for making or breaking corporations; major companies often battle one another through the application of architectural design. These concepts can be utilized on a smaller scale by removing clutter from your mind, your body and your living environment. Obviously a home filled with clutter will cause the natural flow of energy to become blocked and stagnant. The main idea is to open up your living space and decorate your home with things that matter to you. Do your best to avoid purchasing a piece of furniture or art simply because it's on sale when it just doesn't fit with the rest of the room.

I recommend having a basic decorative theme for each room with a central theme running throughout. A theme should hold meaning to you; if you are sharing a home with a spouse or significant other, it should be equally as meaningful to them. It really helps the energy of a room if you feel great about the pieces in it. My fiancé and I wanted our living room space to be welcoming, relaxing and comfortable. We got puffy, cushy matching furniture, soft throw pillows and a cozy throw blanket that's kept next to the sofa. We placed many sacred art objects around the room and set up an entertainment system. We encourage guests to sit back and relax, stretch out on the furniture and enjoy.

Everyone who spends a moment in our living space feels compelled to share with us how comfortable they are and how tranquil and spiritual it feels in our home. Creating a home-space with this special feeling is of immense benefit.

THE FORMAL PRACTICE

- I recommend beginning with a good book on the subject of Feng Shui. You can go online and research it as well, but I recommend purchasing a book for your personal library. Reading is one of the things that sets apart the successful from the unsuccessful.

- Pick one room in your house and become sensitive to the way the room feels. Notice how clutter disrupts the flow and makes it difficult for your mind to relax. Take a piece of paper and write down ten things you notice about the room that could be improved, according to the guidelines of Feng Shui and your personal feeling. Maybe you will need to change the color of the paint on the walls or knock out a wall to open the space. Maybe it's as simple as cleaning up all the clutter or repositioning the furniture to allow for better traffic flow.

- Now that you have a list, make the changes. This may take some time, so consider it a small home improvement project if a lot of changes are warranted.

- Once the changes are made to the room, take some time to soak up the new feelings. Notice what happens mentally and emotionally when you enter and leave. You should feel massive improvements and your home should start to feel more tranquil and inviting.

- Once you take care of this in your home, apply it to your office (if they allow it). Make sure that whatever spaces you spend your time in are suitable. You can even pay attention to your environment. What kind of landscape is around you? Observe how your home interacts with other homes and businesses in your area.

PERSONAL EXPERIENCE

I have read more than a few books on the subject of Feng Shui, as it is a principle contained within the Chinese and Japanese martial arts and Qigong that I study. However, it was while in China for the first time in 2009 that I got some incredible lessons in its depth and effectiveness. During the trip with Solala Towler, author and editor of the *Empty Vessel* magazine, we received some wonderful explanations and examples of Feng Shui principles. I have applied those principles to my home as I described earlier and it makes a huge difference in our living space.

I have discovered the significance of not only understanding the principles of Feng Shui, but in the ability to feel the "energy currents" that are flowing all around us; this allows you to move in harmony with them. This is important in all aspects of our lives, from daily living to martial arts, to health and well-being, and to financial and business success. In the Japanese martial art lineage called *Gyokko ryu Kosshijutsu,* the concept of Feng Shui is called *Fu Sui*—literally "wind and water." One aspect of its meaning is the interaction between the non-physical (wind) and the physical (water). This refers to the interplay between the unseen energies within the body and within all space in the physical realm. Another important concept is in the interaction of wind and water. We must develop a high level of sensitivity for the unending flow of energy currents or patterns in the "empty space" all around us and within all things. Understanding this process helps the practitioner to grasp the concept of Fu Sui as it applies to this ancient martial lineage.

CHALLENGE FIVE
Duality

THE IDEA

The One produces the Two... according to Lao Tzu the "two" represents duality, Heaven and Earth. Today people seem to only understand this as good and bad. This is incorrect. In the dimension of time and space, we have the freedom to choose how we respond to circumstances and events. We should certainly understand what things we enjoy and what things we don't, but that doesn't mean everything we don't enjoy is "bad." Imagine every single day is sunny and warm. You would not have a cool, rainy day to offer contrast and help you appreciate the sunshine and warmth. After enough warm, sunny days, the cool rainy day offers you the pleasure of a different experience. You need the comparison to help clarify your perception of the experience. It would be difficult to appreciate the incredibly pleasing fragrance of fresh cut flowers if you never experienced the odor of skunk spray. Life is not merely duality, things are not only black or white; there is an entire array of grays, or even vibrant colors in-between black and white.

You would likely be suffering from emotional instability if you merely jumped from one extreme emotion to another. Allow your mind to stay open and aware of all the possibilities, not simply the extremes. The idea of this exercise is to become aware of the contrasts in life to understand them in a more expansive manner. When you experience something that you perceive as negative or bad, understand it as an opportunity to gain clarity of your preferences. Do not judge the situation or try to eradicate it, as you will end up attracting more of it to you. Simply acknowledge it and know what it represents; it too shall pass. You will then be better equipped to enjoy a situation you perceive as being pleasurable. You may judge something as negative in the moment, but you will come to understand its positive value or true meaning at a later time. Sometimes, our life lessons present themselves in seemingly negative ways in order to get our attention.

THE FORMAL PRACTICE

- Start with a piece of paper (or hopefully by now you have a journal!). Write two column headers for "Likes" and "Dislikes."
- Begin to write down things you like about yourself and your life; your relationship, your job and level of success, your hobbies, your body, your spiritual development, your level of mental discipline.

- Now do the same with your dislikes. Write them all down and be honest with yourself. Sometimes the honesty can be difficult, but if you can't be honest with yourself, then you can't be honest with anyone else or make any changes.
- Look at the items in the "Like" column and take them in; notice how they make you feel good, maybe even proud.
- Look at the items in the "Dislike" column and take them in; notice how they make you feel. Chances are they aren't very good feelings; the key here is to change them.
- Let's start by changing the tile of "Dislike" to something else. Use another descriptive word like Opportunity, Growth or Change. This morphs it into a neutral term, allowing your perception to shift.
- We need the contrast of like and dislike in order to understand what we enjoy and don't enjoy. Discovering what we don't like gives us the opportunity to change and grow. We only change and grow when we are out of our comfort zone.

PERSONAL EXPERIENCE

This process helped me understand the perceptions of my mind, allowing me to positively shift my mindset. Learning to understand my mental programming was extremely valuable. This helped me take a negative perception, identify it as a valuable element, and see the opportunity to grow and change for the better contained within. Amazing transformation isn't it? I understood that contrast was not as simple as good or bad, and I awakened to the understanding and mental processes of perceptions and beliefs.

CHAPTER FOUR

BEING

When Human Beings Interact With the Energy
of the Heart, the Physical and Spiritual Realms
Rejoice, and Oneness is Manifested

I n this chapter we will explore the third and final phase of the
program known as Being, or humanity. These are the matters of
the heart; those things that make us what we are and who we were
meant to be. By the end of this phase of development, you should be
able to activate your heart center, as well as draw the forces of Heaven
down into you and the forces of Earth up into you. This will allow the
energy to flow freely through you as you are aligned with your place
in the universe. I hope that you truly enjoy this chapter, as it holds
the potential to experience such intense happiness and connections to
yourself, the world around you, and everyone else with whom we share
this time and space reality. This phase places our focus on developing
the ability to feel; not simply as a means of experiencing your emotions,

but the ability to feel your inner body, its processes, and an awareness for your inner consciousness.

Once you have experienced a degree of success in overcoming your ego, you will begin to unlock your ability to open your heart and live a more heart-centered life. The heart center is known as the middle center of awareness. While many people try to fit the energetic body and physical body into the same nice neat package, it doesn't always work out that way. While these two areas do interact, they are not the exact same thing or in the same place. In this case, the physical heart is located slightly left of center, and the energetic heart center or middle dantien is located right in the center, in the mid-point of the body between the chest and back. It is this center that connects humankind to all other living things. The most meaningful moments in life are those that are felt with the heart.

It is through the unification of the energies of Heaven and Earth that you will come to know yourself. As these two forces converge in your body, the heart center can become fully awakened and powerful. For those with psychic vision, this appears as a light in the center of the chest radiating outward in all directions to touch all things, without exception. This is sometimes known as "Christ-Consciousness" and we are all capable of attaining it. Obviously the greatest spiritual masters of the past such as Lao Tzu, Buddha, Mohammad and Jesus all possessed this. In previous chapters I have discussed the Kingdom of Heaven being within; it is within the heart center that you will find it. It is not in any church, temple or shrine; it is within every single one of us. It is within this stage that I will give you the keys you need to unlock the gateway to your heart and enter the Kingdom of Heaven.

Previously, I have mentioned the importance of the "AH" sound, and how it is a sound we tend to naturally make when we are settling in, relaxing or feeling good. The "AH" seed syllable is the vocal vibration for the middle center or heart. Using this particular mantra or sound will help you to get out of your head and open your heart center, as well as connect your consciousness with your heart-space. Here you will be able to experience true *feeling* instead of mind created emotion. The difference is best understood through the feeling of the experience. This is crucial because the new reality we are moving toward will focus on feeling and intuition over thought and information.

"When I let go of what I am, I become what I might be."[1]
— Lao Tzu —

AWAKENED MINDFULNESS

Mindfulness is at the very core of many spiritual systems. Mindfulness is an awakening of our consciousness to a higher level, allowing you to stay in the present moment, and offers a disciplined state of mind that is necessary for spiritual, mental, emotional and physical development and well-being. One of the biggest challenges to developing consistency in your practices is not the drive or desire to perform them, but the lack of mental focus to remember to do them, caused in part by our hectic lives. We are so busy today that the undisciplined mind simply forgets as it focuses on what it deems to be more urgent. Once the mind is properly trained and disciplined, you will be better equipped to focus and remember. The mind will be able to focus on numerous things without needing to come to rest on any single thing. When this occurs you will have a sense of constant awareness for whatever you place your mind on and for the things happening around you. I have found that mindfulness can only occur once the ego has been subdued and mental stillness has been achieved.

MINDFUL LIVING

Life is an amazing gift from the Universal Source. Often people go through life with the unfortunate belief that life is meant to be hard, that it is supposed to be a constant struggle. I contend that life is meant to be an open-hearted, love-filled, blissful grand adventure. I also believe you have to slow down the pace of your life and pay attention to the things around you to come to know this. Combine this with actual exercises designed to help you to develop a higher sense of awareness, and you will begin to become more mindful. Think about it objectively for a moment: look at all the amazing places there are to visit, all the incredible things there are to taste, feel, listen to, and experience in your lifetime. Life is an exciting adventure, meant to be engaged to the fullest.

The physical senses are one way in which we are connected to the Earth. The basic physical senses are directly connected to physical sense organs of our body. In Traditional Chinese Medicine, they take this even deeper to show how the sensory organs are connected to the major organs of the body. The auditory sense of hearing is connected to the ears and then to the kidneys. The visual sense of sight is connected to the eyes and then to the liver. The olfactory sense of smell is connected to the nose and then to the lungs. The gustatory sense of taste is connected to the tongue and then to the heart. The tactile sense of touch is connected to the skin, nerve-endings and brain. Everything is connected; everything is one.

Let's begin with the mindful sense of taste. Most often one thinks merely of the obvious taste of food or drink. The key is to pay closer attention to the usual things you taste; actually experiencing your food or beverage instead of gulping it down in a hurry while watching television, playing on the computer or doing that mountain of work you brought home from the office. Broaden your range of taste to include many additional things you may not normally associate with it. Think about the last time you shared a passionate kiss with your lover. In addition to the love you experience, are you aware of how your lover's kiss tastes? There are other tastes you should become aware of too, like the tastes of foods from other cultures, the taste of the air high atop a mountain. Too often we focus all of our attention on the tastes we like the most and become unwilling to try new ones. Some people feel so strongly about what they do like that they close their mind to anything else. This close-minded mentality then tends to work its way into other sensory areas.

Next we'll examine the mindful sense of hearing. There is the music which you enjoy and the music that you don't, but do you know why you like some and not others? It usually has to do with matching your vibration to the vibrational quality of the music. It is not difficult to understand how higher vibrational music matches the higher vibrations of the people who listen to it; the same goes for lower vibrational music. Usually as you progress through the program you will notice your taste in music changes. What about other sounds, like the cooing of mourning doves at daybreak, the voice of your young daughter saying "I love you Daddy," or the laughter of your grandchild? How about the gentle tapping of the rain on the window as you lay down to sleep, the sounds of ecstasy from your lover, the happy chatter from people across the park, the soothing sound of a small stream bubbling through the forest? There are so many sweet sounds for you to enjoy in life.

We'll move on to the mindful sense of smell. Once again we notice the obvious, such as colognes and perfumes, flowers, foods, and that great new car smell; but what about all the other scents that linger within your experience? Years ago I led a group of martial arts students to a recreational state park where we held a three-day-long training camp. I took the group to a trail in the woods and I asked if anyone could describe the scent of water. One participant, while looking at me as though I was incredibly uneducated, shared that water has no scent because he had never smelled water in his life. I then asked everyone to pay close attention and notice what they smelling. The participants were unaware there was a small lake just through the trees, about ten yards from where we were standing. Some of them began to describe a scent similar to that when it is about to rain, a sense of dampness and the smell of moisture. Once everyone agreed that something smelled different than usual, I took them through the trees and brush to the end of the small lake. I had everyone smell again to realize that water, in Nature, really does have a scent. The heavily treated tap water from your faucet is another story. What is the scent of your favorite flower? Can you describe it? I simply love the scent of roses, jasmine and especially lilacs. Notice what smells trigger memories of past events or of loved ones. Sometimes when I think about my grandpa or feel his presence, I get a very strong smell of coffee. Some of these sensory experiences are beyond verbal depiction, but that does not make your experience of it any less real.

The next sense to be explored is mindful sight. As nearly everyone knows, this is the sense that we tend to be the most aware of and dependent upon. When was the last time you actually used this sense with purpose and gratitude? Make the time in your life to observe; really look at people, places, and things. Truly see them, drink in all of their details, the rich colors and their design by nature. When was the last time you truly looked at your lover? Better yet, when was the last time you looked into their eyes for an extended period of time, studying their eye color, shape, and then going deeper to look into the beauty of their spirit? Now that's seeing. In the hustle and bustle of our incredibly busy and demanding lives we hardly pay attention to important things around us anymore. Our lives are literally going by in a flash and we don't even notice.

Find a place in Nature around you that you enjoy; maybe it's a mountain, a grove of trees, a lake, or a park. Make the time to look closely and be totally present in the moment. Sit for a few minutes just taking in the details of the site itself, studying and appreciating it. Find someone you love or at least care about deeply; it can even be you! Ask the person if you can look at them without rendering them too self conscious or uncomfortable. Now study them, not in a judgmental way, but in an unconditional loving way, to see the divine perfection radiating from them. I do this occasionally with my grandson; I just sit with him and his trains on the floor, watching him concentrate so hard on playing and having fun. I enjoy seeing my fiancé when she is so happy and excited to be on one of our adventures; it melts my heart. Look at all the reasons why you treasure your relationship with these people; these things alone will open your heart.

The next sense is that of touch. Let's expand the understanding of touch to include not only those things that you touch, but also the things that touch you. We are well acquainted with reaching out and touching, but we must also consider all of those things that enter our experience and touch us. Consider the breeze, the sunshine, the touch of someone special in your life as they take your hand in theirs. The sense of touch can be a lot of fun. Here are some enjoyable ways to "get in touch" with this sense. You have heard the old saying of, "You get what you pay for." I personally believe there is a lot of truth in that. Experience it by getting both a cheap shirt and a high quality shirt. Feel the texture of the fabrics in your hand; put them on and feel them against your skin. Feel the difference? Which one makes you feel better by wearing it?

How about touching your lover? I recommend you let them know about this exercise and make sure they are comfortable with you taking some time to touch them with a sense of mindfulness. Gently run your fingertips lightly over their bare skin, feeling it's softness with a tender caress. Now touch their face, their lips, their hair, and their ears; go ahead, be creative and have fun. Enjoy your ability to touch another and to be touched. What a magnificent thing to experience!

Lastly, we will look at the sixth sense of intuition or feeling. This is that strange sensation you get when you know someone is going to say or do something right before they actually do. It is the consciousness of the body that allows us to feel danger and respond before the brain even knows what's happening. In researching the "accepted" version of the sixth sense, I found many people trying to offer analytical answers for this sense. It is much like trying to force a square peg into a round hole because you only believe in squares, having not yet experienced a circle. I like to think of this intuitive sense as a bridge between the outer and the inner. This is still considered a physical sense, as it is developed through heightened sensitivity and awareness of the body, allowing the body to act without the consciousness of the brain. Has someone ever thrown something at you when you were not expecting it, and you suddenly caught or evaded the thrown object before you even realized you'd moved? Another example of this sense is the feeling of "just knowing" something without any rational reason for knowing it. This sense of knowing is perceived through a feeling.

The following example will allow you to see with great clarity how all of the concepts of mindful living intertwine with each other. My fiancé and I use the preparation of a meal as a means to expand and live more mindfully. When we purchase our fresh foods, we make sure we have our vibrations raised and take pleasure in shopping together at our local markets. We buy only fresh, organic, local items that are in season and we often discuss our appreciation for the farmers and fishermen who make the effort to get us such fine foods; this way we put positive, energetic vibrations into the food as we handle it. When it's time to prepare a meal, we put on high vibrational music; I installed an under-the-cabinet CD player system for just this occasion. We have the music softly playing, pour glasses of wine from Napa Valley and work as a team to make the meal. We visit about positive events from our day, making time to stop and enjoy a close embrace and a kiss or two.

We rarely use our freezer or the microwave; instead we eat everything fresh and cook it on the stove or in the oven. We pour our hearts into the efforts of cooking so the food can absorb this loving energy. Our meals turn out beautifully, and even though it is just the two of us, we pay close attention to the detail of presentation. When we sit down to eat we may light a candle for the table, or dim the lights to set the proper feeling. I like to take a moment to feel appreciation for the animal or plant that gave its life so we could be nourished while enjoying an amazing meal, and I will offer a silent prayer before eating. A form of prayer before a meal is used to ask for divine blessing of your food and the people around you, as well as to bring your focus to the experience at hand. We take the time to actually taste and enjoy the food and drink, savoring what we have created together. We even clean up immediately after the meal to avoid the energy attachments of dirty dishes hanging over our heads. We always perform this task as a team, which allows us to have everything clean and put away in mere minutes. How many of the various concepts in this program can you find taking place in this simple act of having a daily meal?

CHOOSE TO BE HAPPY

Being happy *is* a choice. I've taught this truth to many martial and meditative students who tend to believe their happiness is dependent upon someone or something else. This is a serious error that needs to be corrected before any real spiritual growth can begin. You must accept full responsibility for being in complete control of your happiness. You may have to change the way you perceive the world, refraining from making excuses and placing blame, but the fact still remains that it is your choice. I know a number of people who ostensibly like to be miserable, who prefer to mope around all day complaining about the slightest thing. These people have made the conscious choice to be that way. They get the attention they crave as this behavior becomes their identity. These people are lacking a sense of self-empowerment; once they attain it they can make the conscious choice to be happy. Happiness is at the core desire of human experience. Everyone knows in their heart that they want to be happy and want to see others happy as well. This is part of the human condition.

If your basic nature is already that of a happy person, then why not shoot for joy or bliss? One thing I have discovered as a universal truth is that life is meant to be experienced as a joyous, open-hearted, love-filled, grand adventure. Are you living your life the way it was intended? When I was in my twenties it was brought to my attention that I almost never laughed or even smiled. Even when I felt happy inside, there wasn't even a smile visible to others. I could be watching a hilarious movie and not make a sound. I wasn't purposely trying to be that way; I just didn't know better at the time. As I learned the lessons taught to me by some of the most amazing masters of martial arts, meditative arts, and spiritual systems, in addition to my own life lessons, I began to change. Suddenly I was being told that I laughed too much! It felt so good to open up and laugh. It was so freeing that I still openly laugh even if those around me don't get why I am laughing.

I encourage you to smile, laugh, enjoy and feel good! It's not only your right, but your responsibility—to yourself. Laughter is believed to offer such positive effects as balancing blood pressure, stimulating the heart and lungs and boosting the immune system. As we have already learned, the physical reality we live in and the circumstances of our lives are our own mental creations. Why not choose to create fun and positive things in your life? Happiness is not a weakness; it is empowering and will help you connect to the Universal Source in an entirely new way. So smile already! A smile is an incredibly powerful way for human beings to connect with one another.

EMOTIONS & FEELINGS

You must learn how to pay attention to your body and mind and to feel your emotions as they rise and fall. Emotions are a huge determining factor of your success in life, and as I have come to know first-hand, whether you continue to live or die. You must take the time to become mindful of your feelings, understand what triggers certain emotions and know why you react the way you do. Only then can you regain control of your emotions as you transition from reacting to responding. I am not suggesting that you make yourself emotionless; just the opposite. Experiencing our world through emotions is a beautiful and amazing capability that we embody as human beings. The idea is to manage them to avoid living on an emotional rollercoaster.

Emotions are at the very root of your perception. The brain releases chemicals in response to emotions, sending electrical impulses to the nerves that produce physical responses in the muscles. As I trained in a workshop with Qigong Grandmaster Mantak Chia, he echoed this process while acknowledging the importance of our emotions. He shared that everything begins with the emotions, and they are of supreme importance when it comes to your mental and physical health. I intend to help you to better understand the depth of emotions and how you can harness their power to guide yourself through life in a far more conscious way.

When I first opened my martial arts school sixteen years ago, one of the first lessons I taught to my students was to observe their thoughts and the thought processes in their mind over a six- month period. When the time was up, I asked everyone to spend the next six months observing their emotions and the process of feeling them in the body. Love, joy and appreciation are very high vibrational emotions that get you closer to the divine; they connect you to your higher Self as well as to Universal Source. Do your best to steer clear of fear, guilt, shame, anger and disgust, as these are very low vibrational emotions that not only drag you away from divine connections, but help to manifest more of those negative situations into your life.

Many human beings have negative emotions as their baseline experience; this is not healthy or desirable. Ultimately, your base emotion should be joyful and loving, yet level. There are those people who enjoy the negative emotional ride of drama, and there are those who enjoy a blissed-out high; neither of these are completely healthy. The negative emotional addicts risk requiring prescription medication for the problem; the bliss addicts risk losing control over themselves and seeking other forms of drugs to simulate the blissful high of life itself. The ideal emotional place is in the middle, with your emotions in a state of balance.

It is not unusual for people to be ruled by emotions, to be slaves to their raw power. This is a sign of an emotionally unstable person. Unrestrained public outbursts and other rash behaviors are the result of someone who is under the control of their emotions. It is necessary to develop a sense of management over your emotions and to understand what beneficial functions they serve. This does not mean that you become a non-feeling, non-thinking robot. It does mean, however, that you become very aware of your emotions as they arise so you are able to consciously choose how you should best respond in the moment. You still enjoy the free flowing nature of their rise and fall—an important part of the human experience—but you will also gain awareness of your emotions as they come into being and have the mindfulness to choose what is in your best interest. This is the type of self-control that one acquires in order to learn how to maintain a higher vibrational frequency. There are times to let go and allow yourself to feel the extreme excitement of something amazing taking place in your life, but it's still a conscious choice when you do so. There are also times of sorrow, when it's important to allow yourself to feel grief to allow the healing process to begin. This too is still a conscious decision on your part.

These days we have a lot of talk about "emotional scales", a term used by Esther and Jerry Hicks in their wonderful books where they channel Abraham, a non-physical collective entity. Many people offer different examples of emotional scales, ranging in number from twenty to fifty different emotions. I believe this is over-thinking it and not really necessary to your process of growth. The best way to understand and apply the emotional scale is to learn to actually feel each emotion for yourself. Then you can judge for yourself if the scale makes sense for you. Every one of us is unique, and certain emotional qualities may be felt differently within different people. I observe my emotional states for the three highest and three lowest emotions.

While there are countless emotions in the middle, these neutral emotions are not where I desire to remain for long. If I should experience one of these, I recognize it and move back up into the three higher emotions as soon as possible. If you are emotionally in a lower place, then the middle emotions can be a wonderful goal; just don't allow yourself to stop there and get comfortable. Remember this program is about mastery, not mediocrity. The three highest emotions—according to my own personal experience—are love, bliss and appreciation; while the three lowest emotions are fear, guilt and anger. When you live with the three higher emotions present you are vibrating at the highest possible rate for a physical being, closely connected to your Higher Self and to the Universal Source. When you allow outside influences to cause your emotions to sink into other areas, you have lowered your vibration and taken yourself farther away from Universal Source. Here is a short scale (Please refer to Table 4-1) that I developed and use for myself; I hope that it is able to effectively serve you as well.

EXPANSION MASTERY SYSTEM EMOTIONAL SCALE

Love

Bliss

Appreciation

Passion

The entire "in between" range of emotions are here

Jealousy

Blame

Guilt

Anger

Hatred

Since our emotional state is influenced by the electromagnetic field of the Earth and cosmos, I contend that all of these forces directly influence our emotional state. I feel it is imperative to have a practice in place to help you adapt to the new energetic and emotional patterns of the times we are experiencing. In this way, when you become aware that your mood has changed to something undesirable, you posses the mindfulness to change it.

HEART CONNECTION & ONENESS

The heart center is the primary center of experience for a human being. When cared for properly and opened fully, it is the heart that allows a human being to love unconditionally and to maintain a connection with all others in the strongest, purest and truest of ways. It is the open heart that allows us to expand and experience compassion for ourselves and others. By others, I do mean every other person on the planet *without* exception, in addition to every plant, animal, and all other beings in our vast universe. Think of it this way: if at a base level, everyone and everything is made of the same stuff (energy), then we are all brothers and sisters with all of Nature and everything in the universe. The more you learn to open your heart and extend the bright light of your true being in all directions, to shine upon everyone and everything, the more you can begin to connect to the

Christ-Consciousness. From my own experiences and research, it is this deep state of unconditional love, compassion and connection to all others that is at the very heart of the teachings of Jesus and the meaning of "Christ". Reflect on this; are you acting in a way that holds unconditional love and compassion for all others without exception? Are you able to keep your heart open regardless of what experience you have attracted or created in your life? Do you see everyone else, no matter their race, creed, gender, culture, or belief as your complete equal, as your brother or sister on a deep level?

Here is a personal example of having compassion for all things. Where I live, after a rain or in the coolness of night, the snails come out and decide that they must cross the walkways. Of course many of them get squished, likely as either an accident from lack of awareness for what is under one's feet, or on purpose if someone feels the cruel need to step on them. My fiancé and I always take the time to stop, bend down and move the snails off of the walkways in the direction they are heading. We don't think of the snails as being insignificant or judge them for being slow. We simply pick them up and move them to safety. A simple thing, but it illustrates the idea clearly.

Part of the human connection in the physical experience is the relationships we engage in everyday. We are intertwined with family, friends, co-workers, store clerks, and the business or job you identify with in order to make your living. These relationships offer us important social interaction as well as connection to others. I feel a sense of fatherhood from my samurai teacher in Japan, Grandmaster Kenshinsai Machida. He is a kind, loving man and a fierce warrior at the same time; it's truly amazing to experience. When I am in Japan, living in his home or in the esoteric Buddhist temple he operates, he treats me just like his own son. He buys me clothes that match his son's, he feeds me and cares for me; he even tells me when to go to bed. I have a fond memory that has me smiling as I write this; we were sitting around a table in the living room of his home one night talking about samurai martial arts and samurai *shodo* (calligraphy), when he suddenly told me to go to bed and pointed toward the room in the temple were I was staying. I laughed to myself as realized I was 44 years old and getting sent to bed! It really tickled me. Having the utmost respect for this great teacher, I replied by saying "Yes sir, goodnight." I would have given my life to protect my grandfather, and I would do the same for Grandmaster Machida and Grandmaster Hatsumi.

Here is another example pertaining to the Earth. The first time I travelled to China we visited and trained on Wudang Mountain. I was excited to visit there and experience it, but I was amazed at how it felt like home to me. The feeling there was as familiar as my hometown from when I was a child. There were many things that peaked my interest in Wudang leading up to this trip, and I started to feel drawn to those untamed mountain peaks. Signs had shown offering all the usual feelings of synchronicity for years prior to this trip taking place. I felt as though there was a need for me to go there and connect to the energy of the awe-inspiring temples located there. It resonated with me in such a profound way that I told my fiancé we would have to come back and spend even more time there. About two years later, we returned to live in the foothills of Wudang Mountain for an entire month. You see, we need to remember that we are connected to Nature (Earth) as well as to other human beings.

The problem we face is that the heart opens and closes constantly throughout any given day. The heart opens when you speak with someone you love and it closes when your boss yells at you. When the heart closes as a defense against something traumatic, oftentimes it does not just automatically reopen. It may reopen if something amazingly pleasurable or happy happens, but generally it takes a specific process to truly reopen your heart center. I will be providing you with methods that really work as part of this program. Having an open heart center is one of our greatest gifts as humans, and I hope that you get to experience these profound and incredible feelings on a more regular basis because of this program. As you connect to the spiritual nature (Heaven) of your being and to Nature (Earth), you will be filled with such energy that you just can't keep it in; it will be released through your heart center and shared with everyone around you.

The first and most overlooked relationship in your life is the one you have with yourself. Most of the time people allow their relationship with themselves to be handled by the uncontrolled chatter of the ego-mind. Unfortunately, most of these thoughts are negative judgments of ourselves that we end up believing. If you want to develop strong, positive relationships with others in your life, it must start with *you*. You have to be spiritually, physically and mentally/emotionally right with yourself before these relationships can reach their full potential. You must get to know yourself and more importantly, get in touch with yourself; and just maybe even love yourself. This is where it all begins. Have the courage to love yourself!

The trinity view is applied to the relationship with yourself by first looking at your Heaven or spiritual component. Get clear on your spiritual affiliations and beliefs while at the same time keeping your mind open for growth; know within your heart what spiritual paths resonate with you. You need to attain connection to your Higher Self, that Divine part of you that is always offering guidance and assuring that you are always safe and loved. The Earth or physical part of your relationship with yourself is where you learn to get connected to Nature, understanding that you are part of it and not something better than or separate from it. This is also how you see your physical body. You need take care of your physical self through nutrition and exercise. The Being or mental/emotional connection with yourself is extremely important as well. This is where you learn to accept yourself without condition; you recognize the perfection of your physical body and learn to control those random thoughts and mental judgment patterns that run wild in your head. You want to learn to love yourself. Most of us are much harder on ourselves than we ever are on anyone else. The idea is to become free of judgments of ourselves and others.

Romantic relationships are no longer enduring by old world models; they should not be looked upon as hard work, and people are coming to that realization now more than ever. This is part of the change we are experiencing where the old model of "for better or worse, till death do us part," simply doesn't work anymore. Why should your life and the time spent with the person you supposedly love be considered laborious? It seems that anyone who is with the wrong person is now feeling a sense of urging to leave, to get divorced and start again regardless of their age. Those people who are in extremely happy relationships with their spouse or partner are not having these feelings to set things right. The energetic changes from the shift are causing people to feel the need to act on anything amiss in their lives. This is with good reason, as conflict in your romantic relationship causes tension in both parties, making spiritual Expansion an impossible task.

Make sure your romantic relationship is a celebration in partnership. Should a relationship be work simply because you've been together for more than five or ten years? I contend that it should not. We are told by friends, family and professionals that you are supposed to stick it out and work at it no matter what the cost, that it's healthy to argue and fight in order to get things out in the open. Let's face it; if you are in a healthy, loving relationship, you should not have to yell, scream, call each other names, or even consider putting your hands on your spouse in an aggressive way for *any* reason. These are signs of an unhealthy relationship that needs to change. Your relationship with that special person should be a breath-taking experience of joy and appreciation.

In addressing relationships we must consider the "like attracts like" concept of the Law of Attraction. I whole-heartedly believe that in order to find what some may call your "soul mate," you need to find someone who shares the same core fundamental spiritual beliefs. This will allow you to grow together as you stroll down the path of life. To subscribe to the "opposites attract" relationship will, in most cases, end with the two individuals growing apart. Look at it in terms of a life-long friendship, because at its core all relationships have the same essence. Let's say that you have a childhood friend that you went to school with; you played outdoors together and shared birthday parties and sleep-overs. What are the chances of hanging onto that close relationship as you graduate college? Think back to recall how many childhood friends you had that faded into the mists of the past. This doesn't mean that you are no longer friends or that you dislike them; it simply means that you grew apart and went your own separate ways. Some friends do manage to pull this off even while they start a relationship, a career, and a family, and I think that's awesome! In order for that to happen, both friends must have a similar spiritual foundation and share some similar interests and hobbies. This will allow them to grow at the same rate of development, mentally, emotionally and spiritually. Any differences in these key life areas will most likely result in the two friends growing apart and going in different life directions. People come and go in life, it's a simple fact. This is not a bad thing.

Romantic relationships are no different than this. They require the same key components in order to be long-lasting and for both individuals to be truly happy in the relationship. We like to believe the idealistic notion that "love conquers all," and that may get you by for a while; but sooner or later it is not enough and things need to change unless both of you are willing to tolerate unhappiness. If you can manage to fulfill the same qualities in your romantic relationship as you do with your friendships, you have the opportunity to maintain long, happy relationships in all areas of your life. This is the relationship that is the core of your life experience; make it a great one!

Friendships will need to adapt to the new reality as well. As you grow and change, you may find yourself growing apart from some of your current friends or them outgrowing you. It is pointless to resist this; even though it can be sad when it happens, it is the nature of growth and change. Let them go and seek to make new friends that support your life's purpose. I know this sounds cold, but it's really not meant to be. I am not telling you to just write them off, I am saying let them go so you can both grow; but hold them kindly in your heart and should your paths meet again in the future, welcome them sincerely with open arms. I was recently able to do this with a childhood friend and a childhood sweetheart. Close friendships are to be treasured.

The days of clinging and hanging onto someone just because you don't like change are gone. Cherish your friends and serve them however you can; try your best to make their lives better because you are a part of them. Friendships will need to become more honest and respectful with both people truly caring for each other, connecting on a deeper level. Superficial friendships or those that merely allow one or both parties to use the other will slowly fall apart.

Let's examine some ideas of friendships through the trinity. The Heaven or spiritual application is understanding that your friend is an eternal, Divine spiritual being just like you are, and you treat them accordingly. You most likely share core beliefs and you are able to grow together as you walk the path of your lives. The Earth or physical application is the activities and events you experience together. Perhaps you jog or work out together, enjoy meals with one another, or partake in adventures. Maybe they are your martial arts training partner. The Being or mental application is having a deep, heartfelt connection to the person; it is platonic, yet you feel that you would do about anything for them. This is the area where you give emotional comfort when it is needed and offer respect at all times.

There is no exception made for the necessity of change, even in family relationships. Rivalries are no longer a tolerable ingredient of the sibling dynamic. The sibling that is more expansive will not partake in such behavior and usually seek to separate themselves from their brother or sister. Siblings should strive to help each other grow and evolve without a hidden agenda. This will allow the heart connection between siblings to become stronger, with time spent together being treasured. Parental relationships must adapt by parents actually stepping up to raise their children instead of letting them run wild and undisciplined. In order for parents to offer value to the family relationship, they need to establish a heart connection to their children that is strong and loving enough to support them as they become individuals and evolve in their own way. This will have to be done without the over-bearing, controlling behavior that has become common in recent years. Hovering as helicopter mothers, ignoring as disinterested fathers, or acting as friends instead of parents are all things that no longer constitute acceptable, successful parenting practices. Families should be unconditionally supportive and feel the heart connection between each other effortlessly.

Family relationship dynamics through the trinity would apply the Heaven focus of the family members honoring their connection to one another while also honoring the individuality of each member. It would entail supporting the happiness of all the family members unconditionally. The Earth or physical relationship would be found in taking family vacations, picnics and enjoying other activities together. It would also consist of support for physical strengths or weaknesses of a family member. The Being aspect would be relayed through unconditional love, acceptance and support for all members, without judgment, manipulation or control. It would acknowledge the freedom for each member to live their own life purpose and experience their own Expansion.

Business relationships must transform for their own survival. As I have already discussed, the old cycle of the Earth and human nature was masculine or yang, and we are currently progressing into the feminine or yin cycle. This will alter our roles in relationships, how we do business and indeed, how we interact with one another in every area of human affairs. As we enter the feminine cycle, women will take on stronger, more influential roles in society. Men will rediscover the value of feminine attributes, allowing business management, marketing and product demands to change accordingly. Businesses will need to approach their interactions with suppliers, consumers and employees in a considerate and caring manner, and eradicate all self-serving practices.

The trinity view in business would utilize the Heaven application by discarding the old management model of strict rule over faceless employees. Instead, they must give employees respect and self-responsibility, letting them know their participation is valued and appreciated. Companies would increase their charitable practices, supporting local causes or something that is dear to the hearts of the employees. The Earth application is connected to fair profits, the use of quality materials, a clean, inviting work environment, and utilizing green and sustainable practices to protect the environment. The Being area would apply to the safety measures in place at the worksites, the connection that is established between upper management and the rest of the employees and the overall treatment of employees and customers alike. High quality customer service would be of vast importance.

Every type of relationship is a great gift; they are an opportunity to establish heart-centered connections with one another. They are to be valued and honored. We need to re-establish a connection with ourselves and others; to wake up, get off our butts and get back out in to the magnificent world, once again enjoying the interaction with other real live human beings. We must acknowledge each other's presence and be willing to help one another without the expectation of something in return. We need to make friends again, and I don't mean on Facebook; I mean genuine, honest meaningful friendships. And most importantly, we have to get out into the world and seek out the perfect person to share our life with. In order to do all of this, we must get out of our heads and back into our hearts.

THE HUMAN CENTER OF BEING

The middle center, heart center or middle dantien are the names of the middle center of awareness. It is not merely for feeling, but also contains intelligence and memory. This is the center that is extremely powerful for human beings; while we strive to balance all three of these centers of awareness, it is most important to not only open this one, but to live from within it. This is where your original Spirit resides. When you live a heart-centered life, you are living a life of love, compassion, joy and appreciation. This is the power of being human. It is where we experience unconditional love for ourselves and for all other human beings; it is where we connect to all things in the universe.

This is the gateway to the Kingdom of Heaven. It is here that you can go within and know the universal truths. Awakening this middle center is to know Heaven, Earth and your true Self. Do not fall victim to those who might insist that you follow your head instead of your heart; they are leading you down a false path, away from the Divine. Think for yourself. *Know* for yourself! Opening your heart center is supposed to be at the very essence of spiritual and religious practice. When the heart center blossoms like a gorgeous flower, your brightness will radiate in all directions and touch the hearts of all who come in contact with you.

The primary function of the Being challenges is to assist you in re-connecting to both your own sense of self and to others around you, in addition to offering the depths of what a Being represents. If followed with dedication, the challenges will help you stimulate your essence and open your heart to strengthen and balance your heart center. Once these exercises become part of your daily life, they will also begin consciously aligning you with the experience of oneness and a sense of knowing for the purpose of the human experience. You will become a fully integrated human being in full realization of your true potential, with the ability to live in harmony with the forces of the cosmos and Nature.

The challenges in this final stage of the program are designed to help you unify your spiritual Self (Heaven) and your physical Self (Earth) into a completely integrated and unified human Being. In addition, they will guide you on the path of opening your heart center. As you make your way through all nine of the exercises in this section, do your best to notice how each is being influenced by the previous exercises in the Heaven and Earth sections. At this point you should be acutely aware of how all three are intricately interwoven. This interplay is what we are working to balance. Too much spiritual involvement without the proper balance of grounding leads to becoming flighty, lackadaisical or unfocused. Too much physical involvement without a spiritual link leads to becoming bogged down in the illusion of matter and the denial of Divinity.

As you strengthen a connection to yourself and to others, you will begin to develop the ability to pick up on what people around you are feeling, what types of intentions they have and even some of the things they are thinking. I do not consider this to be magic or even anything out of the ordinary; this is what happens when you realize we are all connected. I don't think of this ability as being psychic; I think of it as having a heightened sensitivity. The more in-tune you become with nature and with other human beings, the more you will see this type of ability develop.

BEING CHALLENGES
EXOTERIC CHALLENGES: AWARENESS

CHALLENGE ONE
Giving

THE IDEA

Make sure you are as good at receiving as you are at giving. Most people may read that statement and think it's backwards, and for some it may be. However, many kind-hearted people are great at giving but get very uncomfortable when it comes to receiving. Whichever way that statement applies to you, the secret is to become balanced and receptive to both acts equally. There are people who are so great at receiving that they are considered to be greedy and selfish, as they take from others but never give to anyone. Others may be great at giving but when it comes to getting, they don't know how to be gracious because they don't feel worthy. You can see how neither of these attributes is desirable. Make the time to do some form of charity, something to selflessly help someone else. Give without any sense of need for recognition and if recognition is offered, do your best to evade it. There are many wonderful ways to give to those less fortunate. Giving freely without expectation is one sign that you are living in your heart center.

Some people feel that the act of "giving" is not an important act, but I disagree. I feel giving allows us to connect with others on a heart level. As a word of caution, be aware that many of the so-called "local outreach" programs are giving things to people who abuse the government support systems; investigate before donating and make sure the funds or items are going directly to those who truly need assistance, not to people abusing the system or corporate official middlemen. Also realize there are many types of things you can give. You can give of your time, of your expertise, of your ability to work, of your money, of your friendship. You've got the idea; be intelligent and do the most good that you can. Be creative and find a place to channel your ability to give in a way that feels right for you. Being generous; giving and spiritually evolved does *not* mean allowing yourself to be taken advantage of. Handouts do not help anyone long-term; they simply enable people to feel entitled to more handouts. Give responsibly and in a way that offers long-lasting, self-sustaining benefits.

THE FORMAL PRACTICE

- Ask yourself who you would enjoy helping or who needs help the most at this point in time. Maybe it's a temporary disaster relief fund, or maybe it's to support a children's charity. Do whatever you feel is right for you.
- If you have ever received help for anything or from anyone, find ways to help those who have helped you in the past. Extend the kindness you were shown when you needed it.
- Don't worry about how much. Do what you can afford at the time and if you have no money to give, then donate yourself. Your time is very valuable and appreciated by numerous quality organizations.
- Pay attention to how you feel afterward. Learn to feel the same way when something is given to you as well.

PERSONAL EXPERIENCE

I do my best to make the effort to give of my time and knowledge. I have worked to teach special movement methods to young people who are amputees or otherwise physically challenged, so that they might become empowered by discovering their own strength and potential through enhanced capabilities. I worked it out with Grandmaster Hatsumi to issue them authentic rank in *Bujinkan Budo Taijutsu,* as their lessons included martial arts movement. The first time I worked with the youth group at Camp Yes I Can!, which is an amazing event offered and funded by Wright & Filippis, I realized these young people were giving me much more than I could ever hope to give them. I was so deeply touched by the courageous spirits and positive attitudes of those attending the camp and the staff overseeing the camp. When my friend José and I left the first evening to return to our hotel room, we entered the room and silently sat at the end of our beds. I stared straight ahead, completely unable to speak; I had no words. My heart felt so full and open; it was truly a state of intense bliss. I was overwhelmed with emotion with tears running down my face when I finally summoned the strength to say, "That was one of the most powerful experiences I have ever had. I feel amazing right now!" It was a great honor to work with that entire group. When you give of yourself from your heart, you will quickly know that you are always receiving more than you give.

It is great to offer a little more to people when you are coming from a place of abundance in comparison to their situation. When traveling throughout Egypt and China, I would haggle when making a purchase as is expected, but at other times I gave the price that was being asked. Some of those people cannot feed their families if they don't make any money selling their statues and trinkets, and you can feel when someone is truly in need or if they are simply trying to take advantage of you. I have preformed martial arts demonstrations at senior centers in Japan with Grandmaster Machida and his family and helped them to deliver food to the elderly citizens of his community. I also made sure to make a donation at the Cherry Blossom Festival in San Francisco's Japantown for the disaster relief of the earthquake and tsunami that struck Japan in 2011. These are ways that I enjoy giving, and in every instance I feel that I have received far more than I have given.

CHALLENGE TWO
The Power Of Words / Saying I Love You

THE IDEA
Say "I love you." Sounds simple enough, doesn't it? Well, think about it; how many times in 24 hours does someone tell you that they love you? I hope you hear it often. How often are you telling people that you love them? I hope that's often too. Make it a habit to stay current on telling the special people in your life that you love them. Say it however you can; text message it, email it, write it, say it on the phone or in person, face to face while looking them in the eyes. Be aware of how it makes

you feel when someone tells you that they love you, and how you feel when you tell someone else that you love them. It feels good, right? We are so busy with our demanding lives today that we just don't tell those around us that we love them; we take it for granted that they know. What are waiting for? Share some love! When you say, feel it; don't just mindlessly say the words. Allow the emotional content to charge the words and make a strong heart connection. There is nothing to fear.

This is a great way to get your heart to open and connect to another person's heart; it is very powerful and the very core of how a Being should be living. What an incredibly powerful way to raise your vibration, and theirs as well! This helps others feel good, protected and connected. Know too that you are loved by the Divine. I would also recommend you look yourself right in the eyes via a mirror each day and tell yourself that *you* love you. It's so amazing how we expect others to tell us this, yet we are not comfortable or in most cases incapable of saying it to ourselves. I know it may feel kind of silly at first, but it will be no time at all before you love your Self. A word of warning though, it will raise eyebrows if someone interrupts you kissing your own reflection in the mirror.

THE FORMAL PRACTICE

- Tell the people in your life that you love them. It's that easy. Say the words more often and feel them come from your heart. Even if it "really isn't your thing;" that is the idea after all, to change who you are.
- When you talk on the phone, get in the habit of saying "I love you" before you hang up. Not just family, but to anyone you genuinely love, such as your friends. If there are people that you just don't talk to very often, then text or email them at least every couple weeks just to say that you love them.

PERSONAL EXPERIENCE

I was terrible at this when I was younger. I had a difficult time saying the words. Eventually, I underwent enough spiritual growth to reach a point where I *wanted* to tell people that I loved them, but it just didn't feel right. In truth, it was that I was not yet secure enough in myself to tell them. Since I have undergone a more expansive awakening, I now tell my brother I love him every time we speak or see each other. I told my grandparents I loved them every time I saw them, and am I ever glad that I did. I tell my daughters that I love them whenever we speak on the phone or see each other. Now that I live across the country from them I will randomly text them just to tell them I love them. I tell my grandsons I love them many times throughout one of our phone conversations or Skype sessions, and I end every email that way to friends and family. Of course, I never leave home, go to sleep, finish a phone call or a text with my fiancé without telling her how very much I love and appreciate her. She is great at it too. Even after a number of years together, we both continue to express our love throughout the day whenever we feel inspired to do so. You just never get tired of hearing that from someone, do you? I know my heart jumps every time she tells me that she loves me, and when she looks into my eyes while saying it, I feel like the luckiest man on the planet. There is something happening when it warms your heart; it's called a heart opening!

CHALLENGE THREE
Emotional Quality / Harmonious Relationships

THE IDEA

The first step is to develop a sense of awareness for your emotions, and begin to notice what emotions you are experiencing throughout the day. Begin to notice how one feeling or emotion has a tendency to flow right into another. Notice what causes them to change and how quickly they can do so, but do your best not to judge them. This process alone will begin to take the power away from your emotions and give it back to you.

You need to become mindful to how your emotions actually make you feel mentally and physically. Do you physically tense up when you get angry or frightened? Do you give up and turn into a limp noodle when you feel overpowered or overwhelmed? Does your stomach hurt when you get jealous or feel betrayed? Do you feel lighter when you receive good news? Do you start to gently tremble when you are about to passionately kiss the one you love? Got the idea? Notice the interaction between your emotions and the physical body. Then start to notice the effects on your body when you are experiencing a negative emotion and change that emotion as quickly as you can. Just cancel it out and begin to focus on something that will allow you to feel better. You can create any trigger that works for you, just make sure it is powerful enough to do the job.

Let's apply this to our relationships. I am going to offer examples from a relationship with a partner/lover for the purpose of this example, but in actuality I apply this to every type of relationship I have. Pay attention to how you feel around your spouse or partner. Do you feel kinder and gentler? Do you feel filled with an incredible sense of love and compassion for them? You should feel all of this and more if you are in a relationship with the right person; if you feel negatively around them, I would encourage you to question why. Maybe it's something you need to work on within yourself, or maybe your relationship is simply no longer serving either of you. You will need to decide this for yourself. Pay close attention to the interplay of emotions between the two of you.

As you get into this phase you will begin to develop and apply some empathy. You will become more aware of the feelings of your partner, be able to tell how the things you say and do affect them, and discover how their own issues cause them to feel certain ways. You should flip it around and see how this person influences you too. It is here that you will discover how to take back your personal power, as well as to offer empowerment to the one you love. It will become painfully clear if anyone is attempting to manipulate or control you, and if so, you can learn to become free of these behaviors to reclaim your personal power.

THE FORMAL PRACTICE

- Take a few days to become more aware of what you are feeling at any given moment. The act of stopping to pay attention will begin to bring a sense of awareness for your emotions to the forefront of your mind.

- Now take a few days and become aware of your emotions as they rise and fall, morphing from one to another.

- Write a list of ten emotions you experienced throughout the day. You can write them down as you experience them, or you can recall them later. If you use the recall method, allow the feelings you experienced at the time to resurface so you can understand them better.

- Take three of the emotions you experienced and write how they made you feel mentally in your head, emotionally in your heart, and physically in your body. Ask yourself, "Why did I experience that emotion?" and "How did it make me feel in all three areas?"

- Create a "trigger" for yourself to use when you observe an undesired emotion so that you might change your response and the way you feel.

PERSONAL EXPERIENCES

Back in the early 1990's, I was studying a system of *Tendai Mikkyo* (esoteric Buddhism) with the Blue Lotus Assembly, headed by Stephen K. Hayes, which truly helped to bring these teachings to light for me. I started to review my feelings at the end of each day; I was surprised and more than just a little dismayed and disappointed. The vast majority of my emotions were negative ones. It only took me a minute to realize that I not only wanted to change, but that I needed to change. I did exactly what I described above for you here, and little by little I noticed that I began to experience more positive emotions instead of negative ones. I cannot express how important this truly is to you and your well-being.

Your emotions are directly linked to your thoughts as automated responses, but that is not the entire picture. There's more that has to be attended to than simply your thoughts. I found that my thoughts were a large part of it, but also my beliefs, my perceptions and my past conditioning needed to be addressed as well. Once you become aware of your emotions, you can trace them back to determine their origination point, helping you to understand what needs to be changed in order to feel more positively. I noticed that as I changed these things, I began to feel so much lighter and I started to laugh a lot more often. I also began to feel that the relationship I was in at the time no longer served me. It was very hard to admit, even to myself, but my poor behaviors showed it all too well. I was able to move on to a new relationship that serves us both incredibly well and I am able to experience even more positive, loving emotions, both through giving and receiving.

CHALLENGE FOUR
Unplug From Technology

THE IDEA

Disconnect from technology and clutter in order to reclaim your humanity. I will break this one into two parts for easier understanding, application and practice.

Disconnect from technology. I hear the panic already; your mind is racing, "But what about my…?" and "Oh, I can't possibly do that because I have to…" Remember, no more excuses. Start by setting aside a minimum of three hours on one day and unplug from all forms of technology and communication. You can let someone reliable know you are doing this in case of an emergency. I mean unplug it all; no cell phones, no TV, no radio, no electronic devices, not even a wristwatch. If it has a power source, such as a battery or power cord, it's to be turned off. Ideally, I recommend working up to a full week. Instead of making excuses about why you can't do it for that long or longer, take the opportunity to get away with someone you love and spend some quiet, quality time together. In order to progress you must not see obstacles, you must see opportunities.

Clean the clutter. You really regain a great amount of energy by doing this, and I highly recommend going through your possessions every six months to a year and throwing stuff away, cleaning and reorganizing your living environment. You went through *Feng Shui* concepts in the

Earth level challenges; notice how much easier the energy flows in your home and the positive quality of that energy without the clutter. You may even notice that your nervous system is able to relax and your mind is much calmer. Clutter creates mental and physical stress and tension. See how all of these things interconnect with one another? Clutter can keep you from making advancements in your spiritual practices. Mental clutter prevents you from doing even the most basic of mental exercises. Physical clutter muddies the mind and creates negative energy in the space. It also prevents the natural energy flow in any given space, causing the energy in a cluttered room to stagnate.

THE FORMAL PRACTICE

- As a preliminary exercise, begin by unplugging from the negative news media and toxic people; then start to fill that time and space with positive influences and stimuli.
- Set aside the day in the week that you will unplug from all technology for three hours. I offered a partial list above so you know what to get away from; it's up to you to apply common sense to anything else. Be responsible to yourself and others.
- After you become comfortable with three hours, raise it in increments that challenge you until you can achieve an entire week or more. The longer you go, the greater the effect.
- The second part here is to clear your clutter. Every six months, go through your belongings and get rid of some old things you no longer need. Make sure you find things from each room in your house. You can enhance the earlier challenge of "giving" by donating them to people in need, or at the very least you can recycle them.
- Now clean up your living environment. I trust you are doing this daily and not just every six months. The six months is just for the really big stuff; if you are really good and there is not much clutter to clear, then just pick one thing and get rid of it. It will shake up your ego and nervous system a bit, which is good for both.

PERSONAL EXPERIENCES

In order to begin this experience and make some real changes in myself, I needed to stop all the negative input and conditioning I was experiencing each day. I learned to stop associating with negative people who complained all the time. I know it can sound cold-hearted, but I had to do this (and so do you) for my own well-being. I had to separate myself from toxic people and their behaviors in order to correct my own. Then I cut off all the new media. Let's face it, they are peddling fear and garbage for the herd. Once I eradicated the need to care about how much fear mongering is produced in the name of ratings and mass control, I started to feel even better yet. I don't know about you, but my parents and grandparents had a nightly habit of watching the eleven o'clock news before going to bed. What a huge mistake! This was family conditioning that I set out to break immediately. I then began listening to positive growth CD programs and spending time with positive and successful people.

The month my fiancé and I spent in China made a massive impact on my ability to decompress and be able to begin a completely new life. Unplugging from all technology for that entire month was one of the most powerful experiences and exactly what I needed at the time. I must admit that it was even more profound than I figured it could be. As I have stated earlier, the longer you unplug, the more incredible and beneficial the effects. To be able to set aside all the technology and get back to nature was in itself a truly spiritual experience. I learned to relax, to be unconcerned with who might try to call or email me; it would all wait. I had been attached to my cell phone for years as I cared for my grandparents and my mother, receiving calls all times of the day and night to go to the hospital and handle various needs for them. After years of all that, it felt so unbelievably good to turn that cell phone off and tuck it away in my duffle bag for an entire month.

Everyone has heard that "Cleanliness is next to Godliness," right? It's meant as advice to follow in a bigger way than simply washing your hands. A cluttered, dirty home environment (inside the home and outside around the home) causes clutter in your mind and the minds of anyone living there or even visiting. That's why as people become more sensitive, they understand that they don't like to visit friends or family who live in messy, cluttered, dirty homes.

My grandpa was an amazing man, truly one of the best; yet he lived through the Great Depression and held the belief that you throw nothing away, because you can use it for something else or you might need it later. He passed this on to me. I had to realize that my belief came from someone else's experience, and I needed to actively change those belief patterns in my mind to something more conducive to me and my personal space. When I was packing to move to California, I took the opportunity to throw a great deal of things away. What I didn't throw away, I sold, gave away or donated. Once I unpacked in my new home, I threw away even more stuff. With each item I discarded, I managed to dispose of some of the behaviors I wished to change about myself. Talk about a freeing experience! As I threw things away I also released my mental, emotional, and energetic attachments to those items, the people they were connected to, and the situations surrounding the items. The idea of cleaning clutter is nothing new, but as Lao Tzu put it, "What others teach, I also teach." What I am doing is giving you the practical approach that I used myself and have been teaching to others in order to make *real* progress.

ESOTERIC CHALLENGES: MINDFULNESS

CHALLENGE ONE
Inner Smile—Self-Love & Opening The Heart

THE IDEA
This is a simple and powerful core technique that I learned from Qigong Master Michael Winn and from Grandmaster Mantak Chia. The version each person teaches can vary slightly; you too can personalize it once you are able to attain results and come to feel the benefits. I will present a basic version here in order to get you started. It is important

to have some idea of your body and its parts; after all, it is the vehicle by which you get to experience this lifetime. I will supply you with basic locations here, but part of the exercise is to get to know your body and establish a direct line of communication with the internal side of your physical self.

In a video interview I conducted recently for my blog site, Expansive Expressions, I asked Grandmaster Mantak Chia about the Inner Smile. He stressed the importance of this exercise and indicated that this technique is the essence of all the other exercises in his *Universal Healing Tao System*. The Inner Smile is far more than a visualization or meditation technique; it's a beautiful way to get connected to your physical self.

THE FORMAL PRACTICE

- Begin by finding a safe, quiet place to sit where you won't be disturbed. Have a seat and get comfortable.
- Start by taking three deep breaths, then begin the "Breath Bridge" technique found in Challenge Four of the Heaven section.
- Take your mental focus to your liver. Repeat the same process of smiling to your liver. The liver glows the brightest green you can see in your mind's eye. See it glowing brighter as it smiles back at you. Each time you inhale, see the liver glowing brighter; as you exhale see the glow settle just a bit. Your liver is located on your right side underneath your rib cage.
- Look inward toward your heart and smile to your heart. It's alright here, and even preferred, if you smile physically and not just in your mind. As you smile to your heart, envision it opening and shining light in all directions, touching upon everyone without discrimination or judgment. The heart glows the brightest red you can see in your mind's eye. Now see it glowing brighter as your heart smiles back at you. Each time you inhale, see the heart glow brighter; as you exhale see the glow settle just a bit. Your heart is located slightly left of center behind your sternum and rib cage.

- Take your mental focus to your spleen. Repeat the same process of smiling to your spleen. The spleen glows the brightest yellow you can see in your mind's eye. See it glowing brighter as it smiles back at you. Each time you inhale, see the spleen glowing brighter; as you exhale see the glow settle just a bit. Your spleen is located on the left side of your body under the ribcage.

- Take your mental focus to your lungs. Repeat the same process of smiling to your lungs. The lungs glow the brightest white you can see in your mind's eye. See them glowing brighter as they smile back at you. Each time you inhale, see the lungs glow brighter; as you exhale see the glow settle just a bit. Your lungs are located in your chest behind your sternum and rib cage.

- Take your mental focus to your kidneys. Repeat the same process of smiling to your kidneys. The kidneys glow in dark blue or black, the brightest of either of these colors you can see in your mind's eye. See them glowing brighter as they smile back at you. Each time you inhale, see the kidneys glowing brighter; as you exhale see the glow settle just a bit. Your kidneys are located at the backside of your body between the pelvis and bottom of the ribcage.

- Now, if you have any injury or illness, this is the time to smile to it too. See it in your mind's eye and smile to it as it glows bright gold, the brightest gold possible. Then think about how it felt when it was healthy. Wish it well and see it smiling back at you; then let it go.

- Go back to the heart one last time, smiling to it and seeing it glow bright red as described above.

- Sit quietly and feel your body inside and out. Feel the presence of your mind and feel how great it is to be you. This helps you to develop a sense of unconditional love and compassion for yourself. Reflect upon all the great things you do for yourself, for others and how the lives of others are better because you are part of their experience.

PERSONAL EXPERIENCES

I first went through this process under the direction of Qigong Master Michael Winn and then later I learned it directly from Grandmaster Mantak Chia. It seemed to be a pretty simple experience and yet one with immense power. Using the Inner Smile, I was able to find those areas of myself of which I was not completely accepting, which allowed me to work on them. It also allowed me to establish a direct line of communication with my internal organs. According to Taoist beliefs, each major organ has its own spirit. I still practice this frequently as a quick way to open my heart even further and give positive benefits to my internal physical body.

CHALLENGE TWO
Opening The Heart Center Meditation

THE IDEA

There are many exercises out there for opening the heart center; I read a new way in nearly every book I pick up. The trouble is that the vast majority of these do not contain much substance; others offer incredibly complex methods that may have worked for the author, or so they thought, but have little value to others. Remember that simple is the natural way. The more complex and filled with ritual, the less authentic it tends to be. There are a few good versions out there, but I will provide you with a version that is fairly simple, easy to learn and practice, as well as safe to perform. It has been my experience that the toughest part about a real heart opening exercise is to get the heart to open up in the first place. This can be a real challenge, especially if you have suffered traumatic experiences in your life; getting that door to open can be uncomfortable and even painful. Most people don't realize that opening the heart, the crown and activating the lower abdominal center is uncomfortable in the beginning.

Once you get the heart open, learning how to keep it open is another aspect that must be addressed, as the heart closes so easily. Whenever you get into an uncomfortable situation, your safety feels threatened, or someone says something that hurts your feelings, it causes your heart center to close up as a defense mechanism. Unless you can feel this and purposely reopen it, it will not open again until you feel loved, someone says something that makes you feel good, you feel love for someone else, and so on. I believe Jesus mastered the process of opening the heart and keeping it open no matter the circumstances, even in the face of death.

THE FORMAL PRACTICE

- Begin by setting aside about ten to fifteen minutes every evening for one month. You can make it longer if you like, but do your best to do at least the ten to fifteen minutes. Once you get into the process, it often feels so good you may want to go longer.

- Find a comfortable place to sit or lay down, as long as you do not fall asleep. Relax for a moment and take a few deep breaths. Evaluate your emotional vibration to make sure you are feeling positive. If your emotional vibration is lower than usual, do something to raise it before returning to the exercise.

- Perform the Breath Bridge technique as you have previously to go inward and connect with your inner Self. Look down in your mind's eye and smile to your heart, seeing it smile back at you; thank the heart itself for being healthy, beating and keeping you alive. See your heart glow with a bright golden light that gets stronger with each breath you take. Feel the heart center fill with the power of a higher vibrational frequency. Try to hold the connection between your mind and your heart throughout the entire exercise.

- Recall a time in your life when you can remember how awesome it is to be you. This can be a time that you helped someone, had your first kiss, or were on the receiving end of a warm hug from your mother or father. Now feel that love toward yourself. Say to yourself. "I love me." You can say it as many times as you like or need, just make sure you believe it. Make it genuine, feel your heart begin to open and feel the golden light begin to expand from your heart.

- Extend that feeling of love for someone else in your life. You can also hold this for multiple people at once, or apply it to different people each time you do the exercise. Recall a time when you felt an overwhelmingly strong sense of love for someone. Maybe it's a parent, your child, a dear friend, a lover, your spouse. Feel a sense of unconditional love for the person, the purest love you can imagine. Remember how that felt, feel your heart open a little farther and feel the golden light begin to expand even further outward from your heart.

- Now recall a time when you felt the happiest you have ever felt. Remember what that degree of happiness felt like. Maybe it was when you first fell in love, or the birth of your child, or that special gift you received for a holiday. Remember this feeling of pure bliss and feel your heart opening even more, the golden light of your heart expanding outward even further into the world.

- Remember when you had an experience where either you held a great amount of compassion for someone or someone offered you the gift of compassion. Feel what that was like, feel how right and good it feels to both give and receive compassion. Feel your heart center become even more opened and feel the golden light of your heart shine even brighter and extend even further yet.

- Evoke a time when you felt a deep sense of appreciation for someone; perhaps a friend, family member, or teacher. Maybe it was when someone offered a heartfelt show of appreciation towards you, in the form of gratitude, respect, love or friendship. Recall that feeling of appreciation and then extend the golden light of your heart outward to your friends, family, and teachers as your heart opens even more.

- Now recall a time when someone wronged you or hurt you in some way. Embrace this experience as an opportunity for growth. As you remember this instance, disassociate yourself from those emotions to neutralize them and observe the situation without begin controlled by them. Feel forgiveness toward the person who hurt you and allow whatever happened to dissolve; let it go. Feel the golden light of your heart extend out to reach them as well. Say to them, "I forgive you." Forgiveness is very powerful and it is important to do your best to offer it.

- Now, in your mind's eye, see your heart fully opened and the Divine golden light shining out to cover the entire planet. Every single person without a single exclusion is bathed in the golden light of your heart. Feel it connect to the hearts of every other person, unconditionally, feeling the totality of the universal oneness. Everyone is really doing the best they can. Some are more enlightened than others, but everyone is doing their best. We are all brothers and sisters of the Divine Source.

- Relax and hold that great feeling in your heart. Slowly reverse the process of the Breath Bridge. Start to move around and then open your eyes. Take a moment to collect yourself before jumping up. You are making headway if you come out of the exercise with tears running down your cheeks and a very warm, expansive feeling in your chest.

- Try to hold this feeling of connection for as long as possible after the exercise. The longer you can hold it, the better you will become at living from a place of an open heart.

- **BONUS:** If you get stuck in your progress, you can perform this version to facilitate the process. Find someone you trust and are willing to be completely open and honest with to help you. This other person is going to sit across from you with you facing them. You are going talk about the times you felt self-love, love for others, bliss, compassion, appreciation, forgiveness and unconditional connection to everyone. You are going to talk for three minutes on each topic; you can have your helper time you if you like. Once you open your mouth, do not pause or stop speaking; allow it to just roll out and keep flowing without the mind or ego getting involved.

PERSONAL EXPERIENCES

The first time I experienced this, I was at work in a factory, unloading a truck of nitric acid. The temperature was in the mid-90's outdoors with the sun blazing and high humidity, which is not unusual for a Michigan summer. I was in a head-to-toe rubber acid-resistant suit with a trailing air respirator. I lost so much fluid that day that I literally had over an inch of liquid in my rubber boots by the time I finished unloading the truck. During that time I was hot, miserable and not very excited about the job I was doing. Yet, as my thoughts settled on a happy situation in my life I felt flooded with joy, suddenly so blissful that I ached right in the center of my chest. I felt so light and ecstatic that I knew what it was like to be high on life. If this process can happen under such seemingly miserable conditions, imagine what can ensue if you are sitting comfortably in a pleasant meditation!

As I perform this exercise my heart becomes stronger, bolder and more courageous. It stays open far more often now, in spite of any external circumstances. I am still working on achieving mastery of this exercise, but the progress I've made has been extremely substantial. The technique above is one of the simplest and best practices for achieving real results that I have experienced, without all the silliness they can sometimes contain. It is also one of the most potent, as it doesn't just open the heart center a crack; it has the potential to expand the heart much further.

CHALLENGE THREE
Raise Your Vibrational Frequency

THE IDEA

By this point in the program you should be aware of when your vibrational frequency is up, down or somewhere in between. How do you know? You feel it! I will share with you some personal examples of things that raise my vibration. Hopefully that helps you to recognize the same occurrence in your own experience. When I wake up in the morning with a cool breeze blowing through the window, wrapped up in my nice warm blankets, it reminds me of how I felt as a young teenager on summer vacation; only now it's even better as I have my fiancé to pull in tight and hold while I experience it. How about the taste of fine chocolate or top-quality organic tequila? Or sharing a new life adventure with my fiancé, passing on the practices I hold so dear with loved ones, or learning new esoteric knowledge.

I just cherish the feelings I pick up on from my daughters when they are happy and content. The excitement of my grandson Jordan as he plays with his trains with such focused determination. The feeling I get when I hear his voice on the other end of the receiver when he calls me to tell me "sumpin" or that "he wuvs me really big." Seeing my newest grandson Dallas get excited at the sound of my voice and army crawl over to the iPad to take a closer look as we Skype. Holding my fiancé's hand as we walk along Drake's Beach in Point Reyes National Seashore. The sheer freedom I get from performing martial arts movement while in a state of *mushin* (no mind) and *nagare* (flow). The exhilarating feeling of a good katana (Japanese sword) in my hands. Visually studying the amazing sacred artwork I have framed in our home. The feeling I get while teaching someone when they really get it. Running my fingertips lightly over my fiancé, touching the most exquisite woman on the planet. Laughing with my good friends and students, reading great books by my favorite authors, and buying gifts for people I love. Wow, I could fill entire volumes with the things that raise my vibration; how about you? Why don't you list one hundred things that you know raise your vibration? It really shouldn't be very hard; you may be very surprised how easy this is. After this you will have a small glimpse of just how blessed you really are. I promise.

We live in a world of contrast and we learn from contrast. Write down ten things that lower your vibration. Yes, keep it to only ten please; I know you could easily do more. The problem is that the majority of people focus far more upon the negative than the positive and I am trying to correct those behavior patterns. After you come up with your top ten list, put it aside and focus one more time on the positive list.

After a while you should notice that you are experiencing so much more of the positive list than the negative. Remember, what we think about, we bring about. Focus on the good things and you will attract more of those good things into your life experience.

Here are a few things you should be able to feel for yourself and know, but also know that there are always exceptions to the things I list. Please keep in mind that this is a very condensed list and does not necessarily reflect my personal taste, but it does reflect the results of my research through personal exploration. The vagueness is to encourage you to develop the sensitivity to discern the rest of the details for yourself. (Please refer to Table 4-1).

TOPIC	HIGH VIBRATION	LOW VIBRATION
Music	Classical, Light Rock	Rap, Blues, Metal
Movies	Comedy, Animated	Drama, Horror
Foods	Natural, Organic, Whole Food	Artificial, Packaged, Sweetened
Clothes	Good Quality, Natural Fabric, Clean	Rip Offs, Poor Fit, Dirty
Thoughts	Positive, Healthy	Manipulations, Jealousy
Words	Encouraging, Supportive	Lying, Gossiping
Actions	Helping Others, Exercise	Laziness, Harming Others
Activities	Quiet Walks, Meditation	Stealing, Bar Hopping

Table 4-1

THE FORMAL PRACTICE
- Begin this exercise by getting a piece of paper and writing down all the things that make you feel good when you experience

them. Not just the instant gratification; I am talking about things that leave you feeling good long after you experience them. List as many as you can think of and don't be afraid to be specific. Write as much as you can in three minutes. Do not allow your pen to leave the paper.

- Find some music that you like and listen to it. Feel what it does to your emotional state, how your body physically responds and how it makes your heart feel. Then experiment with various types of music to see how they affect your emotional vibration. You will notice that your taste in things will change as you go through this evolutionary process. Don't resist it, just go for the ride and have fun with it.

- Repeat this same experiment with movies, television shows, and books.

- Pay close attention to the people in your life and the way they affect your emotional vibration. Consider limiting your time with anyone who consistently lowers your vibration and leaves you feeling troubled. Make some new friends who do help raise your vibration, and remember that it's a two way street. If you are not raising their vibration in return, they will not desire your company either.

PERSONAL EXPERIENCES

I have worked with people over the years who were just thoroughly negative. That doesn't mean they weren't nice people or didn't have good hearts; they just weren't happy unless they were complaining or gossiping. Some of these people were negative because they were so unhappy in their lives and didn't believe they could do anything to correct it. I learned to both limit my time around such people and control any conversations that we had, or just evade them altogether. The same went for friends and even martial arts students. Admittedly, I didn't always know how to help raise someone else's vibration effectively, but as I learned this process I got better and better at it. People should be left feeling better that you were around them. I always try to leave my friends, family and students filled with positive, high-level emotional vibrations.

I have practices like the one above in place to maintain my vibrational frequency as high as I desire. When external circumstances cause it to lower a bit, I immediately correct it by raising it back to where it should be. Many of the challenges presented throughout the phases of Heaven, Earth and Being are designed to assist you in raising your vibration, even if the primary focus is on something else entirely. Feeling is the primary key to success.

CHALLENGE FOUR
Overcoming your Own Worst Enemy: The Ego

THE IDEA

This is a difficult exercise for all of us, so don't feel bad if it takes you a lifetime to accomplish this one! Remember that all of these exercises are meant to be a progressive way of life anyway. In martial arts there is a saying that the toughest battle you will ever fight is between your own ears; this refers to the battle you are already in with yourself, every single day, whether you want to or not. Overcoming one's ego is at the very core of self-development, as you simply cannot achieve any level of true spiritual evolution when the ego is still in control of you.

Sometimes this venture is described as *destroying* or *conquering* the ego, but the ego is a part of you that plays the important role of creating your sense of individuality and offers you survival instincts. I don't believe that we would be given a "piece" of ourselves that was meant to be discarded. I feel the same way in how modern medicine is so quick to pull out someone's gallbladder or appendix. The gallbladder connects to one of the longest meridians in the body and has some pretty important digestive functions, and contrary to popular belief, the appendix has important functions in assisting the immune and digestive systems. I don't feel these things should be so easily discarded, unless it is an emergency situation.

The ego is not bad or evil; it serves its valuable purpose for awhile when you are young, but as you evolve and become more spiritually aware, it is time for it to be tamed. The ego will not go quietly; it will fight fiercely to survive. This is an area that defeats even the strongest and most skilled warriors I have known. The best way I know of to overcome the ego is to call it out and keep doing so repeatedly, giving it time out after time out like a spoiled, undisciplined child. The first step is to identify ego-driven behavior; this occurs every time your mind has the need to think that it is better than someone else, has to put someone else down in order to feel better, feels the need for control over others and circumstances, or has the need to be elevated in some way.

Whenever you notice this type of thought pattern emerge, stop it, smile and realize that it is not "your" thought, but your "ego's" thought. Then tell your ego that you see it and will not tolerate its behavior anymore as you change the thought to a more positive one. Here's an example: Your best friend buys a new car that is awesome. Your friend is genuinely excited to show it to you, knowing you can appreciate it. Right away your ego begins to put forth thought patterns that result in negative emotions, such as jealousy and irritation. "How the heck can they afford this car? They will probably lose it soon or wrap it around a tree. I should have a car like that, not them." Those types of thoughts may begin flying through your mind in spite of wanting to be happy for them. The ego plants the seeds; they take root and begin to grow. Now you go back in the house, start to gossip about them and think about how you really don't like them that much anyway. This is how the ego works.

This does not mean you are a bad person; understand that the ego and what you perceive as your thoughts are not really you or your thoughts. You can easily see why it is necessary to overcome this before any real honest evolution as a Being can be made. Whenever this type of situation happens or anything remotely like it takes place, you have to catch it, recognize it and change it. This takes mental awareness, emotional mindfulness and a ton of willpower, but you can do it. As you engage your own ego in battle, you will overcome the larger behavior first and then you will find very subtle ways that it works. One thing I used to do (and honestly still use) to assist me is to put myself in someone else's shoes and understand the situation from their point of view. Maybe that would go something like this: "Wow, I can't believe it, I saved and saved, and finally have enough money to purchase the car of my dreams. I am so excited. Hey, you know who else would like to experience this car? My best friend. I'm going to call them and show it to them; we'll go on a drive so they can enjoy it with me." Everything is more fun when you have someone to share the experience with, right? Then when they arrive, how are you going to act? Are you going to rain on their parade or help them celebrate?

THE FORMAL PRACTICE

- Get a sheet of paper and set aside about ten minutes a day, at the end of the day, for one month. During each session, you will write down any instances you can remember where you acted from your ego. This will be extremely easy once you are able to admit it to yourself; remember, I am speaking from experience.

- As you write down these situations, reflect on them and try to think about how you could have responded more appropriately without the ego dictating your emotional reaction. You may find that you are embarrassed by some of your actions; I know I was. Keep pushing through anyway, as that's another sign of progress. Writing these things down is a way of calling out the ego and exposing it; this is the first step to overcoming it.

- After the one month you should begin to notice an improvement in the way you behave, with your reactions changing into responses. That's awesome! Now take one more month to notice when you act from your ego, but now you must act on correcting it as it is happening. Challenging? You bet! This will call out the ego even further, and that's what it takes to get a handle on it.

- This exercise does not end; the battle with the ego is a constant one that may take years. Do not quit, keep going; you can do it.

PERSONAL EXPERIENCES

I have met my ego face to face in the process of taming it and it was not pleasant. I know how difficult the process can be and how powerful an opponent the ego can be. I have watched literally thousands of people drop out of martial arts of various styles under various teachers. Some of them had good reason; they had to move, cut expenses because they lost their job, or the training simply wasn't right for them. But the vast majority I have witnessed left because the training reached a point that engaged and challenged their ego, and they were not ready for such a battle.

Naturally, the ego-driven student cannot see that they have been pinned to the mat by their own ego; instead the ego tricks them into believing they were somehow wronged by the teacher, style, or organization and they leave with a sense of self-righteousness that is based on a false foundation. I have seen some really talented people leave the training that just days before they claimed they would love for all time, because the ego managed to control them. I think the worst thing about this is that I know they are put back to the beginning and will have to start the battle all over again, which most people are not strong enough to do.

CHALLENGE FIVE
Stilling The Mind / Zero & No Mind Development

THE IDEA

This is a commonly requested technique, as I have had a great number of beginner students approach me and ask for ways to calm their mind. Usually, these people are near tears because of the frantic, unending chatter in their heads that is figuratively and literally driving them insane. Unfortunately, while the method itself is fairly simple, the actual act of practicing it can be extremely challenging. I really recommend that you go easy on yourself with this. Frustration leads to mental tension and more internal dialog. If during this practice you are not having much success at any given time, simply stop, smile to yourself and go do something else; you can try again later.

You need to quiet or still the mind of random thoughts. This exposes the ego and triggers your ability to isolate it and overcome it. Once the ego is overcome, you can effectively become "zero," which is to have no intention, no agenda, and no desire; you simply *be*. The concept of mushin (no-mind) is one that is becoming known as a myth more than an attainable state. This is incorrect, as it is a very attainable, worthy goal for any martial or spiritual seeker. After all, if I can do it, so can you; we are made of the same stuff. The main goal is to perform this practice until you can drop into a deep mediation, turning off your thoughts in an instant.

THE FORMAL PRACTICE

- Begin by finding a safe, secure, comfortable place to perform this exercise. It is critical to be somewhere you will not be disturbed, as being suddenly disrupted can be extremely harsh on the mind with this exercise.
- Have a seat, taking three deep breaths and settle into yourself. Perform the Breath Bridge technique again to go from your outer perspective to your inner perspective.
- Proceed by paying full attention to your breath. Do not try to force it into doing anything. Simply breathe and in and out, keeping this natural process going.
- Now, softy and easily say to yourself, "I breathe in—I breathe out," as you take your breaths and allow that to flow for however long you desire or need.
- Once you can do this for awhile without the mind wandering onto other things, begin to notice the time between the breaths. Then casually start to lengthen the time between the breaths. Just like the space/time between the notes of the shakuhachi flute, the space/time between your breaths is very important. The further you go into the "time" and "space" between

thoughts, the greater the stillness of your mind. Soon you will be able to turn off the thoughts altogether and trust that things will start up again without any issue.

- Allow this point of stillness between your inhalation and exhalation to lengthen at a natural rate, do not force it or your system will rebel by shortening the time in a hurry. You want to subtly sneak up on it.

- Perform this over time until you reach a point where you "fall into" the empty space/time between your breaths. This can take some time to achieve; patience, perseverance and consistency are the keys to succeeding.

- The initial state of mushin resides in that space/time of emptiness between your breaths.

PERSONAL EXPERIENCES

The first time I was able to observe my thoughts, it appeared to me as beautiful indigo-blue electric synapse bouncing around my brain like crazy. Then I watched as one thought would lead to another that I had previously thought was random and unconnected. In reality, these things *are* connected and a word or image of one thought is what usually sparks the next. The first time I was successful with this exercise by stilling my mind for a moment, it startled me so severely that I popped right out of it. I was left thinking, "What if the mind doesn't start up again?" Of course, that's really not a problem here as a general rule.

I used this method with great success many years ago when I took the *Bujinkan Sakki Test*. This test is commonly called the Fifth Degree Black Belt Sword Test, but it is really so much more than that. The object is to go before the Grandmaster as he raises a sword; you put your back to him, sit in the kneeling seated position and close your eyes. At some unknown point in time, the Grandmaster will suddenly cut down toward your head with the sword at full speed and full power. You are expected to perceive the would-be killing stroke and roll out of the position into safety, at least if you want to pass. Sakki translates as "killing intention" and the practitioner is expected to develop the skill to "feel" this, allowing their body to move out of the way without thinking. When I took the test it was performed at the Honbu Dojo in Noda-shi, Japan and administered directly by the Grandmaster, Masaaki Hatsumi. As I was called up, I walked to him and looked him in the eyes; I thought, "It is a good day to die, Sensei. It's alright if you should kill me today," which was something one of the Japanese Shihan (master teacher) had recommended as he helped me prepare. I then turned and sat in the appropriate space so that the Grandmaster did not have to adjust his distancing. I went into the seiza position, tipped my head slightly forward, closed my eyes, and took a deep breath. I listened as a small bird on the dojo windowsill chirped quickly three times, and then slipped into deep meditation with no thoughts happening at all. Bam! Suddenly, the next thing I knew I was rolling backward, upside down in mid-roll and I heard the applause of the others who were there observing.

I completed the back roll and stood up, trying to get my bearings. I had no conscious idea of what just happened. He then patted me on the shoulder, smiled and said "Yes!" I was told by friends observing that I never flinched, but instead moved in harmony with the wooden sword as it came down towards me. This test has been done with a practice sword for a very long time now, but it used to be done with a live blade. One tremendously important fact is this test is supposed to be taken once and only once. To fail and get struck by the sword means you were not ready to take the test and would have died if the sword were an actual blade. It took me only the one time.

This is the idea of the test; to clear your mind, to become zero. To become zero is to have no thoughts, no ego; this frees you to move in a limitless manner in complete harmonious flow with things around you. When your mind is still, the body is not jumpy in anticipation; everything is still. Anyone who flinches or moves with false starts is still too much in their head. The misconception is practitioners believe it is just a matter of sensing the energy of the attack or the attack itself and having the ability to move out of the way quickly enough. The idea is that you perceive the threat without consciously being aware of it, and the body moves to safety without being told to do so by the mind. This type of training will help prepare you to move instinctively without over-thinking everything all the time. It is then you can experience the feeling of being "zero."

CHAPTER FIVE

CREATING HEAVEN ON EARTH

*"Sing like no one's listening, love like you have never been hurt,
dance like nobody's watching, and live like its Heaven on Earth."*
— **Mark Twain** —

arth is a garden paradise, a playground filled with potential
and possibility. The three- dimensional reality of time, space
and matter is where human beings are able to experience the
sensations and emotions of the wondrous physical world. This is where
our non-physical self (spirit) manifests into the physical self (body)
and experiences all the things we cannot as non-physical entities. Look
around at all the wonders openly given to us by the Earth; you have the
vigilant presence of mountain ranges, majestic redwood forests, as well
as an entire aquatic world within the vast oceans and lakes. We have the
benefit of the physical senses to enrich our experience, allowing us to
delight in the bouquet of vibrant blossoms, move to the soothing sounds
of song, and know the loving hearts of others. This world is meant to
sustain life and supply us with everything we need in order to manifest

the experiences we desire in the brief time we have within each visit. Believing in the promise of Heaven only after you pass from this life is a mistake. We are eternal spirit, even while inhabiting these physical bodies, and as such we are able to know Heaven at all times. I know now that we are experiencing Heaven, right here during our time on Earth.

While this may seem bold to some, it is simply a matter of knowing for yourself where we come from and what we truly are. We come from the Universal Source, existing as a small piece of that Source. We are part of a collective whole while still having our individual consciousness as a spirit or energy. We know the comfort of pure love of the Divine while in our non-physical, formless state. We are presented with the opportunity to take pleasure in a brief existence in physical form that we can know as ourselves. This brief time in the physical realm is an amazing gift that allows us to experience Heaven in an exhilarating and tangible way right here on Earth. We are given the ability to manifest the experience we choose to engage in, while being supplied with life lessons designed to augment the Expansions of our Higher-Self. Life lessons are the challenges given to us by the Universal Source. Living a life of Heaven on Earth is what the experience is meant to be. Once the connection to your Higher Self has been clearly reestablished this will become evident.

Living a life of Heaven on Earth is to live from your heart. It is to take each step on the path with an open and unconditionally loving heart. It is the ability to feel and connect with the hearts of all others; to know the burning intensity of passion from the heart of your lover, manifested into physical touch and the soothing sound of their voice as they whisper, "I love you." To experience the innocent, loving heart of a child or grandchild as they wrap their tiny fingers around your index finger in an attempt to hold your hand and look up at you. It is to recognize your own loving, forgiving heart and to feel a genuine sense of Divine love for your Self. This is Heaven on Earth and it is meant to be shared with everyone, without exception; to hold in our hearts the love and compassion for all other beings, remembering that we are all portions of the Universal Source. We are all one. The Kingdom of Heaven is within; it's within your heart, and when you can open the gateway of your heart you will experience Heaven. It will then be manifested outward into the world and into your daily experience.

Creating a life of Heaven on Earth is not the monumental task you may first believe it to be. As you begin to accept responsibility for yourself and your life you will develop more awareness, more mindfulness and far more sensitivity for the world you enjoy. As you accomplish this and connect to your place in the universe, you will begin to actively and consciously create the life you desire to experience. Once you take action and apply these lessons to your life, you will stop and look around one day in the not-so-distant future, realizing that life could not possibly get any better. That's when it will! It really doesn't take long to begin to feel that you are living in Heaven on Earth. As you hold this experience, all new things and events will present themselves to you in the expanded experience that you are here to enjoy.

When you awaken every morning, I encourage you to give yourself a moment before jumping out of bed. Take those few minutes to reflect upon how blessed you are to have another magnificent day in this life! Get excited about it and prepare to engage it with every ounce of energy you possess. Consider all the people and things in your life that you genuinely appreciate. Think about how grateful you are until you feel tears of bliss spontaneously gently cascading down the sides of your face, until you feel your heart open and swell with the joy that it brings. As you hold this feeling of appreciation in your heart, you will attract even more reasons to feel grateful. When it's time to get up and start the day, I recommend that you proceed to an altar, a sacred place in your home, or even walk outside to be with Nature; whatever resonates best for you. This is a very personal thing between you and the Divine; it's your intimate time together. While this is your personal time with the Universal Source, it is also an extraordinary time to share with someone who is closest to you. These practices are more powerful when you perform them along side someone special in your life. It intensifies every aspect of the practice, offering a far more potent and fruitful experience for you both. As you connect more profoundly with the Universal

Source, you will begin to know the Divine nature of yourself and know it of that special person in your life as well. I often refer to my fiancé as *Angel*, not only as a term of affection, but because I can truly see and feel her Divinity. I hope you are able to recognize this quality in the special person you are sharing your life experience with. Once you can acknowledge this in your own reflection, it becomes much easier to see in others.

If performed consistently, these practices will set the stage for the wonderful events of your day and set into motion the creation of the remarkable life you desire. As you apply the teachings of Heaven, Earth and Being you will begin moving through life with a far greater degree of consciousness and balance. You will come to know your Higher Self, the consciousness of your spirit. You will feel more alive, more awake and more connected to everything and everyone around you. As this transpires you will begin to realize that you are living a life of Heaven on Earth. I have come to believe through my own life experience that this is the way we were all meant to live our lives. While this does require courage and effort on our part, it is a small price to pay for such a divinely-inspired, breath-taking adventure. Beginning the courageous journey of creating your life of purpose may require incredible amounts of inner strength. But believe in yourself and your right to live a life where you are consciously engaging your life lessons and soon you will be living a life of Heaven on Earth.

It helps greatly to have a clear impression of what Heaven on Earth looks like. What would Heaven on Earth be for you? Would it be having someone special to love, treasure and share your life with or having a job that you find stimulating and exciting? How about living in the most breathtakingly perfect place? I recommend spending some time to get a very lucid mental picture on what your life would look like if it was Heaven on Earth. You must be clear on it before you can possibly hope to create it; allow yourself to feel the emotions of living this dream life as you picture it in your mind. How terrific would you feel to have that perfect someone, to have an incredibly rewarding career, and to live in a beautiful home in the most perfect location? It would feel unbelievably extraordinary, wouldn't it!? It's okay to let yourself experience the emotional sensation of that life. Just evade the trap of your mind to flipping to the negative and thinking that it could never happen to you; because it can. Stay positive and hold the feeling of what it would be like to live your vision of Heaven on Earth.

For the majority of people, finding that exceptional someone, their life's soul-mate, would help them to feel as though they were living in paradise. Maybe this is a factor in creating your own personal Heaven on Earth experience. This is a fundamental drive for most human beings. I feel it is first necessary to experience self-love and self-sufficiency as you become the person you were meant to be. Once this is firmly in place, you have a wonderful platform from which to attract that special someone into your field of experience. The first mistake people usually make is to look to someone else to make them feel loved, secure or to take care of them. This is unfair for the other person and usually results in failure. You must love yourself, be secure in who you are and be able and willing to completely care for yourself before looking to find someone to share your life with. The primary idea is to mutually *share* these qualities with someone. That is a healthy relationship, and life is much more magical when you have someone to share it with whom you deeply love.

If you can establish a relationship with someone who shares the same spiritual and fundamental outlook on life as you do, then you are off to a great start. You can both grow, change, and experience evolutionary wonders of personal transformation together, helping one another along the way. It's a very blessed and beautiful experience of unity. If we are spiritual Beings (and we are) having a physical experience, doesn't this make complete sense? Take the time to discuss these issues with the other person *at the beginning* of a relationship. Living a heart-centered life does not mean acting impulsively, but instead knowing in your heart what is right for you. First get your Self right; then you will be ready to attract an amazing person into your life who wants to share the stroll down the path of life with you. Please don't try to change yourself for someone else; this dishonest approach does not allow you to live from a place of authenticity, and you both deserve better. Get out into your community to meet other like-minded people. Allow for some Divine intervention; give the universe a chance to move things around and create an opportunity for you to run into that special person. The best place to run into someone who will fit with you will be at places and events that are of interest to you.

A relationship is not the only topic of attention in creating your divinely inspired life experience. By following the guidance in this book and adding in a few ideas of your own, you have every opportunity to begin living your life that will be nothing short of Heaven on Earth. Living in Heaven on Earth is your choice, just as it is your choice to be happy. Change your mental perspective and your entire life will change. Once you grasp this in your heart and know it as truth, then you open the doorway to experiencing Heaven on Earth as it was meant to be.

THE INTERACTION OF HEAVEN, EARTH & BEING

The forces of Heaven, Earth and Being are engaged in a constant state of dance-like interaction. These three natural forces play in harmony with each other to create a universe of balance, beauty and wonder. As you become not only self-realized, but fully actualized, you will begin to not only see these interactions, but to feel them as well. Science helps us to understand how the cosmic forces of Heaven interact with the Earth. The divinity of Heaven as the Universal Source is ultimately responsible for the creation of the Earth and human Beings, as well as all other things. We come to know ourselves as smaller pieces of the same energy that is the Universal Source. The physical body is in itself a manifestation of the Earth. Look around you and marvel at the intricate tapestry that has been woven with the strands of Heaven, Earth and Being (humanity). Experience the magic of the gleaming evening sun setting over a majestic mountain top and feel your heart center open like a stunning blossom. Know the divine nature of love as you hold the hand of someone you adore, feeling your heart connect to theirs as you share this adventure in time and space.

You will soon know for yourself how within each one of the three (Heaven, Earth and Being), there exists the other two. From this you will begin to know the truth of *oneness* and experience real, life-changing Expansion. Once you know this for yourself your life will change forever. You will see the exquisite in every flower petal, you will feel the splendor in the simple act of a kiss and you will sense the magnificence of the enchanting gift that is life. You will know the divine perfection of everything that exists. The time has arrived to combine the energies of Heaven and Earth inside us to stimulate the opening of our hearts, allowing them to radiate in all directions and to shine upon the Ten Thousand Beings. This is the direction of the human race's evolution as we awaken to our place between Heaven and Earth.

THE NEW WORLD REALITY

The reality of our time is that the world is in a state of vast transformation. Humanity has reached a crossroads; we now have the choice to evolve or to resist this natural state of growth. It will then be the choice of every individual on the planet to either step forward and take part in this rare opportunity, or to make the decision to avoid it, ignore it or not believe it. Free will can be a tremendous gift or it can be the equivalent of a child with a loaded gun. We must choose wisely as sometimes there is no second chance and no do-over. While this will present the human species with unique challenges, I whole-heartedly feel this time will bring the astonishing opportunity for all humankind to become fully conscious Beings in complete harmony with Heaven and Earth.

I would like to paint a prospective picture of the future for you. I am not claiming to know exactly how things will play out in this cosmic event, but I will offer you a glance into some possibilities, which I feel are very real. I have seen fleeting look of things in flashes of insight during my Qigong and meditation practices. Some of these ideas are the reflection of various martial and spiritual masters that I've had the great honor to train with. Whatever the source of this inspiration, I would like to present something to stimulate your imagination. To envision it and feel it will help us all to create it and live it as our collective reality.

Imagine a time in the very near future when all the things that once served the greater good of humankind are no longer effective. Imagine that all of these policies, organizations and systems either disintegrate or transform by making changes to better fit with a new era. Envision a world where we count on our leadership to offer honesty and full transparency as they act for the true good of the collective people, willing to be at the forefront of any challenge. Human beings are no longer separated by ethnicity, culture, creed, class or country; they are all connected through the heart. Corporations make their products and profits by applying sustainable practices to protect and honor the Earth. These same companies treat their employees with respect and gratitude for their contributions. Customer service means everything and companies enjoy greater success due to all new levels of benefit they provide for their customers. The companies that make the most profit are those acting for the genuine greater good of the people; not those willing to sacrifice the public's health in order to receive larger management bonuses. The employees offer an honest attempt to perform at their best and take pride in their efforts. People throughout the world begin to awaken and come to know their true place in the universe; they reclaim their connection to the Heavens and Universal Source while also respecting the Earth and its resources. They re-establish a deep respect for their physical bodies inside and out and find their way into their heart centers. Joyfulness is the normal state of all people; hatred and violence fade away into the shadows, soon to become nothing more than myth.

Imagine nearly every person taking control and responsibility for their health, no longer relying on potentially harmful medications. People are naturally health-oriented and in-tune to their bodies. Everyone acts with genuine kindness, compassion and appreciation for one another without exception. This same time offers us the ability to enjoy new levels of technology in limited doses while we all remain closely connected to the forces of Nature. Imagine the collective consciousness blossoming as it unfolds with a sense of enlightened consciousness that the human race has never known or experienced before. Imagine that your "job" is your life's purpose and you are consciously able to succeed at your life-lessons, allowing you to expand your consciousness as the universe expands in harmony with you. Take a moment to sit back and picture this, making sure to feel what it might be like to live in that environment. The ability to emotionally and vibrationally connect to this vision of reality is the first step in actively creating it.

I know this is the type of world I would like to see my children and grandchildren experience. I also know this sort of transformation will not come quickly or easily; change of this magnitude will most likely be foreshadowed by great challenge and struggle. To navigate these changes successfully will require the opening of our heart centers. Not merely some of us, but all of us; every single person on the planet must switch off their head and switch on their heart-light. This will allow us to evade adversity and make the transition into the new reality. I know I have made my choice, and I encourage all of you to make yours as well. Making the choice to accept your role in humanity as a fully activated Being begins with your ability to take a single action; to decide that today is the day you get up and take charge of yourself and your life.

THE FEELING OF BLISS

I refer to the feeling of "bliss" throughout this book. This term can sometimes carry a negative connotation, due to those who become blissed-out and sacrifice their grounding. I am referring to the term bliss as one of the highest vibrational frequencies a human being can experience. Bliss is a feeling that is alongside appreciation in its high vibrational quality. These feelings are the direct products of love, and love is *the* highest vibration possible. Love is the Universal Source. True bliss is the sustainable sensation of experiencing the Divine. It is a feeling beyond happiness and joy, and causes you to tear up for no reason other than feeling so completely uplifted. As you learn to hold your vibrational frequency at these higher emotional levels you will feel the type of bliss that I am talking about. This is also why I have included some high quality methods for grounding yourself. Through the Expansion Mastery System, you may experience such intense states of bliss that you need to be properly grounded to maintain a sense of balance. The higher (vibrationally) that you go, the deeper you need to be grounded. This allows you to feel bliss without effects of being spacey.

Happiness is at the essence of all human desire. I have experienced many esoteric Buddhist, Taoist and esoteric Western practices designed to show you that happiness is at the heart of what you truly desire. While I agree with this, I also feel that happiness, once attained, should be upgraded to joy, and your state of joyousness should aim for bliss. Why not shoot for the stars? While the analytical differences of these emotional states might be minimal, their vibrational quality differences are substantial. When you feel happy you smile and laugh and bounce around. It's a good feeling. When you are feeling joy you have a wider smile and your laugh comes from somewhere deeper. It's a great feeling. However, when you experience the feeling of bliss, you feel the initial ache in your chest as your heart opens and radiates out of your chest in every direction. You feel a sense of light-heartedness that cannot be described, only experienced. You are smiling all the time and infecting others with your smile. You are laughing from deep in your soul and you see the humor is everything, no longer taking yourself so seriously. This is an ecstatic feeling! It is a feeling that takes you into a state of direct connection to the love of the Divine.

APPLYING THE CHALLENGES AND GOING BEYOND

The challenges presented through the Expansion Mastery System are designed to offer you a firm foundation of practical methods to facilitate your personal Expansion. They were designed to offer you challenges for growth in the same way that the Universal Source offers life lessons or personal challenges for Expansion. Follow them closely and practice them often. You should be able to perceive the positive effects relatively soon, if not immediately. I would advise you to follow the program in the order of which it has been laid out, at least in the beginning. Allow yourself to go through each challenge and be patient with yourself as you undertake the journey. After you spend time with each challenge and you are able to internalize them, feel free to practice any one you wish whenever it feels appropriate to do so. You will even be able to modify them in order to best fit you and your own Expansion. Striving to create Heaven on Earth means becoming a leader of your own destiny, not a blind-faith follower of what someone else dictates. Develop a foundation and then expand by making slight personal changes to the original exercises. You do not want to become stuck in these practices; they are meant to be uplifting and enjoyable. If you find yourself becoming too heavily dependent upon a particular exercise and it is no longer yielding results, then let it go for a while, replacing it with another. The new practice may be just what you need in order to reach the next echelon of your Expansion. Becoming overly dependent upon a routine will lead to resistance, causing regression rather than Expansion. Do what supports your creation of Heaven on Earth and you will soon be experiencing the life of your dreams.

CHAPTER SIX

SPIRITUAL WARRIOR

"Link yourself to heaven and earth; stand in the very center with your heart receptive to the resounding mountain echo."
— **Morihei Ueshiba / John Stevens** —
The Essence of Aikido

A *Spiritual Warrior* is someone who moves forward in their spiritual evolution and Expansion, even in the face of very difficult choices. They do what they must to follow the path of spiritual advancement, no matter how hard it may be. The Spiritual Warrior lives from a place of non-attachment and will change everything in their life if need be in the pursuit of spiritual Expansion. I have found that once you seriously begin seeking the spiritual path, you will eventually be faced with the decision of graduating from a Spiritual Seeker to that of a Spiritual Warrior. It is only by passing through these stages can you become a Spiritual Master. The Spiritual Seeker is one who is just starting or dabbling in spiritual or religious teachings. They read and attend seminars and workshops, practice many different systems and techniques and begin to make some real progress. Sooner or later though they will be faced with the decision to remain a Seeker without making any further discernable advancement, or to become a Spiritual Warrior, understanding what it is to rely on their own Divine nature for what they need. The professional Spiritual Seeker continues through life experimenting in this and that, going from one New Age fad to the next, lost in the fog in fear of truly discovering their Divine nature and personal power. They continue to rely on others to make their decisions for them and are easily thrown at the first hint of distress or improvement.

The Spiritual Warrior, on the other hand, forges ahead into the great mist of the unknown, doing what must be done in order to keep making progress. For the Spiritual Warrior, there is no stopping or stalling out, because they know that to stop or stall means to go backwards in their evolution. This is seen as simply unacceptable. They begin to gather all the techniques of value, the ones that really serve them, learning to rely on a base system that serves their greater progress. More than likely they are open to drawing from numerous systems of spirituality and religion as they grow enough to realize for themselves what is true and honestly helping them. Great respect for the truth of all systems is recognized and reflected in their personal practice. These are the people that shine brightly and gravitate toward tranquility and serenity instead of drama and egotism. The Spiritual Warrior develops the personal strength to take full responsibility for all their choices and actions, and applies their skills in ways that allow others around them to feel safe. The Spiritual Warrior diligently practices for their own advancement, as well as to protect others and offer help and healing to those who really need it.

While it is not necessary to be a martial artist or to even care about swords, the lessons from these practices can be applied by and be of great assistance to everyone. One translation of the Japanese term known as *Bujin* is "Divine Warrior." This is seen in the martial arts organization of the *Bujinkan*, headed by Grandmaster Masaaki Hatsumi. This type of warrior never tires in their pursuit to create a clear connection to their Divine nature, their Higher Self, and their sense of oneness with the Universal Source. The symbol often used by these warriors and the ninja shadow warriors of Japan is the *kanji* or ideogram for "Nin," which is loosely translated to mean patience, perseverance, or to endure. This Japanese character consists of two individual characters placed one on top of the other. The upper character is the kanji for blade, or more specifically, the sharp edge of the sword. The lower kanji means heart. Jointly, this refers to a sword being held over your heart.

One way to look at this is that together it refers to remaining strong and true to your heart when someone attempts to keep you from your path, even with a sword. To remain true to your heart is to remain true to your spirit. While there are a great number of interpretations of this, I have come to know it as the ability to keep a pure, sincere heart, even in the face of adversity; to remain true to what you hold in your heart, the seat of the original spirit, even under the threat of death. Here lies the paradox of needing the heart to be both immovable and free at the same time. Furthermore, I feel this speaks of the resolute strength that is required of the heart in the journey to spiritual growth and Expansion. Through my own training in martial arts and various spiritual systems, I personally hold the meaning to be found in the methods of *muto dori* (no-sword capture— to evade, counter and capture the sword of an attacker when you are unarmed). When practicing the methods of being unarmed while another person attacks you with the sword, the challenge is to be able to evade the sword cut, neutralize the threat, and maintain a constantly open heart center filled with joy and love while you do so.

As you may well imagine, this is a monumental task, as the heart center typically closes upon threat of danger. In many esoteric systems the heart is referred to as a flower. Just as there are flowers which close in the darkness of the night, only to reopen again in the morning light, so too does the heart center react. Through spiritual training and growth it becomes possible for the heart to stay open even in the darkness, shining its light upon the world. To have the heart center remain open under potentially dangerous circumstances necessitates a supremely pure and unshakable heart. This is teaching the warrior to have the ability to move freely without tension, to receive without resistance, to evade without anger or the need for revenge. It is keeping the Divine connection at all times, no matter the circumstance, and living from your heart center without allowing it to be affected by negativity. Would you be able to remain light-hearted as you stared death in the eye? Could you smile a sincere smile even as someone was attempting to harm you? Would you be able to remain compassionate even though someone else meant to do you harm? I have come to know that the heart must come first. Even for the warrior, the heart is the most precious of gifts and developing the heart center is more important than developing the weapons skills. The warrior must establish inner balance by having solid spiritual practices in place alongside their fighting skills.

The methods of muto dori (no-sword capture) are said to be extremely high-level techniques. It doesn't take much to comprehend this, as truly having the skill to live through a real sword attack by a highly trained sword master seems to be the stuff of fantasy. It was, however, a real skill that was utilized by ancient warriors. I experienced the essence of *having the blade over my heart* both literally and figuratively by needing to go under the blade for emergency open heart surgery. A bit ironic isn't it? During my period of recovery, after my brain began to reconnect to my body and my nervous system adjusted, I drafted a letter to Grandmaster Hatsumi. I shared a couple things with him from that experience that I have never shared with another living soul. I thanked him from the bottom of my heart for giving me the skills I needed to survive that experience. He responded by sending me a hand masterfully drawn picture of *Kurikara*, the sword of the esoteric Buddhist deity Fudo Myo-O (the Immovable Light King) along with a blessing of good health. It is now one of the great treasures in my collection of Divine artwork. This is the meaning of a spiritual or Divine Warrior. This is how I have come to know it through my own life experiences.

I didn't realize it at the time, but that experience was just preparing me for what I had to do next as a Spiritual Warrior. During my recovery, my perspective on life began to go through a major shift. It was here that

I heard the voice of my Higher Self and the need to evolve spiritually to all new levels. It was clear to me that this calling was to take place now or never. Such a thing would require a complete alteration of my life; everything would have to change in order for me to experience the spiritual transformation that I needed. I recognized that this calling, this need to become the person I might be, was a direct result of the planetary evolutionary shift that is happening. After a few years of inner and outer turmoil I made the conscious decision to move forward, to answer the call of my Higher Self and to expand into who I might become. I know better than most that change is difficult, but I also know that it is the path for growth and the rewards are well worth the effort. Making serious changes in your life also requires the strength and resolve of a warrior.

Another aspect of the Spiritual Warrior is reflected in the twenty-second chapter of the Tao Te Ching written by Lao Tzu and is also reflected in the King James Version of the Bible. This is the idea that is phrased well in the Bible (Matthew 5:5) and contains the most widely known expression, "Blessed are the meek, for they shall inherit the earth." While there are many ways to interpret this statement, I would like to share my understanding of it. The "meek" are those on the spiritual path who have overcome their ego. Meek does not mean to be "weak" as many interpret it, but instead it actually refers to having spiritual strength, with the ability to live one's life in authenticity from the heart center.

> "Therefore the sage embraces the one. Because he does not display himself, people can see his light. Because he has nothing to prove, people can trust his words. Because he does not know who he is, people can recognize themselves in him. Because he has no goal in mind, everything he does succeeds."

— Lao Tzu —

Chapter 22 of the Tao Te Ching

(translation from *Living the Wisdom of the Tao*, by Dr. Wayne W. Dyer)

As the Spiritual Warrior rises ever higher in energetic vibration, reaching upward toward that of the Divine, those around him with low vibration will be threatened by his very presence. Feelings of insecurity from their false beliefs and anger from being shown their shortcomings will consume their hearts, closing the hidden door even further. They are trapped in a vicious cycle where their lower vibrations cause negative emotions, and those negative emotions perpetuate the lowering of vibrations even further. In the mirror of the Spiritual Warrior's heart, her bliss reflects their unhappiness, her love reflects their fears, her gratitude reflects their intolerance, and her divine truths reflect their ignorance. It is through the distaste of their own reflected image that they must decide to accept change and embrace growth, to allow their vibrations to rise and their hearts to open fully and completely, to be filled with true freedom, love, bliss and appreciation. After all, this is how the Spiritual Warrior began his quest too. This is the love and service of the Spiritual Warrior.

DEVELOP THE STRENGTH OF THE WARRIOR, THE COMPASSION OF A HEALER AND THE SPIRITUAL WISDOM OF THE SAGE

The Warrior, the Healer and the Sage—these are the three facets of a human being who has become complete. Most people fragment themselves to focus all their intention purely on one area of life. The truth is that human beings, men and women alike, are made to be all three at the same time. The development of all three areas of Being is a sign of a complete, open and honestly shared system, whether it be martial arts, a healing system, or a religious or spiritual system. The ancient fighting systems contained healing techniques, as well as spiritual teachings to help balance the warrior. Over time, these things were splintered; today people believe they are getting a complete system if they learn just one of these areas. The unfortunate truth is that they are not.

The healer learned their methods could be used to harm someone if the need was to arise; they referred to this as "reverse medicine." Healing was directly linked to the Divine, so these ancient healers were generally spiritual in nature and had spiritual practices intertwined with their healing practices. Some spiritual practitioners, such as monks and priests, remained as purists and refused to fight as they knew it could lower their vibration to do so, but they usually had healing skills. These healing skills manifested as a by-product of many of the spiritual practices; examples of such things can be found in the monastic circle walking methods of many religions. The same circle walking methods can be found in certain schools of *Baguazhang*, a Chinese martial art. Other monks were fierce warriors when need be, utilizing their fighting skills to protect the ancient teachings and the temples that housed them. Finding a balance in all three aspects of Healer, Warrior and Spiritual Sage allows you to live through the trinity and see the world through the three-fold lens. It also develops and gives free reign to your potential and power as a fully actualized human being.

In order to succeed on your spiritual journey, you will need the heart and spirit of a warrior. This will enable you to keep forging forward, even when life challenges your very core beliefs. As soon as you think you understand what's going on and what to believe, you may be forced to change those beliefs once again. That's just how it works. In order to help you I will present tactics and techniques for transforming yourself into a "Spiritual Warrior." Not as someone who goes out and fights to prove their way is the one right way, but to transform you into someone who simply does not know how to give up or quit. You will be powerful enough to keep moving forward and overcome any walls that rise in your way. Remember you will need to hold the compassion of a healer in order to be easy on yourself, evade frustration and allow your Self to heal. You will also learn to hold compassion in your heart for others around you. Once you let go of such judgments, your vibration will rise, as compassion is a product of the emotion of love. Throughout the process, you will be gradually unfolding the spiritual wisdom of the great sages within your Self. You will begin to understand the depth of the words of the world's great spiritual masters throughout the ages. You will come to feel the truth of their teachings and embody them within yourself.

OVERCOMING THE SYMPTOMS OF CHANGE

Earlier I spoke of the symptoms people are experiencing in this time of great change and transition. These symptoms are signs that things are changing. All of these symptoms are present to tell you changes are required in yourself and your life in order to effectively pass through this shift. Physical tension and resistance, negative emotions and internal energy blockages are just some of the afflictions that will make passing through this shift a very challenging experience. After my surgery I felt depressed and unsettled; I couldn't shake the feeling that the life I was living was not meant for me. Through the ability to hear the guidance of my inner voice or Higher Self, I came to know I needed to change. I'd developed several poor behaviors requiring reversal if I were to make this transformational shift into a spiritually-based life. It is difficult on family and friends when they cannot possibly fathom the depth of what is happening, but I summoned my Warrior Spirit and did what I had to do. I hope after all the smoke clears and the dust settles, these people will be able to let go of undeserved blame and accept the truth of what has happened. This was necessary for me to become a better person and evolve as someone walking the path of personal transformation, in order to serve as a messenger to others in the world at this time when messengers are needed.

Many people are experiencing different varieties of symptoms at this very moment. The types of stress on the physical body are similar to the stresses on the mind from the amount of common computer usage. I will share some of the "symptoms" that I have encountered over the years with myself and others. You may argue these are things people commonly experience; however, there is a noticeable increase in their occurrence and they are happening for no detectible reason. I do recommend consulting your health care professional should you experience any of these effects. Do not merely dismiss them as energy symptoms that will subside in time; some of these things do, but others may manifest into or already be something much more tangible and potentially harmful. This is not medical advice or a diagnosis of any sort, but is offered as a way to understand what could be happening if any of these things are unusual for you. I've often heard the phrase, "The tests came back normal, we don't know what's causing this," when I've pursued medical care in the doctor's office. The exercises in this system will help you to alleviate these types of symptoms, assuming they are energy related. You need energy practices to counteract the effects of energy-based symptoms.

HUMAN HEALTH SYMPTOMS OF IMPENDING CHANGE

Physical Symptoms:
- Increase in headaches, migraines, brain tumors, brain cancer
- Increase in body aches, fatigue, and feelings of being drained of energy
- Fibromyalgia
- Increase in vertigo
- Increase in sinus pain and pressure in the face and head
- Seizures or seizure-like activity
- Dizziness, sudden disturbances in equilibrium, passing out
- Pressure and pain in the joints; joints crack and pop excessively
- Difficulty moving quickly; walking is slow and labored
- Restless, irritating feelings in the extremities

Mental Symptoms:
- Difficulty with mental focus and clarity
- Difficulty with memory
- Difficulty making choices and decisions
- Notable increase in mental illness and functioning mental illnesses
- Notable increase in violence for no apparent reason, followed by aimless wandering

Emotional Symptoms:
- Increase in depression and depression-related illnesses

- Increase in emotional breakdowns, meltdowns and other emotional instability
- Feelings of needing to find your life's purpose and live it
- Feelings of being easily overwhelmed, having too many choices
- Feelings of general uneasiness, uncertainty, being lost, empty, disconnected and unfulfilled
- Feelings of needing more from life

PLANETARY SYMPTOMS OF IMPENDING CHANGE

- Instability and unpredictability of the Earth's electromagnetic field patterns and strength
- The feeling of familiar environments changing; things just don't feel the same
- Extreme weather pattern changes, global warming
- Fish, sea stars, abalone, birds and insects dying in large numbers for unexplained reasons
- The sky being washed out instead of bright blue in certain areas and times
- The loss of vibrancy of color in trees and plant life in certain areas
- The various alignments of planets, magnetic poles shifting, and other galactic events

MYTHS, LEGENDS & HALF-TRUTHS

In this section I will present you with certain myths that are floating around disguised as the truth. I intend to expose some of these myths to illustrate the new reality, preventing the deception that is so commonly accepted as truth in our world. Most of these myths or half-truths are perpetuated by the media; after being placed in front of the eyes and ears of the general public long enough, they become accepted as truth. This does not make them true; it merely creates and spreads false beliefs. After stepping outside the box of the "accepted norm" and separating myself from the herd mentality, I was able to see how these types of "memes" are spread and the danger they pose to everyone. A meme, in case you are not yet familiar with the term, is basically a thought, belief, or behavior that is spread throughout a culture from person to person. A meme can travel through thought, belief, gossip, media, social media, and other forms of human interaction. The awakened individual is able to think more clearly for themselves and not follow the mass control and cultural beliefs of the herd.

MYTH #1—You Have To Have A Near-Death Experience In Order To Awaken

No, of course you don't. Experiencing a near-death trauma is absolutely unnecessary to achieve substantial spiritual growth. Spiritual Expansion is about the celebration of life! While undergoing a near-death or severely traumatic experience may act as a catalyst in the awakening process, it is not needed or recommended. The challenges provided in the Expansion Mastery System will, when performed correctly and consistently, guide you through the process of rapid spiritual growth. Many of these exercises are designed to serve as a metaphorical death experience as well as a resurrection. Most spiritual systems have this concept in place in some safely guided form of symbolic practice. The simple nightly act of falling asleep is meant to serve this same idea.

The ancient Egyptians were very spiritually advanced, knowing how to take a person through a process that mimicked death in order for them to better and more fully appreciate life. The Egyptians had a set of rites they were taken through that were designed to allow them the experience of death and resurrection, and to experience for themselves that they were both spirit and body. The functions of such rituals were to open the person's heart and ignite their passion for life. It is of interest to point out, that within the pyramids there are three chambers that are aligned in the very centerline of the pyramid. The middle chamber is the one that resonates with the heart center when you chant the syllable "Ah."

I have been taught that martial artists are supposed to experience a similar effect every time they get thrown to the ground, only to rise again and continue training (living). I set up a particular event for my martial arts students in a way where they had the opportunity to experience this and then apply that feeling to their daily practice. There seems to be something in our being that changes when we go through a truly life-threatening experience. It's much deeper than the simple recognition of our own mortality. Something shifts in the core of our being; a sort of mental-emotional, vibrational shift that allows us to see things differently, as if an encounter with death allows us to more vibrantly appreciate life and find our life's purpose.

MYTH #2—In Relationships, Opposites Attract

Yes they do, in magnetic poles and in a larger sense to human beings. The Law of Polarity is a universal truth, applying to the grander scheme of the relationship concept as far as the attraction of male and female, or two different human beings. However, when we drill down into the actual details of a relationship, we see the Law of Attraction applies more readily. The concept of a harmonious relationship is then accomplished through the Law of Attraction, or like attracts like. The old world reality of Opposites Attract is simply no longer valid. Working hard at a relationship, engaging in arguments and speaking to one another in harsh, aggravated tones, putting up with the other person; none of these things have a place in a truly healthy, happy, and harmonious relationship. This may have been okay in relationships of the old paradigm, but it certainly does not apply any more. We are learning more and more how the concept of "like attracts like" is the way to best achieve the ability to manifest, as well as to create healthy, long-lasting relationships.

MYTH #3 —It Takes Lifetimes of Meditation to Achieve This Type of Change

While meditation is extremely valuable and serves a great purpose, there have been very few people who've attained enlightenment by sitting on their butt. The ancient Chinese knew this, which is why they applied circle walking and other moving meditational techniques. For the diligent practitioner, success will come in this lifetime if you are consistent in your efforts and have a great practice. I have found that sometimes this idea of impossibility is placed in front of a practitioner to help them let go of impatience. If you think that it cannot be attained, then you will not be impatient about achieving results. However, if you believe that it will not happen in this lifetime, chances are it won't.

MYTH #4—You Are Supposed to Stay Close to Family and Spouses, Even if They Are Toxic

This is completely unreasonable and untrue. Blood is thicker than water, right? Not when it is toxic. Remaining in a toxic family environment or toxic relationship is never good; it drastically lowers your vibration. There is no law saying you have to remain with relatives who treat you disrespectfully or behave badly. There is no good reason to remain in an environment where you are subjected to mental, emotional or physical abuse, nor should you remain in a relationship where you are kept from growing spiritually. While it is always a sad situation, separating yourself from toxic relatives or spouses is often the right move to make. Every single person has the right to be happy and to advance spiritually.

When separating yourself from someone, I have learned to always leave the door open for them in case they become willing to change their toxic behaviors and begin treating you with respect. At this point I do everything I can to welcome them back with open arms. In most cases, this will allow both of you to expand in the ways that each of you needs but cannot accomplish when your energies are closely linked. There is a saying that "time heals all wounds," but I believe it should be stated that "time and space heal all wounds." Allowing some space opens the gateway to the potential of the energy field all around us.

MYTH #5—You Should Think With Your Head and Not With Your Heart

This is true to the extent that you *should* do your thinking with your head. Leave the heart to do the feeling. The mistake made here is believing the brain in the head is the only source of intelligence in the body. Science has proven this to be untrue. Every one of the trillions of cells in our body has intelligence. The heart is considered to be a very intelligent organ and is also the seat for our sense of feeling. Your original spirit is connected to this center and listening to your heart is actually great advice. The key is to know when to use each of these. I hear some people claim that following your heart and emotions will get you into trouble; this is true only when you have no conscious connection to them and they are controlling you.

I cannot stress enough how significant it is to live from your heart center. It is essential to develop your sensitivity to the subtle energies around you. In the same way, you can feel if you should trust someone or if a certain place just feels bad to you; you should hone this ability to guide you. It is far more accurate than your intellectual reasoning. Making decisions based upon how you feel instead of what you think is the true approach of the human being. This sensitivity is designed to keep us safe and guide us to our life's purpose. Always thinking without feeling will push you away from your purpose, back into the mentality of the herd.

SHARING EXPERIENCES: POSITIVE RESULTS

I feel it's only fair if I begin this section with some of my own successes. I will also include some experiences that have been shared with me by students of my methods and this program. I have changed a great deal over the years, but not as much as I have over the last few. I am living an entirely different life and I feel as though I am an entirely different person. That person I am now is the person I always wanted to be, knowing deep down they were inside me just waiting for the opportunity to be free.

Result #1

I went way out on a limb at the end of one of my most attended martial arts classes by reproducing my personal vision board on a dry erase board I used to write and draw martial principles for the class. I told the entire class that these things were what I intended to do with my life in the very near future. I even listed them in the specific order they needed to happen in order to pull off the bigger picture. I laid everything I believed in on the line and out in the open for them all to see. I then stated, "If any one of these things fail to happen correctly or even on time, then everything else will fall apart. If that happens, then everything I believe to be true is wrong." I literally called myself out, laid my soul bare in front of all these people who followed my instruction, some for more than a decade; it would have been pretty embarrassing had I failed. The fact that every single thing on that list occurred as I described it, in the exact order and within the timeframe it needed to, proves, at least to me, that this stuff is very real, very powerful and within the natural abilities of human beings. Keep in mind this had to be done in two weeks! Here is the list:

1. Have my fiancé get the perfect day shift nursing job in California
2. Find a beautiful apartment in Marin County, California, and secure it in the two days we had to fly out and apartment hunt
3. Pack everything from our apartment, the martial arts school and my old house
4. Get the P.O.D. delivered, loaded and picked up within three days
5. Have our car transported from Michigan to California
6. Take care of all loose ends, closing bank accounts, leaving jobs, etc.
7. Spend the winter living and training on Wudang Mountain, China
8. Get Visas for China, arriving on time before our departure
9. Get all travel arrangements set for China, as well as inner China flights
10. Celebrate the holidays before having to leave

You may read one of these examples and say to yourself, "Surely those could just all be coincidences." But with numerous results all in the same area, I am sure you will agree that coincidence is more farfetched than the truth. Please understand as well that there are many other examples I could have shared with you here in addition to these.

Result #2

I had planned on moving to California with my fiancé as soon as she was able to get a job in the Bay Area. In the meantime, I had to sell two homes after the passing of my grandparents and my mother, during the worst times in the housing market and in Michigan to boot. My realtor did a wonderful job helping me with this task. My fiancé got a great job in California and we decided to leave Michigan, but I had still not sold my mother's house and we were leaving in a couple weeks. We set out to "manifest" a buyer and a deal for the house, and out of nowhere it happened. It seemed the city of Kalamazoo decided to begin a new program, never in existence before, where they would buy moderate income homes to fix up and offer to first-time homeowners, helping them learn to manage house payments and responsibilities. The deal went through without a hitch. Now here is an additional manifestation within the larger one: the house was old and my step-father made nearly all the repairs himself over the years; let's just say it was not up to code. There was no way I could have sold the house any other way without investing more money in it than it was worth.

Result #3

I decided during my first visit to China that I wanted to return for an extended stay on Wudang Mountain to train in Qigong and martial arts. There were hotels in the area and some minor martial art academies, but nothing I found felt right and the hotels would be very expensive to stay in for an extended trip. The San Feng Pai Academy did not exist at that time, but came into being and started accepting live-in students just a few months before we were to leave Michigan. I just happened to get an email with all of the information when we were trying to decide where to go before moving to California. All of the arrangements were made and we set off to live in the foothills of Wudang Mountain for a month at the brand new facility. The school was overseen by an incredible Taoist Master who happens to be the source and teacher of many other masters on Wudang Mountain.

Result #4

When I left my job of 23 years I also gave up my health insurance; quite a risk for someone with a history of open heart surgery. There is a bit of faith that comes into the entire process. So, there I was in China for a month without any health insurance, then upon returning to the states I went straight to California where I proceeded to live without health insurance. I knew I needed it so I began checking around, but found out that I was considered to be "uninsurable". Yet, there was a program, which had just started up just in the beginning of the year that would cover me at a very affordable rate.

I would like to offer some additional results from people who have been applying the things I teach through the Expansion Mastery System. These acquired skills of increased sensitivity to one's own self, the intentions of others and to the subtle energies of their environment have been used to keep people safe. In some instances, it has saved their lives, allowing them to return home safely to their families. These are skills that are available to all human beings, but we seem to have forgotten how to activate them. This is an important part of Expansion Mastery.

Result #5

I have always had a strong "intuition," as I used to call it. I just never really understood how to listen to it. Robert has helped me to not only 'listen" to my sense of understanding, but he has really helped me to "feel" my way through life. I can give you countless examples of how he has changed my life by helping me to understand and trust what I am sensing. Rather though, I will give you a crystal clear example of how his teachings literally saved my life. Earlier today

I was heading up I-75 just before the Zilwaukee Bridge, passing a huge tandem semi. There was a very tight shoulder with a concrete retaining wall on my other side. As I was in the process of passing this truck, already dead center next to him, I felt the need to get out of this space. The feeling was as if something was physically pushing me to the right. There was a pressure from the inside and a feeling of dread. I had thoughts of knowing this truck was going to run into me. These feelings and thoughts happened instantaneously. Two seconds later the driver turned into my lane, right toward me and he still didn't see me. Thank God I listened to my sense of danger as I was already halfway onto the shoulder beeping the horn to get his attention when he had turned toward me. He finally noticed me as I passed his cab and then he reacted by jerking the wheel and going back into his own lane. Thank you Robert, for teaching me how to feel these things. You saved my life. —**José V.**

Result #6

The most important thing Robert has shared with me so far is the understanding that *you* are in control of your life. Thoughts, words, actions, emotions, beliefs and your own happiness are all your control. Happiness really is your choice. For me, this really came out dynamically when I became depressed and suicidal. For two weeks I was bitter and sad about my life and on a couple of occasions I attempted to take my own life. What kept bringing me back was a repeating thought of, "You are in control; happiness is a choice." I was fighting myself constantly until one day after another attempt at taking my life, I summed up the courage (which Robert shared was a necessary component of life) and I finally made the *decision* to be happy. After that, my life took on a whole new light! It was like my eyes opened for the first time. I became filled with appreciation for all that Robert had shared with me. Every day was awesome, and new, and fresh and blissful! Then I applied the *consciousness* part of Robert's teachings and I popped up to a whole new level! It was like seeing the world in full color after having been wearing sunglasses all my life.

Since I applied the *alignment* idea, I started experiencing the life of my dreams. All of the concepts he shares have drastically transformed my life from existing to living! —**Mason H**.

Result #7

One summer I found myself on a multi-day hike in the Southwest Colorado high country. I hiked about ten miles and climbed some interesting cliffs. Early evening I arrived at my planned campsite. Machin Lake is a beautiful setting at about twelve thousand feet. It is a remote location. I was preparing camp when I felt my stomach sharply sink and little shivers go up and down my spine. I looked and listened, but nothing suggested danger. There were miles of thick forest below me and fifteen hundred foot cliffs to the south with icy top ledges. While I enjoyed the beauty of the place, I knew that something didn't feel right. I decided to listen to my gut and move on. The least logical way to go was up. Nightfall was setting in and thunder clouds were gathering. As I rushed up a nearby couloir I realized it was too late to wonder about the sanity of my decision. I managed to clear the icy ledge and find shelter before the hail fell. I kept wondering what possessed me to move away from Machin Lake?

The next morning I went back down to the lake. It was out of my way, but I had to know. To my surprise there were many fresh bear tracks around the very spot where I was going to set up camp. I counted at least four to five black bears and some of the tracks were the biggest I had ever seen. It seems that the bear had the same dinner plans as me, fresh trout from the lake. Bears are not after people, especially in the high country, but you never know when you might end up between a momma bear and her cubs. It takes experience, but in the wilderness one quickly learns the value of trusting your gut feeling and higher sense before listening to your logical brain. The awareness that Robert refers to kicks in and stays turned on just like eyes and ears. In addition to safety and survival, it helps to feel, appreciate and enjoy nature on a whole new level. I am very happy that my awareness has become so sharp as a result of Robert's training. It has kept me safe and happy many, many times. —**Mike Z.**

SPIRITUAL SPEED-BUMPS: OBSTACLES ALONG THE PATH OF THE SPIRITUAL WARRIOR

You will most likely discover the need to become a Spiritual Warrior as you walk the path of your own truth. This does not mean that you will have to practice martial arts or become a soldier, but it does imply that you will need to be resilient and stay true to yourself. All too often people around you will not be comfortable with you making advancements in your spiritual quest. This is not always a malicious objective, but simply due to fearing you might change and they might not have you in their life in the exact same capacity that you have been up until this point. Be as gentle as you can with the people in your life, but do not allow them to halt you on your journey. You must be strong enough and focused enough to keep going.

I have helped guide thousands of martial and meditative students around common mistakes that can result in lengthy delays and plateaus for long periods of time. It is common for the person doing their best to raise their vibration and become a unified being to not initially notice the effects it has on those around them. As you go through this process of self-actualization and unification, your vibrational frequency will begin to rise. This will not go unnoticed by those in your life, and you should expect two very different types of feedback. Eventually, you can expect random statements from friends and family members that you have changed, and hopefully they state that it's for the better. They may praise you for the transformations they notice and may even encourage you to keep doing what you are doing, even though they don't understand exactly what you are going through.

It is a wonderful situation when you have a spouse or special person in your life who desires to expand with you. It must be noted though that if you do not have a similar spiritual foundation and your partner does not desire to grow at the same time, they cannot be coerced or forced to do so. You cannot force another to grow, they have to want it in their heart and desire it for themselves; and indeed they may not be ready for it. The person resisting growth will usually become angry and seek blame as the life they've become comfortable with crumbles around them. While this is a difficult period for both people, it is important to stay true to yourself and keep going. Hopefully, such a scenario plays out to allow the other person to experience necessary life lessons to spark their Expansion while freeing you to experience your own. The common mistake is reconciliation out of guilt, pity, or to take the path of least resistance. Going back to that spouse or significant other will instantly halt your progress and ultimately result in an unhappy home life for you both. Once you acknowledge and commit to your call to expand, it is devastating to stop the process, and it is impossible to move forward with someone constantly pulling you back.

This same situation applies to family members. They may also give you positive feedback and support. If they have higher vibrations themselves, they will be thrilled for you and more than eager to support you. If you lack spiritually evolved siblings, parents, or children then you may run into a difficult situation. They may react out of fear as the family dynamic changes, feeling they are losing control over you and the family model they have created. This can cause siblings to exert their control and influence over you in an attempt to put you in your place. It may result in parents increasing their dominance, and when they realize they can't control you, they back away altogether to avoid dealing with it. The mistake here is the same. Giving in to the demands of your family members will stop your growth in its tracks. You need the freedom to walk your own path, and you know what is best for you better than anyone. Do not give in to the pressures that family members may place on you, but make sure they know you love them, keep them in your heart and always leave the door open for the future.

Be aware of distraction that may cross your path. The information age has presented people with a wide array of mindless distractions as a way to ease mental fatigue. These distractions, such as surfing the web, will prevent you from being as productive as you can be. Television and other forms of perceived relaxation will also serve as distractions, as does talking on your cell phone constantly or playing video games for hours on end. Beware of things that suck the life out of your productivity.

You will most likely find yourself going against the grain of the "accepted" social convention. This should not be a surprise when you look at the mentality of the herd. Are they spiritual expanding? Of course not, they are caught up in the mindless drama that keeps them from making any progress or even noticing what is happening around them. To me, it is reminiscent of the blinders they put on horses. Once you step outside the circus of mass control, you may initially find life to be a bit lonely. It is important to keep on your path and eventually you will attract other like-minded people to you that will encourage mutual support. Breaking free from social convention is quite an eye-opening experience; it can be a bit frightening at first, but soon you will be amazed how the world looks when you can see clearly and distinguish truths for yourself.

FLUID BELIEFS, FLUID NERVOUS SYSTEM, FLUID MIND, FLUID BREATH

The higher levels of achievement in martial and spiritual arts include a sense of what the Japanese call *nagare* (flow). This sense of fluidity is extremely important and a quality held dear by masters and grandmasters. The ability for one to achieve a sense of continuous, relaxed flow in their physical movement is a desired level of accomplishment. To do this one also needs to develop kinesthetic awareness. To move your body this way is to flow with the energy currents that move the wind and water. The sharp, jerky style movement of most hard-style martial arts is a direct contrast to this concept. Tai Chi, Baguazhang, Aikijujutsu and Budo Taijutsu are examples of martial arts that use this form of flowing movement. Some forms of dance and ice skating also rely on this fluid motion to display its grace and beauty.

Here I will be addressing the fluidity that you can't see, unless it is reflected in someone's physical movement. I am going to address the fluidity of the mind, nervous system, breath and beliefs. Developing a fluid mind is crucial to your spiritual advancement. This mindset allows the mind to move freely about while retaining a sense of focus. Your mind does not focus so intently on one thing that you because oblivious of everything else in your immediate environment. The fluid mind allows you to move seamlessly from one position to another or one movement to another without pausing. It allows your mind to stay in a greater state of Expansion and respond to multiple points of attention instead of just one singular point. You are also able to clear and still the mind more quickly in order to hear the voice of the Divine. Achieving a level of fluidity in the mind allows you to mentally adapt to situations more quickly and easily as they unfold. This is extremely beneficial for martial, healing and spiritual applications.

The concept of a fluid nervous system is quite an in-depth topic. The fluid nervous system allows you to physically move without the tension that would result in hesitation or stuttering within your movement. A fluid nervous system permits you to physical flow with a relaxed sense of grace from one position to another. Today, it is common for people to suffer from a completely shorted-out nervous system. With all the over-stimulation, information and computer work, it's no wonder that people are overly tense and easily overwhelmed. Moving with this sense of freedom is very difficult to attain, as there are only a handful of techniques that I am aware of which actually work to release the buildup of "tension" in one's nervous system. It is easy to tell when someone is suffering from an over-stimulated nervous system by checking the eyes. The eyes are said to be a gateway to the soul, but they also serve as a gateway into the nervous system. You can observe the tension through the hardness of the eyes or if they have become wide and protruding.

The breath serves as an activator for the nerves, so developing methods for breathing fluidly serves to assist the nervous system in becoming and remaining fluid. The first step in creating fluid breath is to avoid holding your breath. Try to notice when you experience any form of stress and observe your natural tendency to hold your breath. This is a good practice to learn to recognize when your breath is being held, to release it and breathe deeply to relax. The next step is to coordinate your breath with your body movement. Many top-rated professional speakers also learn to coordinate their breath with their speech patterns in order to flow and pause at the proper points in their dialogue. Learn to be able to move, jump, punch, and speak while coordinating your breath with those movements to act in a naturally synchronized manner. It is important to allow the body movements, the nervous system and the breath to work in conjunction with one another without needing to place conscious thought on the process. Once resistance is eliminated you will not only feel that you are moving lighter and with purpose, but with a new level of grace, awareness and natural power.

I would really like to focus more on fluid beliefs. It is imperative for your beliefs to remain in a fluid state, open to alteration with new knowledge or experience, in order for you to grow and expand. Because your beliefs will be constantly challenged when you are involved in a true spiritual awakening, it is imperative to break persistent patterns of thought. Therefore, you cannot afford to have your beliefs be immovable; this will make certain you do not change, grow or expand. When a new experience or reliable knowledge renders your current belief obsolete, you must be able to adapt and flow with the new belief in order to make this transition less traumatic on the mind. Allow your beliefs to take form, yet not to become concrete and unchangeable. It is actually natural that your beliefs should change as you expand spiritually. There are so many things that we just do not understand, even through science. Fluid beliefs are important in both science and spirituality. By keeping your beliefs fluid you will find your mind can remain open, making your expansion much easier. A closed mind results in contraction, as it keeps a person small and prohibits growth.

If a different perspective is offered and you become agitated or resistant, then your beliefs are not in a state of fluidity. You will immediately feel your nervous system, mind and breath become stressed. A belief is the result of a person's formed perception; their interpretation based on their current level of understanding. It only makes sense that a person's life experiences would bring about change in their beliefs as they continue to learn and grow. Beliefs should constantly require "updating" if you are learning new things. Just as the gentle river flows, bending and winding around the banks without interruption even when it encounters obstacles – so too should your beliefs flow, with the same gentle, constant motion and ability to change freely.

In order to assist in keeping your thoughts fluid, it is imperative to keep a broader perspective and forming opinions based on your need to control and keep the ego feeling secure. It is more beneficial to realize that upon hearing something for the first time, you may only understand a small degree of the depth of the topic and you need to keep your mind open to new or additional information. The need to feel as though you know it all is nothing more than a cheap trick being played on the undisciplined mind by the ego. Beliefs can be very challenging to change once you form them. Be mindful of this.

There is a concept within the ancient martial and spiritual traditions, including Zen Buddhism called *shoshin* (beginner's mind). Tracing this concept back we see that it had the original meaning of "heart-mind." In Taoist practice, the heart is considered to be the seat of the spirit as well as the cognitive mind. The character for *Xin* (in Chinese) or *Shin* (in Japanese) literally means "heart-mind." This mindset teaches us to hold on to the desire to learn new things, to retain that insatiable thirst for knowledge that one has when they just begin something new and exciting. To keep this open frame of mind will help you to remain capable of growing and learning new things, even once you have become very accomplished. All too often in these traditions, shoshin is viewed as a beginner's level concept. This is definitely not true; shoshin requires self-observation and a constant mindfulness of one's mental and emotional state. This aids in keeping the ego at bay and allows the practitioner to enjoy even those methods they have performed tens of thousands of times through keeping a fresh perspective of the exercise. It also serves to continue an excitement for learning so that you do not lose the enthusiasm you had when you first stepped foot on the path.

The beginner's heart-mind is very helpful in creating a fluid mind and fluid beliefs, because you do your best to make no assumptions that you already know all the layers to everything. One popular statement that I hear thrown about is "Been there, done that." This is an example of the opposite of shoshin. The mind that has "been there and done that" is closed and unable to grow, forever locked in its shallow understanding. In martial arts, the use of shoshin allows the warrior to move naturally and respond instead of reacting. It is this state of mind that promotes extended daily practice without the ego arising to either stop your progress or take credit for what has not yet been accomplished.

> *"When one practices discipline and moves from the beginner's territory to immovable wisdom, one makes a return and falls back to the level of the beginner."*
> **— Takuan Soho —**

I learned through more than three decades of martial arts training that your level of understanding and sense of knowing will change dramatically from year to year, especially in the beginning. Look at how many things we have been taught to believe, only to find out later that it is incorrect. Everything that was believed to have been "scientifically tested" seems to change with time. As technology improves, we learn that the limitations of the previous technology did not allow us to make the valid discoveries that we thought it did.

I find it fascinating how various organizations—from corporations to churches—attempt to influence and control our interpretations, perceptions and beliefs in order to control the sheeple herds. I am using the term "sheeple" here as a humorous yet accurate way to describe the masses who, out of fear and lack of knowing who and what to trust, mindlessly follow the trends, fads and whatever they are told to think or feel without taking responsibility for themselves. Of course not everyone is being underhanded; our families, friends, teachers and others are simply sharing the best knowledge they have with what their perceptions and beliefs have to offer. In this manner, even though what they may have offered was not fact, it was well meaning and not at all maliciously deceptive. It is crucial to understand the difference. This is why it is extremely important for human beings to once again learn how to think, and more importantly, *feel* for themselves, stepping outside of such blatant disinformation.

NO MIND

I would like to present a brief look at the concept of *mushin* (no-mind), which has been addressed earlier in this book. No-mind is a different state than beginner's heart-mind. No-mind is usually understood as bringing the mind to a point where the thoughts become still. It is a moment when the mind is not thinking, not allowing the uncontrolled random thoughts generated by the ego to run rampant. When there is stillness of the mind, when it is void of thought, the ego is quiet and the heart can begin to be heard. It is during the suspension of thought that the consciousness of the heart-mind is free to assume the leading role. This is a good basic understanding, but it has layers of deeper meaning and greater skill. It is at this basic level that one beings to experience moments of inner peace and tranquility. This can be a highly profound event in itself, as so many people are burdened with the constant chatter running wild in their mind.

Another level of no-mind is to understand that once you still the mind, it is then possible to hear the Divine voice of your Higher Self, or of Universal Source. Martial artists may see it as a challenge to still move from this mindset, but when you drop the consciousness down into the lower abdomen, it happens as if on auto-pilot. Most spiritual practitioners do not have to address the issue of moving while in this state because they are most likely seated in their practice. Once the continuous, uncontrolled thought patterns are slowed down and brought to a still point, the loud voice of the ego becomes barely audible and the voice of the Divine can be heard. This level is all about communication with your Higher Self.

I want to share another, even deeper level that I have attained with this concept. When you clear your mind, still your thoughts and move with a more divinely inspired flow, you may find yourself aware of an entirely different plane of consciousness. I have experienced this several times with various masters, and it has allowed me to receive teachings that others do not normally receive, as well as special privileges. I have encountered this type of "no-mind dimension" while training in Japan with Grandmaster Machida, the result of which was to be the first recipient of an award regarding this skill. I also encountered it in China while practicing push-hands with Grandmaster Zhong Yun Long. Grandmaster Hatsumi is most often within this realm while he is demonstrating his incredible movement. It's difficult to put into words, but it is like moving in two dimensions at once. It's as if your physical self is moving in the time and space reality, and your consciousness and energy body is in another reality. It is here that you have the ability to fully understand someone else's intentions without the hindrance of language barriers or miscommunication. One way to know if this experience is real for you is that it happens to both people; it cannot be claimed by one person while the other is unaware of what just happened.

The level we are discussing allows for a teaching method that is referred to as *jikiden* (direct transmission). Grandmaster Machida refers to me as his *jikideshi* or direct transmission disciple. This application of direct transmission takes place from heart to heart, mind to mind, and consciousness to consciousness. Obviously, the student of the martial or spiritual arts must be open and receptive to this form of transmission in order for it to be effective. This level of teaching is rare to find, but it is the most effective form of transmission from one person to another.

CHAPTER SEVEN

TO LOVE,
APPRECIATE
& SERVE

"Acting in the service of others, from the purity of your heart, is to walk hand in hand with the Divine."

I would like to discuss three very important areas of the human experience. These three things have tremendous influence and can help any human being to regain a sense of self-empowerment. I know this very well, because it has done just that for me and others I've shared it with. While these three concepts are certainly nothing new, I will present them in a way that may offer you some new insights and depth. Once you are actively aware of them and can stay mindful of them, you may notice a massive shift in your sense of personal empowerment and greater life experience. I cannot offer you a more pure example of a spiritual life experience than extending unconditional love, in a constant state of appreciation, with the ability serve humanity in a way that truly makes a difference for everyone involved. I feel that this is the potential for greatness of the collective human race. These three concepts will generate more Expansion than anything else you could do. I would like to look at each of these concepts in order to better equip you with the knowledge of creating this experience for yourself.

When humanity begins to lose the qualities of love, appreciation and a desire to serve others, we begin our descent into the downward spiral of dehumanization. This leads us to live an ego- centered life that keeps us separated from the Universal Source. It also separates us from Nature, from being connected to others and being connected to our true sense of Self. Living this life would be the more accurate definition of hell. This is the current direction of the human species, but there is great anticipation among many who believe that we can turn this downward spiral upside down. We have no more time to sit back and ignore the things that are going on around us. We must stand up, shake the cobwebs from our minds, rub the sleep from our eyes, and actively participate in our lives. We can change the course of current events to spiral us upward to the highest reaches of humanity, to higher levels of being that have never been experienced in human history. This would take us in the direction of living from the heart center, where love is the default emotion of every person on the planet. From this we would expand and openly share our appreciation with others for even the smallest of interactions, carrying this sense of appreciation in our hearts, allowing us to become even closer to the Divine and experience Heaven on Earth.

THE POWER OF LOVING OPENLY & UNCONDITIONALLY

Love is the very essence of the Universal Source. Therefore it is the very essence of our nature; we are at our most powerful when we act from love. Love is not only an extremely powerful emotion within the human experience, but it is at the root of our Divine nature as a Being. We are here in time and space, which means we get to have a concentrated, amazingly powerful experience filled with love. We get to feel it, to hold it in our hearts and embrace it. This is one of the Divine gifts of being in a human body.

I have been involved in teaching and training people for over three decades and during this time I have always remained a student, participating in a large number of self-improvement seminars. One thing I continually notice is there are so many people in attendance who are frantically trying to find that special someone in their lives, someone to share their love. Many times these lonely people openly weep in a matter of seconds when they speak about their desire. This is a powerful and emotional quest they are on, and let's face it; some people just don't have the keys to attract positive relationships into their lives, let alone *any* relationship. You can tell they have a good heart and are just filled with desire to love and be loved; so why is a loving relationship so elusive? I believe I can offer some down-to-earth explanations that aren't surrounded by all kinds of confusing psychological exploration.

The first matter is that you need to develop self-love. You will have a hard time finding someone to genuinely love you if you do not love yourself first. Once you are capable of feeling unconditional love for yourself, you will appear more desirable to others as a person they want to love. Don't make it some difficult thing you have to do or go through; loving yourself doesn't have to be that complicated, especially when you get your head out of the way and feel with your heart. Some people have it all backwards; you cannot wait for someone to love you and to accept you for who you are until you do it yourself. How could you expect someone else to truly love you when you are not capable of loving yourself? It is not up to someone else; it's not their responsibility, its 100-percent yours.

The second matter is to cultivate your self-confidence, self-respect and general sense of worthiness. You may notice these things begin to arise in your experience when you resolve the first issue. Many people talk themselves into believing they will feel more love for themselves when they get better looking, or lose the weight they desire, or when they accomplish some other goal that they place in their own way. As you develop the honest ability to love yourself for who you are right here and now, then you will feel self-confidence, self-respect and a true sense of worthiness. This does not mean to accept the flaws in your character or appearance that you can change for your own benefit. Too often, people look at the idea of accepting themselves as a way to get out of improving themselves. This is not the idea. If you need to be more accepting of others, then make the effort to become more accepting of others. If you need to lose excess weight, then make the effort to lose the weight—your health will benefit from your efforts too.

It's all Expansion; it's all raising your personal vibration higher and higher. Try a simple exercise. Write down ten things in detail that you desire in a companion and lover. Now, look at it from the perspective of the other person. Do you fit the top ten things that that type of person would be writing on their list for their companion? If you don't, then this lets you know what to begin working on in regards to yourself. How could you possibly expect someone so amazing to be attracted to someone who is willing to be less amazing? The answer is simple; you shouldn't, couldn't and wouldn't. At this point you have two clear options; the first is to lower your standards. This is not the recommended route, but it is the one so many decide upon. The second option is you can raise yourself to new levels; then you would be amazed at how quickly a person like the one you wrote about shows up in your life and is interested in you, as if by magic.

The third matter is that you need to open your heart. Many people I meet have closed heart centers because they have been hurt in the past by what they perceive as rejection, being taken advantage of, or being abused. This sometimes requires a high degree of courage to overcome; it helps to have and apply the Warrior Spirit. In some ways it's as easy as making the conscious decision to do so; in other ways it's difficult to overcome the obstacles that may be in front of you. I am very aware that some people have been through very challenging and negative experiences. However, it is the people who cannot rise above such life experiences that remain in a low vibrational state, controlled by their own past in a victim state. You have to decide whether you are going to be imprisoned in your past, or experience a new and exciting day truly living in the present.

Free yourself from the victim mentality; it is impossible to love yourself and someone else when you are focused on being the victim and blaming others for the circumstances of your life. While that may be the easy way out, it keeps your vibration low and results in you attracting and creating the same undesirable people and situations into your life over and over. If you recall from earlier in the book, I explained how love, appreciation and bliss are the three highest vibrations of the human experience. The things you think, the things you believe, the emotions you feel, the intentions you have, the things you say and the things you do must all be of the highest vibrational quality possible in order for you to achieve positive, long-lasting change and the ability to consciously create the life you desire.

Grandmaster Masaaki Hatsumi often speaks of *Magakoro*. Magakoro means to have a sincere or true heart. When we open our hearts, they radiate outward and touch the hearts of others. This is the meaning of sincerity or having a sincere heart. When you have the ability to open your own heart and have it expand enough to communicate with the hearts of others, then you will be in a position to establish sincere relationships. He also teaches us to develop the ability to perform martial arts techniques without closing our hand tightly or even at all. On the surface, this serves to make sure the practitioner is remaining relaxed in their movement. On a deeper level, there is the understanding that the hands are expressing what is in the heart. The hands are the external manifestations of the heart. Keeping your hands open during a stressful situation indicates that you can hold an open heart center, even during negative life situations. This offers some insights into a person's handshake. The person who feels the need to squeeze your hand is trying to close their hand; this is usually the result of the ego and a closed heart. The person who has an extremely loose handshake shows their lack of desire to have an open, honest connection with you. The person who has a solid, yet comfortable handshake is the person who is offering you a sincere interaction.

THE POWER OF APPRECIATION

Appreciation, gratitude and giving thanks are all very crucial in your personal Expansion. A strong, confident person is ready, willing and able to show their heartfelt appreciation whenever the opportunity arises. Appreciation truly is power; it is like fuel for your Expansion. Appreciation is also a significant part of nearly every facet of the human experience. When you feel appreciation for someone or something, it raises your vibration to a very high level. Start looking for all the things in your life that deserve to be appreciated. I encourage you to express those feelings and allow yourself to experience them fully within your mind and body. The more you appreciate, the more likely those people and things will show up in your experience to appreciate. Once this process is set into motion it doesn't take long to realize that everything in your life is a great gift worthy of your appreciation.

Appreciation tends to have an impressive quality of igniting your passion, yet offering a calm, centered effect that is very soothing. This is the connection of Heaven and Earth. Having the feelings of appreciation are one thing, but actually sharing those feelings with others or expressing them in some way can be an entirely different matter. It is vitally important to feel the emotion of appreciation and hold it in your heart; it will surely help your heart to open. It is equally important to project that appreciation in a way that it can be shared with the world. Maybe it is as simple as telling someone "thank you" for holding a door open for you or as profound as a prayer said aloud.

I have found in busier societies, one of the first things to disappear is the personal connection between beings. They look out for only themselves and stop looking out for each other. People lose their sense of awareness for others as they become self-absorbed; the next stage is to go deeper into their heads, and they even lose their sense of awareness for themselves. This takes them farther away from Universal Source; it takes them farther away from their connection to Nature (Earth) and ultimately away from their sense of Being. When I run into a clerk who is having a bad day, I usually try to make them smile or engage them with a positive statement of some sort. It doesn't always work, but I have found that if the person is truly just having a bad day then they generally perk up and smile. I can literally feel them lighten up. It's great to be able to affect another person in such a positive way. It's the same in hospitals; how often do you hear patients talking to their nurses in a disrespectful way, ordering them around like they are personal servants? That sort of treatment of others is the sign of a very low vibrational frequency; discomfort and fear are still not excuses to treat others rudely. When you live your life with politeness and respect, and look out for others every bit as much as you look out for yourself, you are manifesting the spirit of appreciation into your life.

THE POWER OF SERVING OTHERS

"Everybody can be great… because anybody can serve.
You don't have to have a college degree to serve. You only
need a heart full of grace. A soul generated by love."
— **Martin Luther King, Jr.** —

I believe the desire to serve others is an inherent one that comes from our true selves or spirit. It is through service to others that the Universal Source is able to serve you in return. One of the most powerful experiences I've had while serving was while teaching a summer camp in Upper Michigan with my friend José. As I mentioned earlier, our purpose was to teach special movements for balance, centering, sensitivity and even some martial arts to a group of wonderful young people who just happened to also all be amputees. I owe them a debt of gratitude for allowing me to expand through serving them.

We were only there for the day, but it was an amazing experience that opened my heart farther than it had ever been opened before. At the end of the day one young lady approached us and said she had not had the courage to get out of her wheelchair until she was inspired by what we were doing; it looked fun and she wanted to be a part of it. This young woman was about sixteen years old and had been severely burned all over her body in a house fire. She was only a baby at the time, and that horrific incident was also where she lost her legs. Of anyone I have ever met, this outstanding, strong young woman had a lot about which to feel victimized. Yet, she got out of her wheelchair for the first time and learned to walk on her prosthetics in order to "play" with all of us. Her courage and spirit inspires me so much that every time I think of her, I can't help but feel a swell of emotion in my heart. She pushed herself to participate in everything we did that day, even though her legs were very sore. This is an example of a true Warrior Spirit. I saw her in attendance at additional events we've taught; she has gotten very tough and can do some amazing martial arts based movement on her prosthetics. I have since put her through a martial arts rank test and awarded her the rank of eighth kyu, a green belt in Bujinkan Budo Taijutsu. Should you ever have the good fortune to meet her, whatever you do, do not give her cause to put a wristlock on you!

A young man attending the camp lost a portion of his body to a flesh eating disease. He happened to love angels and spoke to me over lunch about his affinity for them. He asked my permission to like them because it didn't seem like a "manly" thing to do. I told him that I loved angels myself and I thought it was absolutely fine for him to do so as well. I noticed that he kept looking at the t-shirt I was wearing; it was a simple t-shirt with a tiger and Japanese characters on it. He asked if he could trace it or draw it for his website because it looked strong; at that time he had not known what it was like to feel personal strength himself. Of course, that would change shortly. He trained all day with us; he became very tired and fatigued but kept pushing himself, and he was able to do some movement and techniques that left us sore. I removed my shirt and gave it to the young man for doing such an amazing job and trying so hard throughout the day. I was later told his father had contacted the company who puts on the camp each year and told them his son had changed; he was more confident and happier than he'd ever seen him in his whole life.

Another young man about sixteen who'd lost both legs told us we just made his dream come true. Do you have any idea how great it feels to have someone tell you that? His dream was to be able to twirl the nunchaku like martial arts legend Bruce Lee. We shared such an experience not in the form of learning how to use a weapon in order to feel power over another or harm someone else, but instead as an amazing tool of empowerment and transformation. We focused on teaching him to master his body and his physical and mental coordination in order to harmonize the actions between his mind, body and the padded nunchaku. Actually, nunchaku began as a farmer's tool, not as a weapon. As he began to get the simple twirling methods we shared with him, he began to feel as though he could do the things he liked just like everyone else. He never once mentioned anything about striking someone or hurting them with the nunchaku; he was too focused on learning how to get them to move properly within his own body movement. The focus of self-mastery is incredible; when you don't allow yourself to become frustrated or discouraged, you keep your vibration high and think of self-mastery instead of harming others. José and I were incredibly honored to work with these fine young people.

Being a martial arts instructor for a few decades and owning my own school for over sixteen years has allowed me to serve others in a multitude of ways. I was able to watch many personal transformations take place and it was always exciting and rewarding. Occasionally I would run into the person who kept asking to be changed, but resisted so strongly that they were not capable of the change. That was when I learned very clearly that I could not possibly change someone else; I could merely point the way to that change. The victim mentality would immerge as "Here, fix me!" or "I want to change, so change me; I shouldn't have to do it myself." You can clearly see that in either case, success is not an option at that moment. No one can do it for you; you have to truly want it and then let nothing stop you from attaining it. I served in the best ways I knew how at the time, I gave them tools to apply much like those in this book, and they did the rest.

I didn't realize it at the time, but they were all offering me tools of transformation as well. I was still learning, growing and desiring to expand during my time as an instructor and school owner. I surely did not pass every life lesson the first time around as they presented themselves to me, but eventually I succeeded and went on to meet the next. I can see now how any negative experience with someone was an opportunity for me to grow; it was not just about their personal growth and Expansion, but my own as well. Those teaching are still learning; they are merely farther along the path and are able to point to the path for those who cannot see it yet. It is and always has been up to the student to take action. There comes a point where the teacher, parent, or leader reaches the end of their participation in a person's growth for the time being, and the individual must walk alone through the rest. It is the unique personal journey of each and every one of us.

Ask yourself three questions: Am I *ready* to learn and grow? Am I *willing* to learn, change and grow? Am I *able* to learn, change and grow? After taking a moment to search your soul for the answers, you may have a better idea of where you are in your journey. If you answer in the negative to any of the three questions, then no one can possibly assist you yet as you are not willing to allow it. Once you are on your way, you need to know that this is your journey and nothing can stop you unless you let it. Over time you realize that by serving others you end up serving yourself in ways you never imagined.

Being in service to others is part of our fundamental programming as a Divine being. I heard it put best by Dr. Wayne W. Dyer when he said "The inner mantra of the ego which I have had to learn to shed and tame is, "What's in it for me?" But the mantra of the Higher Self, the God-realized Self is, "How may I serve?" This realization to serve happens when the ego has been sufficiently subdued and you are now responding from the place of your heart center. Imagine yourself truly attaining the level where you could receive inspiration to serve others without any hidden selfish agenda lurking about in the dark recesses of your mind. How wonderful and pure must that feel? Human beings are at their absolute best when they are acting in service of others while expecting nothing in return. This is the act of giving from the heart.

The ancient warriors of Japan knew how important this was. I find it particularly amazing that some of the most prevailing and powerful warriors in human history acted from a place of service to their fellow man. Indeed, the term samurai literally means "to serve." My sword teacher is a direct descendant of a samurai family, as he shares the ancient fighting arts of the famous Aizu Clan. His grandmother was actually a full samurai and expert with the naginata, a halberd pole arm. Grandmaster Machida, even though aging himself, still acts with kindness, compassion and service to others. He and his family spend much of their time preparing food and delivering it to the elderly in their area. They participate in serving the good people of their community as a way to serve and give of themselves. I have never seen the slightest hint of any expectation to receive anything in return for these actions. This great warrior has a fierce spirit that is one of the strongest I have ever encountered, yet his heart is filled with kindness and love for his fellow being. What a great paradox is life!

The Japanese shadow warrior traditions have another title as well. It is used in the Bujinkan organization for those who are fifth degree black belt or higher. This term of *Shidoshi* refers to a "knight," as a "teacher of the warrior ways of life and death." It is a title one traditionally receives after passing the sword test performed by Grandmaster Masaaki Hatsumi. This title helps us to remember the serious nature of the fighting skills being learned, and to uphold the responsibility of having the lives and deaths of those you teach in your hands. This reminds the instructor to have compassion while teaching, to take care of their student's health so they can continue to live and learn. It also teaches the instructor to keep an awareness and ability to take life at any moment should the need arise to protect and defend. This reflects the vital nature of training in the past, and by keeping this mindset and awareness alive, we are able to train our spirits to walk the fine line between life and death, whether that is the life or death of an attacker or our own.

It is not uncommon for people, especially those with limited funds and not so limited egos, to rationalize that to be in service of others means to give things away without charge. While there is something to be said for experiencing true poverty, there is nothing wrong with someone making a living doing what they love while they serve others. The key to this is always putting service first and profits second, offering all they can in value and service while acting from their heart. There is little that feels better than to be of service to another human being and receiving appreciation in response. This is a natural energy exchange that is extremely powerful. We must reach a point in our world culture where we once again make the time to serve others without the expectation of personal gain. We need to act from a sense of empowerment where we are not afraid to give openly to those around us. This will happen when we live from our heart center.

CHAPTER EIGHT

COMMON MISTAKES AND HOW TO EVADE THEM

"There are two mistakes one can make along the road to truth...
not going all the way, and not starting."
— Siddhartha Gautama —

I will share some of the known pitfalls you may encounter and how to evade making the same mistakes as myself and others who have traveled this path before you. You may encounter some new and unique issues that are part of your individual experience, which are there to provide you with opportunity and life lessons. As you progress on the spiritual path, you will become aware of how important your responses are to your progress. Some of this will be reflected by the situations that you attract into your life experience. Changing your perceptions and interpretations to hold a positive response to obstacles by seeing them as opportunities will serve you well. Do your best to evade negative initial reactions by being in control of your ego and random thoughts. It also helps to know how to manage your emotions in these cases. See every single thing that gets in your way as the golden opportunity that it is, even if you don't completely understand how it could be at the time.

The spiritual path is the same as any activity that requires skill, perseverance and patience to succeed. The difference here is that the stakes are higher and these pitfalls can set you back months or even years if you mistakenly fall into them. Some can result in knocking you off the path of Expansion completely. Over the period of time I have been teaching and training others in martial arts, I have found that people tend to make the same basic mistakes. These are particular patterns that emerge, as humans are creatures of habit. The following are the major mistakes I have noticed in those I have worked with over the years, as well as some of the mistakes I personally made on my own spiritual path. I hope to save you time, effort and serious amounts of frustration through presenting these topics.

THE 3 MOST COMMON SPIRITUAL (HEAVENLY) MISTAKES

NUMBER ONE MISTAKE: The closed, controlled mind

The biggest mistake in this area is allowing religious or spiritual beliefs to close your mind, prohibit your learning and bring your Expansion to a screeching halt. It is vitally important to keep an open mind and allow your beliefs to change with a sense of fluidity. This is part of the evolution; you will change what you believe based on your experiences and the truths you discover for yourself. You must break free from the bonds that restrain you due to the interpretation of someone else.

You truly do have all the answers in your own heart just waiting for you to know them as truth. The entire concept of "This way is the only way," is completely absurd; it is arrogant and causes a greater connection to the ego than to the Universal Source. I caution you against the old idea that something is right just because it is accepted by mainstream society, or that you have to believe a certain way to fit in with all your friends and family. This is nothing more than herd mentality. The herd does not think for itself; it goes in the direction it is told, without question, and unfortunately it is usually led by the spiritually blind. There is great value to living in your own truth. However, you must also be wary of going against society just for the sake of being different, as this is just an opposite herd mentality. Choose your direction from what lies within.

NUMBER TWO MISTAKE: Becoming a "space case"

Working so much on your spiritual Self that you neglect your physical self will upset your sense of balance. Always make sure you work on grounding yourself before performing spiritual methods. As you make more progress spiritually, you will need to ground yourself all the more. The stronger you are connected to the Earth, the higher you can reach into the Heavens. It's about balance. It is a common mistake to shift all your focus to the spiritual when you rationalize that you are not your body. The truth of the matter is that while your essence is spiritual and is not your physical form, your physical form is still a time, space and matter manifestation of your spirit. It houses your heart center, which makes it your personal temple; to neglect your temple is to move yourself away from the Divine connection. Being grounded is a necessity.

Your body, the physical *you* is a great gift from God that should be cared for and appreciated for the limited time that you have it. Care for it, nurture it, and enjoy every moment you are able to live through it; just don't get overly attached to it, as it is only a temporary vehicle. As we age it may seem a bit more confining, but this is necessary in order to help us want to feel the sense of freedom we experience in the process called death. Death is merely a transition of our spirit from our current physical form that results in complete freedom and direct connection to the Universal Source. There is no true death, for your essence is energy, and energy cannot be destroyed. It is a time to return to the Source of all things, hopefully having expanded greatly in the short time you had in the wonderful playground of time and space.

NUMBER THREE MISTAKE:
Having blind faith in a belief system

This is by far the most common mistake made by those on a spiritual or religious path. Blind faith is another trait of the herd mentality and should be evaded at all costs. Learn the truth of "what is" from your own efforts in seeking knowledge and experiences. Blind faith is another form of laying down your sense of self-empowerment. Becoming disempowered is not the way to spiritual Expansion; it actually causes contraction in a myriad of ways. While there does come a point where trust and faith will be a necessary factor in your advancement, blind faith is never the right method. Always have the courage to think for yourself. Over time you will develop the capacity to *feel* what it right and what is not right for you. This feeling will present itself to you in a sense of knowing within your heart, and your heart does not lie. This should be your basis of faith; this type of faith will greatly empower you and guide you in the right direction. It will give you truer answers than you could find in any religious institution, because it allows you to get the answers you seek directly from the Universal Source. Remember that you already have all the answers and knowledge inside, you merely have to remember how to access it. Be courageous enough to strike out on your own path of truth and live your life from a place of authenticity.

THE 3 MOST COMMON
PHYSICAL (EARTHLY) MISTAKES

NUMBER ONE MISTAKE: Being stuck in your head

The information age has produced an epidemic that has overtaken the general public and caused everyone to be so stuck in their heads that they have lost contact with their bodies. With this also comes a loss of awareness for their environment and disconnection from Nature and the Divine. You need to get out of your head and back into your body, where you can connect to Heaven and Earth. You need to be able to feel your body inside and out, to re-establish your connection to it, developing kinesthetic awareness and cellular consciousness. This will lead you to the ability to drop your mind to your lower abdomen (dantien) and awaken the mind of the lower center. Once this has taken place you will feel the desire to move, to exercise, to experience this life through the senses once again. There is a real life out there far better than any virtual reality that could be created. The goal of inhabiting a human body is to expand your sense of consciousness to experience paradise. That's the true greatness of being human and living in the reality of time, space and matter. Embrace the experience, don't hide from it; after all, you asked for it in the first place.

Go for walks and other activities to get your awareness into your legs and feet. If you have some sort of limitation that prevents you from doing this, then get your awareness into any area of your body that is possible. Whenever you feel yourself becoming overly centered and stuck in your head, simply unplug from technology for awhile and get out into Nature. This is a quick fix that works absolute wonders. I would recommend this as a daily activity, especially if your job or career requires you to exert an excessive amount of mental concentration. At the end of the workday, make the time to go out in the yard, walk in the nearby woods, or take a leisurely stroll through a local park. Just a few minutes nearly every day will help counter the effects of having to be in your head. You may notice that your mental stability and clarity improves as well. Make sure to escape the day-to-day grind that gets you stuck in your head.

NUMBER TWO MISTAKE: Not realizing your intimate connection to the Earth

It seems to be uncommon for people today to understand that they are indeed directly connected to the Earth. Not through an actual physical cord or physical attachment, but through the energetic fields of the planet. The magnetic and electrical fields of the Earth directly correlate and interact with those of every human being. Understanding this is the first step to developing awareness for it. The next step is to become sensitive enough to feel it for yourself. It is very possible to do this; while these forces may seem subtle, they are also very powerful.

We are all connected, as we are all created from the same Divine energy and the same base elements. Through this acknowledgement you will begin to awaken to the common sense of living a more natural life that is in ideal harmony with the environment. Maintaining the mindset that you are separate or better than the Earth is not only arrogant, but it also serves to keep you separate from any Divine connection. Become aware of the Laws of Nature and include them in your daily life.

NUMBER THREE MISTAKE:
Having an unhealthy view of your body

This takes on a couple different meanings and plays a more important role than you might first expect. The first and most obvious is having a negative image of your physical body. Sedentary lifestyles, medications, lack of connection to our bodies, poor eating habits and even poorer nutrition in the foods we consume contribute to the body losing its essential, healthy shape. This is why we have the phrase, "out of shape," to refer to the physical condition of the body losing its form. It seems common to belittle thin people as a means of personal acceptance for being overweight, but this is not solving the issue, it is merely the act of placing blame, making excuses and attempting to take the path of disempowerment. The path of empowerment appears in the form of exercise, proper diet and living a physically conscious lifestyle. It is a matter of taking mental and physical responsibility for oneself. Of course, it is just as unhealthy to be too skinny; as always, it is about balance.

Some people end up hating their body, and this creates more physical disconnection. This is not the healthy answer either. Feeling self-conscious or unhappy with your body is the mind's way of letting us know that the body has been neglected and requires attention. Remember, the body is the physical representation and reflection of your spiritual condition; it's your temple. If your temple is in disrepair, then take active measures to correct the problem. We have an entire spectrum of outstanding nutritionists and dieticians at our disposal; seek their help to assist you in finding the correct programs to fit your individual needs. This is not simply about your physical looks; it's about your mental condition due to self perception, in addition to your health and well-being. Take proper care of your body and it will provide you with an amazing physical experience here on Earth. I feel that it is important to accept yourself right now the way you are while taking positive steps to "get in shape."

The second meaning is found in how we are told as children that certain parts of our body are *dirty* or *bad*; this especially applies to our sexual organs and waste functions. We need to accept and embrace our entire body without any exceptions. Everything serves a function in the body; it's amazing and complex. Nothing about the body should be looked at as dirty or disgusting; this sends negative messages to the body and causes physical disconnection. The *entire* body is a Divine gift of perfection and should be appreciated.

THE 3 MOST COMMON CONNECTION (BEING) MISTAKES

NUMBER ONE MISTAKE: Unplugging from others

The biggest mistake in the area of Being is that of disconnection from other human beings. Do your best to call or talk face-to-face whenever possible in place of emailing, texting or online chatting. I was probably one of the worst offenders in this; my nervous system became so shorted that I just didn't want to interact with anyone any more than I had to at times. I was fortunate I had my martial arts school to keep me involved with others so I didn't become a hermit. I was far too quick to write people off as a way of not having to deal with them anymore, because I didn't have enough energy for strenuous interactions. This was a tragic mistake on my behalf and one that I hope you may avoid.

Stay connected and don't write people off or avoid contact with them; that doesn't mean that you must stay under the thumb of controlling, toxic people, as it is those types that you may need to separate yourself from. But all too often the disconnection comes from anger, an ego-driven response, or some other unfortunate situation of miscommunication. I live without regrets and I take ownership of my actions. However, if there was something I could change, it would be how hastily and easily I would write people off when I was younger. I have been on the giving and receiving end of this and both are painful. The heart center is slammed tightly shut on both sides of this action, and that is not beneficial to anyone. This is a sign of living a life that is still involved with the ego. I consciously choose how much time to spend with various people in my life, but I avoid shutting them out anymore. The more positive and expansive people are, the more time, attention and energy they get from me.

NUMBER TWO MISTAKE:
Not completely subduing the ego

I have witnessed many people begin to make real progress in overcoming their ego, just to fall victim to believing they have succeeded when they haven't. I've worked with people who explain to me they've been working on ego-related practices for a matter of weeks now, and they feel they have got it beat. It never fails that shortly thereafter they've been defeated by their ego while buying into their own delusion of having won the battle. The only shortcut I am aware of to overcome the ego is to know about the tricks it tries in an attempt to sucker-punch you when your true self is not looking. When you begin to believe you are getting the best of it, don't believe it; that's when you want to start working on it with even more intensity. Don't become a victim of the ego's fear. Keep going, keep pushing and when the ego resists, you need to fight back even harder yourself. One good sign that you are making progress in the battle with the ego is that you stop taking yourself so seriously and "lighten up."

One of the greatest signposts on the path of overcoming the ego is when your base thoughts lean toward the idea of unconditionally serving others. Be cautious of getting pulled back into the ego-driven activities that culture deems as acceptable. The three primary sources of ego-driven activity revolve around competitive sports, politics and religion. Any activity that sparks the thoughts, feelings and attitude that you are superior in any way is working to build the strength of the ego.

A spirit-realized life cannot exist in the same reality as an ego-connected life. Ego disconnects you from God or the Universal Source and prevents you from reconnecting until you get it tamed. The choice is yours. Do you wish to live the life of the ego or the life of the spirit?

NUMBER THREE MISTAKE: Lack of compassion

This trap has been catching more and more people due to the social disconnection caused by technology, poor economic conditions and so on. It is amazing how little compassion many people have for their fellow human being today. As people focus so intensely on their own busy lives, financial concerns and other personal issues that do not usually include spiritual growth, they have lost their sense of compassion for themselves and for others. You must cultivate a sense of compassion for the Ten Thousand Beings. In other words, cultivate compassion for everyone and everything. I observe three mindsets in regards to this: someone is indifferent and they completely ignore others around them, they set out to act in a malicious manner toward others, or they have compassion and consideration for others around them. If you notice yourself ignoring someone else because you are busy or frightened, catch yourself and cultivate feelings of compassion for the other person. Look at others as you walk by them and acknowledge them. If someone needs a hand, offer them yours. Compassion is directly linked to your heart and its ability to open. Compassion is one of the primary characteristics we see in the great spiritual masters.

Compassion for others is at the core of spiritual growth. However, we must never forget that it starts from within. It is difficult at best to feel true compassion for others when you are incapable of feeling compassion for yourself. As you learn to foster compassion for your own self, it begins to radiate outward from your center and touch those around you. As you overcome the ego, open your heart center and experience love and appreciation, you will notice yourself naturally transform into a more compassionate person. Compassion is said to be the primary essence of spiritual and religious systems, and it is a central practice among those who haven't lost sight of that. Compassion is simply an extension of love.

THE 3 MOST GENERALIZED COMMON MISTAKES

NUMBER ONE MISTAKE: Inconsistency

Unfortunately, some of you may not even begin this program. That's alright; it's not your time because you are not ready for it right now. Some of you will begin and then get drawn back into the distractions of the internet, television, video games, sports, politics and additional activities which draw your focus from spiritual advancement. Some of you will begin, make real progress and then become frightened by the truth of your experience, retreating back into your old habits and beliefs. Others of you will jump in with both feet to get started and never stop, changing your lives forever!

All the paths of inconsistency spell failure no matter what spin the ego attempts to put on it. The only path to success is through consistent, relentless practice. Once you start, keep going! It's alright if you miss a day due to something out of the ordinary, but you must jump right back in the next day. Success requires consistency; there is simply no way around it. The most harmful thing you can do to yourself is begin the program, start to experience results by kicking in the Expansion process, and then stop it. I have witnessed this time and again; it is destructive to one's Being.

Sticking with something is very difficult for people these days, especially with faster-paced lives, the need for constant entertainment, and relentlessly focusing on the newest thing to have or do. The most beneficial thing you can do for yourself at this moment in time is to slow down, relax and take a few deep breaths; then set your focus clearly on the goal of Spiritual Expansion. You are not in competition with anyone, not even yourself. Allow things to come when it is the proper time and just keep moving forward, doing a little more each day. One big key to success is to enjoy what you are doing.

NUMBER TWO MISTAKE: Thinking you already know

This is a huge mistake made by people with even the best of intentions. When someone starts to tell or show us something, our brain associates it with something we have already experienced or learned as a means to comprehend and categorize the new information. This type of unconscious mental behavior is largely responsible for stunting our learning capabilities. Just because something sounds familiar does not mean you know it, at least not completely and as deeply as you could. There are always deeper levels of understanding that will unlock your ability to truly *know* a topic.

Thinking you already know something completely is the ego at work. Don't fall for this trap of arrogance, and don't allow others to build your ego by telling you how great you are or how much you know. All too often the ego takes these compliments to heart, throws humility to the wind and closes the mind in order to revel in the praise of well meaning friends, family and fans. Take the compliments and appreciate the sentiment behind them, but do not take them as food for the ego. Use compliments as a way to know that you are making positive progress.

NUMBER THREE MISTAKE: Self-serving relationships

This applies to all of your relationships—friends, family, work colleagues, and all the rest. This too is a product of the ego, as well as the stress of overly-busy lives. By this point, you should be getting a very clear picture for how the ego works against your Expansion. We are so busy and rushed all the time that we focus on what we need from interactions with others, without considering what we have to offer the other person. We must learn to enter into any relationship or interaction with the primary concern of what you have to offer someone else. Enter with honesty and a sense of openness; without manipulation or with the mindset of taking what the other person has to offer you. None of these things will lead to a happy, healthy relationship. Take the time to check your heart and make sure you are entering into relationships by contemplating what you can offer the other person. Be a person of value who has the desire to serve, and you will establish more positive, long-lasting bonds with those around you. It's simply a matter of being mindful and remembering to give as well as receive.

In addition, when you are enter into an interaction with someone else and you think only about how beneficial it will be for you, you are limiting what can come into your reality. When you are focused on getting a certain result, you may very well miss other types of benefits. In order to know the blessings being bestowed upon you, you must be open to receiving them. When your mind is fixed on what you think you want, you close yourself off from receiving what others have to offer you and what gifts the Universal Source is attempting to provide. When you enter an interaction with the thought of, "How can I best be of service?" you retain a sense of openness that allows you to recognize and receive the gifts that are being brought into your experience.

By evading these and other potholes on the path of personal Expansion, you can embrace a more productive evolutionary journey. As I stated above and will reiterate yet again, be cautious for other mistakes that could appear out of nowhere. I have provided you with only three examples for each category, and while they are the three most common mistakes that I have witnessed within my own experience, the possibility exists that you could have something unique manifest in your own experience. Sometimes, these potholes are actually disguised life-lessons, and sometimes they are traps laid by the ego. Learn to distinguish one from the other. Life-lessons at first encounter may seem like terrible circumstances, but it is usually through great challenge and strife that we are able to make the most powerful changes in ourselves. It is merely an opportunity placed there for you in order to learn a personal lesson. Don't allow yourself to become irritated, frustrated or discouraged. Hold the Warrior Spirit and forge on. There is only one direction now, and that's forward!

CHAPTER NINE

MASTERY

"To know others is wisdom, but to know one's self is enlightenment. Those who conquer others require great power. But to conquer one's self requires inner strength."
— Lao Tzu / Solala Towler —
The 33rd verse of the Tao Te Ching

O ne spring day about twelve years ago, I was training in Japan at the *honbu dojo* (headquarters training hall) of Grandmaster Hatsumi. During a break, he held a small informal meeting for the *Shidoshi-Kai* instructors guild members. One instructor asked him what we could do to develop the ability to be more like him. His answer was, as usual, both simple and mysteriously profound. He replied, "To do what I do, you must do what I did and continue to do." I took these words to heart back then and have kept them close ever since, using this advice to make major advances, and I continue to use them to further my complete Expansion. Mastery is not a destination that you achieve; true mastery is an ongoing process towards personal

232

perfection. I make a daily effort to maintain my progress and to aspire to new heights.

Mastery is not a term I throw out there lightly, as I know how much intense effort it takes to truly master something. The most difficult thing in life to master remains to be ourselves. The vast majority of real masters I know will not usually allow themselves to acknowledge that they have attained mastery. They are humble, sure, but there's another reason for this. They know if they allow themselves to begin thinking of themselves as masters, they will stop learning and growing. I don't know anyone who has truly attained the level of mastery who would allow that to happen. This is another reason why spiritual mastery is a path of "pathlessness," because if you allow yourself to think about actually being a master, you stop your Expansion. Mastery is a continuous process with no end. To achieve mastery you can never, ever quit – for any reason. I know that you are committed to piercing the veil of excellence and going for absolute mastery, and I applaud you. To master yourself is a lofty achievement indeed.

"One can have no smaller or greater
mastery than mastery of oneself."
— Leonardo Da Vinci —

The Expansion Mastery System supplies the practitioner with everything they need to begin to reestablish their Divine connection. As you practice these foundational exercises within the program, you will find yourself discovering new layers of knowledge and experience within the techniques. You will also have prepared your internal body to support more masterful techniques. With all the research and training I have conducted, I have found that there are three very highly effective practices for this time of amazing transformation. Once you have successfully established your foundation, I recommend moving into one (or more) of the three methods that I will share with you here in the Mastery section. These practices are internal energy based practices, or Qigong. I have found these three techniques to be the most effective for harmonizing with the changing electromagnetic field of the Earth, as well as offering the additional benefits of well-being.

The first exemplary method is called Pangu Mystical Qigong, which I learned from the founder, Master Ou and his lovely daughter Olivia. This is an easy and effective form with multiple levels of learning, such as the Moving, Non-Moving, Healing and Advanced Forms. It only requires about 15 minutes to complete, or 25 minutes if you give it the time it truly deserves. I find great enjoyment practicing this wonderful form in Nature, and I perform it outdoors both in the early morning and evening to connect to the sun and moon. The Pangu form has also been shown to have powerful results in a way array of areas. An article published in the *Alternative Therapies in Health and Medicine* journal studied the effects of the Pangu form of Qigong on individuals going through detoxification, specifically from heroin addiction. This study showed a statistically significant reduction in withdrawal symptoms, anxiety scores, and in drug levels in urine at a more rapid pace than both the control group receiving basic medical care and the other test group receiving a detoxification drug. This suggests that Qigong practice may accelerate the detoxification process, reduce symptoms, and shorten recovery time.

> *"A person's spirit/soul is like heaven; the body is like earth. The spirit/soul provides vital intelligence; the body provides material elements. Therefore, when spirit and flesh unite harmoniously, a complete person results. One cannot live without matter, nor without spirit. When mind and intention are united, perfection results."*
>
> **— Master Wenwei Ou —**
> Excerpt from Harmony of Heaven, Earth and Humanity
> *Pan Gu Mystical Qigong*

The second method is called the Primordial Wuji Gong. I have learned the Wuji Gong form from a number of practitioners, such as Michael Winn and Solala Towler. I was certified as an instructor in the Wuji Gong form by Master Michael Winn in 2009. Both of my formal teachers learned it directly from Master Zhu Hui, who in turn learned it from a 106 year-old Taoist Master named Li Tong. Master Li Tong lived on Wudang Mountain in China, traveling by foot throughout China to perform healing techniques on those in need. I had the pleasure of practicing this form on a stone platform high on the mountain above the Purple Heaven Temple where it is said to have been created by Chang San Feng, who is also thought to be the creator of Tai Chi Chuan. It is considered to be a "Grandmaster's form," which indicates that it is of the highest level and quality. This form is the embodiment of Taoist theory. It focuses on uniting the practitioner with the forces of Heaven and Earth through the activation of the microcosmic orbit, the macrocosmic orbit, inner alchemy, fire and water alchemy, the eight trigrams (Bagua), the five elements of Feng Shui and more. It can be done in as little as 15 minutes or for better results, about 30 minutes. I have been fortunate enough to practice this form in many sacred locations throughout the world, such as on the mountains of Wudang, the Great Wall of China, and in many sacred Taoist temples throughout China.

The third and final method is called the Microcosmic Orbit. I have learned this remarkably powerful technique from many instructors as well, including Master Michael Winn, Grandmaster Mantak Chia, and a number of martial arts teachers. In a recent workshop I attended with Grandmaster Chia, he explained how his teacher passed this technique on to him with the instruction that it was to be used to help with these changing times we are experiencing. That instruction was given to him over four decades ago in light of what was to come, offering little doubt as to its importance. I will detail a basic version of this technique so you may practice it once you have completed the challenges from the Heaven, Earth and Being sections. I would caution you against skipping those exercises to jump right into the Orbit, especially if you have never had any formal face-to-face transmission from a qualified instructor. The other techniques I offered will help prepare you for the Microcosmic Orbit. The Orbit is also referred to as the *Small Heavenly Round* or *Small Heavenly Cycle*, depending upon the teacher and system. The primary goal is to practice it diligently enough that eventually it happens naturally and spontaneously, without your conscious direction. I cannot adequately stress the significance of becoming proficient in this technique.

BONUS MASTERY EXERCISE:
The Microcosmic Orbit

- Begin by finding a quiet place where you will not be disturbed while you perform this practice. It is best to do this without the risk of a sudden interruption.
- Sit comfortably and quietly, with your spine straight. Begin to relax both your body and your mind while settling into your seated position. You can sit in a chair or on the ground.
- Use the Breath Bridge breathing technique taught in the Heaven chapter in order to bridge your focus from the external to the internal. Relax, breathe and go within. Make sure that you are using the abdominal breathing that was taught in that section as well. Do your best to continue the abdominal breathing throughout the entire exercise.
- Begin by placing your focus in the upper center of awareness (upper dantien) in the head and watch this center as it glows a bright golden color. See the golden light pulse in coordination with your breath. See the golden light get brighter with every breath you draw in.
- In your mind's eye, trace your awareness as you drop it down through the vagus nerve to the heart center (middle dantien). See the heart glowing with a bright golden light, pulsing with your breath.
- Now trace your awareness as you bring your consciousness down into the lower center (lower dantien). The lower center is pulsing with your breath and glowing with a bright golden light. Compact that golden light into a sphere of glowing golden energy.
- Gently place your tongue against your upper pallet behind the top teeth, and then gently tighten the anus sphincter of

the perineum. Do your best to remain mindful of these two placements throughout the exercise. Both should be gentle, do not over squeeze the anal sphincter.

- Now see the golden light sphere as it begins to spin forward. Make sure the sphere is a comfortable size for you. Allow it to spin in place. When you feel ready, allow the golden sphere to exit the lower abdomen and begin to travel downward through the Conception Vessel down the front centerline of your body. Gently exhale as it drops down.

- The golden sphere first travels down the body to the sexual organs, then passes by the perineum. As it goes past the perineum, see the golden sphere travel around your coccyx and inhale as it begins its upward ascent through the Governor Channel up your spine. It travels past the door of life (ming men), between your kidneys, up through the spine between the shoulder blades, then up to the neck, to the top or crown of the head, and over the head, where it once again rejoins the Conception Vessel. Here the golden sphere begins its downward descent. Exhale as the sphere begins to travel downward.

- See the golden sphere as it cascades down the front of your face, down through the throat, down through the chest, past the heart and into the abdomen.

- Allow the golden sphere to keep rotating on this path to complete 72 rotation cycles. Trace the sphere with the awareness of your consciousness and feel it travel through your body. Remember to continue to breathe from the abdomen and stay relaxed. As the sphere spins through the orbit it will break up energy blockages and old patterns that you no longer need.

- *Caution:* Never make an attempt to force the flow of the sphere. And never, ever stop the sphere in front or behind the heart. Start and stop the flow at the lower abdomen. Remember to inhale as the sphere ascends up the back and exhale as it descends down the front.

- After you have completed the desired number of cycles, whether you performed the spin three, nine, eighteen, thirty-six or seventy-two times, slow it down and prepare to return the sphere to the lower abdominal center.
- See the sphere travel down and stop in front of the lower abdominal center just below the navel. The glowing golden sphere will then return inside to the lower center in the abdomen or dantien. There it will glow brightly for a moment while you relax and breathe. Condense this sphere into an intense little ball where you will store it in the lower center.
- Sit quietly for a moment and just feel your body inside and out. Relax your tongue, allowing it to rest normally in the mouth. Release any tension in the perineum that you may have and relax. Then, when you are ready, repeat the Breath Bridge technique to reconnect with the external world. Tip your head slightly down to protect your eyes and slowly open your eyes. Take a moment to allow the energy to settle before standing up. Standing up too quickly can have adverse affects.

KNOWLEDGE & EXPERIENCE

Mastery requires two primary components; that of knowledge and experience. Knowledge is the first step, the point in the process when you find out something exists of which you'd had no prior awareness. Set out to gain knowledge and awareness. Knowledge is *understanding*. This can be accomplished in a variety of ways depending upon what serves you best. You can listen to an audio series, attend seminars, read books, or find a teacher. I personally do all of these and more. We have all heard the phrase, "Knowledge is power," right? This is a very true statement and I believe that no one book or perspective holds all the answers. The key to knowledge is thinking for yourself. It is great to be open to someone else's interpretation of something, as they may offer you fresh or expanded insights.

Experience is the second step, allowing you to develop a sense of inner knowing. It is through the actual experience of performing a practice that we gain the skill and insights not included in a book. More importantly, we establish a deep, personal sense of knowing and mindfulness. We are able to grasp finer details in ways that they apply to our own individual identities through feeling. These are details that are outside the box of conventional knowledge. It is experience that allows us to really know something in our "Inner Being." Experience is *knowing*. To have a deep sense of knowing for something is far different than having knowledge of it. This knowing comes from your Higher Self. True power lies in the bringing together of these two forces. When knowledge and experience are balanced, then you are on the path toward mastery.

KNOW YOURSELF AS DIVINE

As a species of extraordinary beings, it is time to mature. It is time to grow up and accept our Divinity as spiritual beings enjoying a physical experience. We are here on Earth to enjoy and learn; not to desecrate the gift of life we received from the Universal Source. The time has come to stop putting ourselves down in an attempt to feel more humble and appease a God who would punish us for simply being what God created in the first place. We are not sinners; we are Divine beings originating from the Universal Source, and we are doing the very best that we can.

When I was a small child my family went to church regularly; there was one song called *Amazing Grace*, which includes the lyrics "that saved a wretch like me." Whenever we got to that part of the song it just felt bad to me. Keep in mind that I was only five or six years old; children that age are still strongly and naturally connected to the Universal Source. It felt wrong to say that line in the song and I had the tendency to skip over that part. It was a beautiful song, except for that line. I was confused; why would I come to church to worship God and then make myself feel bad? It made no sense to me. I can recall thinking, "Why should I say that about myself? It means I'm being a bad boy and I'm at church being good." When you pay attention and think for yourself, you begin to notice these things. Follow these feelings when you experience them; you know what feels right in your heart.

Young children maintain this direct connection to the Universal Source for many years. As the ego develops we end up separating ourselves from our Source, and this is why there is a need for actual spiritual practices to re-establish our connection to the Universal Source. It is far more beneficial to know yourself as Divine then it is to know yourself as a sinner. Say the word to yourself while you hold a sense of mindfulness to *feel* what happens to your mind, your body and your heart as you say the word. For me, I feel pangs of shame, guilt, twinges of discomfort in my stomach, and a sense that I have done something very bad. Ask any child who understands what the word is supposed to mean what they feel when they say it. Observe their body language as well as the expression of their eyes and the tone of their words. To make spiritual advancement, always refer to yourself in positive ways. It is okay to accept that you are a Divine Being; now you just have to go about acting like it!

GETTING STARTED: HERE'S THE FIRST THING YOU MUST DO

The very first thing you must do in the overall process is enter into the mind-set of the Beginners Mind (shoshin). You will need to prepare your mind to begin a new adventure and be open to the experience of learning. Take a moment to read the section on shoshin again and apply it to your own mental state. Then ask yourself this one question. "Am I ready to learn, willing to change, able to grow, and 100-percent committed to succeeding in my own personal Expansion?" Don't be in a hurry to answer; take your time and really grasp the totality of the question. When you can answer with a resounding "Yes!" then you are ready to dive in and begin the journey of the time of your life. Once you are fully committed to experiencing your personal Expansion, you must be ready to step outside of the confinement of the herd. You must be prepared to walk your own authentic path.

You will need to prepare your mind. Slow down, take a deep breath and take a moment to reawaken, shaking off the numbness of technology. Here are some other "call to action" items for you to help you prepare a solid foundation and set the framework for success.

1. Prepare your mind (shoshin) to accept this challenge. Know that you can and will succeed.
2. Relax your physical body and your mind. Progress begins with the ability to relax.
3. Achieve a sense of knowing that you are an Eternal Divine Spiritual Being.
4. Choose a single "challenge" and take action. It all begins with a single step.
5. Learn to manage your thoughts and emotions. Develop a higher sense of feeling.
6. Develop a sense of awareness and exercise it daily.
7. Achieve a mental state of mindfulness; this will lead you to mastery.
8. Become a Spiritual Warrior. Have the unshakable courage it takes to succeed.
9. Keep going! Never stop. To stop is not to hold onto what you have, it is to go backwards.

MY PERSONAL DAILY ROUTINE: FORMULA FOR SUCCESS

I apply a daily formula that I believe is crucial to experiencing ongoing success. It has worked wonders for me. The formula is not magic in and of itself, and I recommend that each of you come up with your own personal version of this formula. The basic essence is to begin each day with a renewed connection to Heaven. This includes spiritual and subtle energy practices to achieve a clearer connection to my higher self. Then I strengthen the awareness of the Earth. This is when I address my physical workouts and get active outdoors. The entire time I am being mindful of my heart and connection to others.

Remember to own the process by customizing it to fit your time constraints and Expansion needs. You are welcome to copy mine in the beginning to get you started if you like. When I feel things are becoming a bit complacent I change things up within my routine; this is not meant to be fixed, it is meant to be *felt*. There are certain things that I consider to be essential – at least for me. There are other things that I consider necessary to perform on a regular basis but not really on a daily basis. Realize that you can make your daily routine shorter than mine; just maintain some form of the core formula. Mine was not always as extensive as it is now, but these days I am able to live the life of Heaven, Earth and Being to an incredible extent.

Daily:

1. I awaken and before getting up or even moving, I lie in bed and give appreciation for the ability to enjoy another day. I observe my fiancé as she sleeps and I instantly know how blessed I am. Then I reflect upon all the other people, places, things, and events I appreciate. I do this until I really feel my heart open just a bit more, which always results in becoming teary-eyed. I try to include at least one person whom I am finding difficulty with in the past or present and develop a sense of forgiveness and appreciation for them as well. This is a great way to get your vibration up for the day. Once I feel this immense amount of appreciation, I rise out of bed.

2. I get up and stand before the altars in our bedroom and offer prayer. In my prayer, I offer appreciation and ask for guidance. I make sure that I feel my personal connection to the Universal Source. Sometimes I do this standing and sometimes I perform my prayer in the kneeling position called seiza. I will sometimes perform the Silver Strand in front of the altars as I offer blessings and count my own. I also take a moment to focus on coordinating my thoughts, feelings, words and actions for the day.

3. I go outdoors onto the deck or even into the park and just connect to Nature; I feel the cool breeze, smell the ocean air, feel the warmth of the sun on my skin and look around, drinking

in the beauty of where I live. I especially enjoy the mountains. I offer appreciation for the wonderful area I am blessed to live in and acknowledge the elements and seasonal cycles. I then open my heart center even more. I begin hydrating myself at this point and continue throughout the day. These first three steps can be done in a matter of about ten minutes if you are rushed for time, but I like to spend about an hour or so with these when I can.

4. I then begin an energy workout. I stretch my body using an advanced set of the stretching exercises I offer in this program, perform some *Tao Yin* exercises and spinal cord breathing. I then go into a couple of specific Qigong forms, including the Pangu form. I open my energy system and get everything flowing properly on the inside. I end by practicing an I-Chuan posture before grabbing a shower. I take the time in the shower to feel appreciation for the ability to practice good hygiene. I feel any negative thoughts or emotions being washed away, while feeling fresh and renewed.

5. I get to work on my writing and business development.

6. I remain mindful throughout the day to maintain a sense of high vibration. I steer clear of things that I feel lower it. I can't escape everything that lowers my vibration and I don't try. I just stay aware of it enough to feel if it begins to lower, and I correct the situation to raise it back up. I have discovered that my own behaviors effect my vibration in a negative way far more than those of any outside forces anyway. If I do have my vibration lowered by some external situation, I immediately set out to raise it back up.

7. In the afternoon I do a physical workout. I like the intense cardio programs. I may add more exercises by going to the gym if I am feeling it, or I will stay home and work out on the Bowflex. I also enjoy swimming as a mid-day exercise.

8. I continue working more on my writing and business development.

9. I do my best to tell people around me that I love them throughout the day and think loving thoughts about those whom I do not get to interact with.

10. I like to end the evening by walking out into the park and looking up at the night sky. I get in touch with the stars and the vastness of the universe. Then I do a set or two of Qigong forms, practice the microcosmic orbit, and sometime just sit afterward with my fiancé and enjoy the night. We like to stand outdoors after we have finished the Qigong practice with my arm around her, pulling her close as we look up at the stars, delight in taking full, deep breaths of the nighttime ocean air and experiencing Heaven, Earth and each other.

11. Afterward, I may go inside and read something inspiring or work on various esoteric spiritual techniques so that I may better apply them to my life experience.

12. I make sure to get a proper amount of rest, going to bed at the correct times for brain health and rejuvenation. I like to send appreciation to the universe and bless my life and others in my life before falling asleep. I occasionally perform an additional Non-Moving Pangu Qigong form right before drifting off.

If you have a keen sense of observation as well as the ability to connect to the material here, you may notice a pattern emerge within my daily formula. The first four exercises relate to Heaven, the mid-day exercises relate to Earth, and then other exercises throughout the day relate to the Being. The remaining exercises at the end of the day relate more to the Heaven area, which is a great way to wrap up the day, raise your vibration and connect to the Divine before going to sleep. It's the same goal as saying your prayers before you go to sleep.

Weekly:

I may replace something from the daily routine with the exercises that you see listed below, or if there is time to be made, I add these things to what I already do. I do not make this a rigid practice, because then I lack the freedom to be spontaneous and move with the energies around me. I look for Divine inspiration to decide what I should be doing, while keeping the basic structure so I benefit from the consistency of the practice. Try not to become too stuck in one routine as you will become unable to adapt when your Higher Self directs you and your practices. This is all dependent upon the day and what I am currently placing my focus on, or an area I am addressing where I need to make progress. Here are just a few things that are normally factored into my weekly schedule.

1. I practice additional martial arts training. I draw from various Japanese and Chinese systems.
2. I may engage in mountain hiking, long walks on the beach, or swimming in the ocean.
3. I attend seminars and workshops for spiritual expansion, martial arts, healing, health, and Qigong.
4. Once a week we sit and study esoteric teachings.
5. Once every two weeks, I teach a martial arts group. This session lasts between three to four hours of intense training and study.
6. We listen to self-improvement audio programs by our favorite authors.
7. I may take a single practice from the Expansion Mastery System and explore it more deeply.
8. We look for additional learning experiences such as nutritional workshops, workshops on health and healing and other methods to empower ourselves with knowledge to take full responsibility for our health and well-being.
9. We schedule things that we simply find enjoyable to raise our vibration. Maybe it's a visit to the San Francisco Asian Art Museum, attending a concert, tequila tasting or some other relaxing, enjoyable event.

The primary goal is to begin with a daily schedule that is easy and enjoyable enough that you are willing and able to perform it without being distracted. You must get this in place in order to make real, life-changing progress. Start simple, adding to it as you progress. One mistake people make is being too overzealous in the beginning, creating a daily practice that is too complex. This usually leads to burnout and eventual failure. Be patient, start easy and work up to new levels. You will find this not only easy to continue, but enjoyable and more beneficial.

Ultimately, what you are after is to have many of these challenges and exercises to simply become part of who you are and what you normally do in a day. Once you attain this level, the practices will be a natural part of your day and no longer something that you "have to do." This is what we are striving for. In this way, it is integrated enough into your being and consciousness that you have not only made great changes in your life, but you have *become* them.

Heaven, Earth and Being (humanity) is the key to knowing the universe! It is the ultimate expression of Divine connection, love and life. It's the essential balance of benevolence and inner strength. This truth is well known by martial masters, spiritually enlightened leaders, and those who are most proficient in the internal energy and healing methods. It is acknowledged and accepted within the most secret, esoteric teachings from both the East and the West. The harmony of Heaven, Earth and Being is the sacred point where these masters reside. When a human being moves in harmony with Heaven and Earth, other human beings, and their own spirit, body and heart, they are then living as they were meant to live. It is then that you will gain the ability to view life through the eyes of Heaven.

AFTERWORD

LIVING A FULLY ENGAGED life of love and continuous growth is the pinnacle of the human experience. To live as a completely conscious being filled with love, bliss and appreciation is to know what it is to be rich beyond imagination. Being fully awakened to your intimate connection to Heaven, Earth and your own heart is to experience the Divine right here and now. The concept of Heaven, Earth and Being is a map of sorts. It's a map that guides each of us to deeply know the three aspects of our self and achieve complete balance as a being on this path of pathlessness. I feel now, for the first time in my life, that I am truly living. This is to live in harmony with Nature, over-flowing with love for all beings and knowing deep within that you are eternal and Divine. To hold a sense of knowing for all these things is to live a fully engaged life. Don't procrastinate and allow the gift of your life to slip carelessly through your grasping fingers. Open your hands and heart, expand your sense of self and begin to enthusiastically embrace the gift of a fully engaged life.

Expansion requires more than most people are willing to give of themselves. It requires great strength and determination, and at times you may feel as though you are making sacrifices in order to live authentically. Above all else, you must keep going. Living a life of Expansion demands a constant state of mindfulness; to purposefully seek knowledge and experience so that you may have fluid growth and come to know the truths of your heart and the Universe. While the demands are great, the rewards are far greater. Be bold. Be courageous. Be ready to answer the call of your life's purpose and to live a life of Heaven on Earth!

I have felt the deep inner longings to continue on my spiritual quest, no matter what the costs; and there have been costs, I assure you. Yet, I have lived with no regrets. Some of the greatest moments in my life have taken place because I made the choice to live a life of spiritual Expansion. I not only heard, but actually listened to the voice of my Higher Self demanding that I intensify my efforts for spiritual growth. Then it became of choice of living my own authentic life or living for others, as they wanted me to live. I tried to ignore this voice and do what I thought was right according to what social convention dictated. As a result, it nearly killed me. I was blessed enough to be granted the opportunity to make the necessary changes in my life and begin again. This time I placed my spiritual Expansion as the primary and conscious purpose in my life.

The Expansion Mastery System is presented here for everyone to do what they must in order to accept this time of great transformation that we are in, and to expand without the dramatic endeavor of a near-death experience. Do not fear swimming against the current of the conventional social norm. This is a trap that will wither your soul and brand you as one of the herd. It is now that you must live a purposeful, engaged life as someone consciously aware of who they are and why they are here. Living life to the fullest does not imply indulging in senseless, self-gratifying behaviors. It refers to living more openly and honestly from your heart center while remaining fully conscious of your relationship to the spiritual and physical worlds.

I have now dedicated myself to helping others to attain what I have as I continue striving for my own personal mastery. We, as the human species, have reached a point in time when these deep-seeded feelings calling for change and transformation from within can no longer be ignored. We must walk through life with our eyes wide open, with clarity of vision, and know that we are living in the time of a great planetary and consciousness shift. Now is the time to take action and reclaim a fully conscious role in our lives! Now is the time to be completely present and fully engaged! Now is our time to Expand!

I am sitting here at my desk enjoying the fresh scent of the Pacific Ocean, the cooing of the mourning doves, and the tender warmth of the morning California sun. Today is just seven days away from my 48th birthday. My heart is open, filled with love and shining brightly to all who would accept its light. My eyes are filling with the tears of bliss for what has become my blessed life. I sincerely hope the Expansion Mastery System is able to positively impact your life and that through this work I have been able to touch your heart in a spectacular way. It is time for all of us to grow and mature as a species, as if our existence might depend on it. I send my heartfelt love and appreciation to every single one of you, and I wish for all of you to experience a fully engaged, magical, miraculous life filled with love, bliss and appreciation! Have the time of your life – because you are!

If you are interested in following my free weekly lessons from the Expansion Mastery System, please visit my website at www.expansionmastery.com. I would love to hear from you so please feel free to leave comments. The blog is designed to create a positive community of expanding beings where we can all learn from one another and connect through our hearts. There will soon be instructional videos and audio on the site, which cover everything in the Expansion Mastery book. I will also be offering video and audio courses of the challenges covered here and additional advanced material. If you want more details or require clearer, guided methods of the challenges, you can find them at my website. Keep going!

Robert D. Bessler
June 7th, 2012
Year of the Dragon

BIBLIOGRAPHY

Bible. King James edition. www.kingjamesbibleonline.org

Braden, Gregg. *Secrets Of The Lost Mode Of Prayer*. United States: Hay House, Inc., 2008.

Canfield, Jack. *The Success Principles*. New York: HarperCollins Publisher, 2005.

Dyer, Dr. Wayne W. *Excuses Begone!* United States: Hay House, Inc. 2009.

Frantzis, B.K.. *Relaxing Into Your Being*. California: Clarity Press, 1998.

Goodman, Richard L.. *The Tao Te Ching in Translation*. Hong Kong/ Taiwan: Windstone Press, 2010.

Hatsumi, Masaaki. *The Essence Of Budo: The Secret Teachings of the Grandmaster*. Kodansha Intn., 2011.

Hicks, Esther & Jerry. *The Amazing Power Of Deliberate Intent*. United States: Hay House Inc., 2006.

Kamchuen, Master Lam. *Master Lam's Walking Qigong*. London: Gaia Books, 2006.

Li, Ming, Chen, Kevin, PhD, and Mo, Zhixian, MD. "Use of Qigong in the Detoxification of Heroin Addicts." *Alternative Therapies in Health and Medicine,* January-February 2002.

Lubicz, Schwaller de, R.A. *Esoterism & Symbol.* Vermont: Inner Traditions International, 1985.

Lubicz, Schwaller de, R.A. *The Temple Of Man*. Vermont: Inner Traditions International, 1977.

Osho. *Joy, The happiness That Comes From Within*. New York: St. Martin's Press, 2008.

Ou, Master Wenwei. *Pan Gu Mystaical Qigong*. United States: Unique Publications, 1999.

Phillips, Dr. Tony. Science @ NASA. *Earth's Inconstant Magnetic Field*. 2003.

Ray, James Arthur. *Practical Spirituality*. California: SunArk Press, 2005.

Steine, Bronwen and Fran. *The Japanese Art Of Reiki*. New York: O Books, 2005.

Stevens, John. (Ueshiba, Morihei). *The Essence of Aikido*. Tokyo: Kodansha, 1999.

Towler, Solala. *Tales From the Tao*. London: Watkins, 2005.

Towler, Solala. *Chuang Tzu: The Inner Chapters*. London: Watkins, 2011.

Tzu, Lao. *Tao Te Ching*. 2500 BCE.

RESOURCE PAGE

Bible. King James edition. www.kingjamesbibleonline.org
Dr. Mark Hyman: www.drhyman.com
Dr. Wayne Dyer: www.drwaynedyer.com
Grandmaster Mantak Chia: www.universal-tao.com
Heartmath Institute: www.heartmath.org
Master Wen Wei Ou: www.pangu.org
Merriam Webster Dictionary. www.Merriam-Webster.com
Michael Winn: www.healingdao.com
NASA: www.nasa.gov
Osho: www.osho.com
Solala Towler: www.communityawake.com

Printed in the USA
CPSIA information can be obtained
at www.ICGtesting.com
JSHW022213140824
68134JS00018B/1038